THE AGE OF KIPLING

THE AGE OF KIPLING

Edited by John Gross

Simon and Schuster . New York

Published by Simon and Schuster, Rockefeller Center
630 Fifth Avenue, New York, N.Y. 10020

Kim – the Finest Story about India in English
by Nirad C. Chaudhuri first appeared in *Encounter*, April 1957
Kipling's First Novel by Betty Miller
first appeared in the *Cornhill Magazine*, Spring 1956
These two articles are reproduced by kind permission of the proprietors
of *Encounter* and John Murray Publishers

First U.S. Printing

SBN 671-21405-5

Library of Congress Catalog Card Number: 72-83900

Printed in England by C. Tinling & Co. Ltd.

Contents

List of Illustrations

List of Illustrations

Acknowledgments

The editor and publishers wish to record their gratitude for permission received from owners, agents and photographers to reproduce the following list of illustrations (numbers refer to pictures; italic numbers to colour illustrations):

Lord Baldwin (and H. E. Jones and Son, Photographers) 2, 4, 10, 24, *51*; Department of the Environment 9; Haileybury College Governing Council 13, 15; R. E. Harbord, Esq., (and John Freeman, Photographers) 12, 17, 18, 19, 22, 62, 88; Heinemann Publishers 69, 71 (and Mansell Coll.); F. Cabot Holbrook and Howard C. Rice, Jr 43, 46, 47, 48, 49, 50; Houghton Library, Harvard College (Henry James Archive) 42; Imperial War Museum, London 66, 68, 83; India Office Library, London (and R. B. Fleming, Photographers) 3, 27, 28, 29; Roger Lancelyn Green, Esq. 11, 26, 44; City of Leeds Art Gallery (and Gilchrist Bros, Photographers) 23; Raymond Mander and Joe Mitchenson Theatre Collection (and John Freeman, Photographers) 52, 84, 85, 86; Mansell Collection 25, 40, 55, 82; Mary Evans Library 16, 39, 57; National Film Archives 89, 92, 93, 94, 95, 96, 97, 98, 99; National Portrait Gallery 72; Art Gallery of New South Wales *90*; Popperfoto 61; Press Association Ltd 63, 74; Princeton University Library (photo Willard Starks) 45; Private Collection (and A. and C. Cooper, Photographers) *53*; Radio Times Hulton Library 14, 20, 21, 30, 31, 32, 33, 38, 41, 56, *59*, 60, 64, 67, 70, 73, 75, 76, 77, 78, 79, 80, 81, 87, 93; The Royal Commonwealth Society and the Kipling Society (and John Freeman, Photographers) 1 (Courtesy of R. E. Harbord), 5 (Courtesy of R. E. Harbord), 7, 8, 34, 35, 36, 37, 54, *58*; The Scout Association 65; Victoria and Albert Museum (and John Freeman, Photographers) 6

Foreword

Kipling is a writer who in many ways lends himself to over-simplification, and he is still no doubt most commonly thought of, not without reason, as a kind of cartoon-figure, a handy textbook symbol of the Empire that was. Yet he was in fact far more contradictory and many-sided than either friends or foes generally gave him credit for being during his own lifetime, and if the essays in this collection range widely both in theme and approach, it is in an effort to capture something of his complexity and versatility. The man who emerges may often have chosen to take a bold or even crude line, but it was not through any lack of subtlety in his own make-up; he may have had among his other gifts an almost unequalled talent for coining slogans and catchphrases, but he himself defies any easy formula or summing-up.

For a start, there is the paradox of his being at once one of the most public and the most intimate of writers. He may have requested (or admonished) his readers

> Seek not to question other than
> The books I leave behind,

but the more one ponders those works the more forcefully one becomes aware of the personality behind them, and the more curious, inevitably, about the experience by which it was shaped. That means going back to where 'it all began', as the late Betty Miller does in an essay which unravels the childhood origins of the emotions at work in *The Light that Failed*, and by implication much else in Kipling besides. Janet Adam Smith takes up the story somewhat later in Kipling's schooldays with her account of how the often unexpected realities of Westward Ho! were gradually transmuted into the myth of *Stalky and Co.*, while Lord Baldwin's sketch of John Lockwood Kipling reminds us that if the writer's childhood left its deep scars it was also a source of strength, not least on account of his father's artistry and feeling for things Indian.

On India itself, Michael Edwardes and Philip Mason discuss Kipling's treatment of the army and the civil administration respectively (to all intents and purposes he could be said to have reclaimed the common soldier for literature, although his relative failure to do imaginative justice to the Indian Civil Service is almost as revealing in its way), and James Morris's evocation of Simla conjures up the curious blend of parochialism and world power which inspired so much of his early work. His deepest intuitions about India, however, went beyond the Raj and the politics of the day: they are explored here by N. C. Chaudhuri with an authority which perhaps no non-Indian could hope to achieve.

The essays which deal with Kipling after his return from India, though they roughly follow the chronological pattern of his career, also provide a good many suggestive links and contrasts. For example, Leon Edel's essay, fleshing out the hitherto rather shadowy figure of Wolcott Balestier, while it leads on naturally to Louis Cornell's account of Kipling's experiences in America, also throws some picturesque side-lights on the early development of Kipling's reputation, which is discussed at greater length by J. I. M. Stewart. Mr Cornell in turn helps to explain Kipling's determination to identify himself in large measure with the English land-owning gentry, which is appraised by Roger Lancelyn Green; he points forward, indirectly, to Kipling's posthumous fate at the hands of Hollywood, analysed by Philip French; and he raises questions which converge with some of Eric Stokes' final speculations in his general assessment of Kipling's imperial ethos. But for that matter Mr Green leaves one wondering about what happened to the more urban and less classbound figure portrayed by Colin MacInnes in his essay on Kipling and the music halls, and Professor Stokes is as relevant to the more ostensibly literary contributions as what Robert Conquest has to say about Kipling's poetry is to debate over his politics.

Again, it adds something to our understanding of both essays, and of Kipling, if we read George Shepperson on the Boer War in conjunction with Bernard Bergonzi on the First World War; Alan Sandison, on Kipling and Haggard, has an opportunity to discuss some of the larger literary issues implicit in the friendship which John Raymond describes, necessarily more briefly, in his account of Kipling's later years; and Gillian Avery leads us back, as any consideration of Kipling as a children's writer must, to reflections on the childhood where 'it all began'.

It would not be quite accurate to call the result of all this a composite portrait. There are too many disagreements between individual contributors for that; but then unanimity, in the case of a writer as controversial as Kipling, is not to be looked for. That the controversies still smoulder, on the other hand, is itself a tribute to his vitality – and on this last, at any rate, all the contributors are at one. He remains a haunting, unsettling presence, with whom we still have to come to terms.

John Gross

Betty Miller
KIPLING'S FIRST NOVEL

So we settled it all when the storm was done
　　As comfy as comfy could be;
And I was to wait in the barn, my dears,
　　Because I was only three,
And Teddy would run to the rainbow's foot,
　　Because he was five and a man –
And that's how it all began, my dears,
　　And that's how it all began!

WHAT began? The story of *The Light that Failed*, a novel which, with *Barrack Room Ballads* and a handful of short stories, was the first fruit of Kipling's return to England, and his recent separation from the family circle at Lahore. *The Light that Failed* is primarily a story of sex antagonism; and in placing the verse just quoted at the head of his opening chapter, Kipling has himself defined the origin of that situation: placed it at a specific moment in his own childhood: when he was five and his sister was only three.

It was at this age that a cataclysmic change took place in the life of the imperious small boy. Up till that moment, living in Bombay with his adoring parents, despot and darling of the Indian servants who attended him, he had been, unquestionably, a spoilt and a precocious child: and some inkling of what he then was, or felt himself to be, may be gathered from the repetition, in so many early stories of his, from *Tod's Amendment* to *Kim*, of that situation, patently dear to Kipling's heart, in which a small boy nonchalantly reveals himself superior in wisdom and in courage alike to the soldiers and statesmen who unsuspectingly patronize his nursery.

Brusquely, on two separate occasions in his childhood, this life of unlimited love and admiration received a severe check. Rudyard Kipling was not yet three years old when he first accompanied his mother to England, where, soon afterwards, a daughter was born to her. (Kipling's reaction to this event is not on record, but one recalls a short story in which a small boy, neglected by his parents, observes the adoration lavished on a playmate, a little girl who wears, habitually, a big blue sash. Concluding that it is the sash which is responsible for so enviable a popularity, he tries to borrow it, in order to render himself equally acceptable in the eyes of his own parents.) Three years later, with no idea of the gulf towards which he then travelled, little Rudyard was once more on his way to England. Like other Anglo-Indian parents, the Kiplings had succumbed to the necessity of transferring their children to a more equable climate. What has never been made clear, however, is why they chose to board them out with a couple unknown to either of them save through the newspaper advertisement which served so conspicuously to entangle the destinies of the two families concerned. Nor, it seems, except for the most nebulous of hints, could they bring themselves to warn the children of what was to come: with the result that brother and sister awoke one morning in a mean little house on the outskirts of Southsea to find that their parents had gone back to India, leaving them in a strange and uncongenial country, in the care of an even stranger and more uncongenial woman whom they were told to call Aunty Rosa.

What Rudyard Kipling suffered for six years at the hands of this woman he was later to describe, and in memorable terms. None the less, bearing in mind the fact that his sister has put it on record that the picture painted in 'Baa Baa Black Sheep' is in some respects an exaggerated one, it is possible to suggest that the persecution which the youthful Kipling endured at Southsea was to him less of an ordeal than the inexplicable reversal of the supremacy he had hitherto enjoyed as the only son in the house of his parents in Bombay. At Southsea, in the House of Desolation, as he called it, not only were there no servants to do his bidding; for the first time he was systematically bullied and beaten by a woman whom he regarded as one of a lower caste than himself. It is necessary to re-read a short story, 'The Son of his Father', to appreciate something of what this meant to an Anglo-Indian child, and to Rudyard Kipling in particular. In this story, a white boy – yet another of Kipling's Terrible Toddlers – beaten by his father for some trivial offence, attempts to commit suicide, not because his father has beaten him, but because the chastisement took place in the presence of a woman, his native foster-mother. The child refuses, in consequence, to obey the woman's orders, or to eat from her hand: and when (at his command) she is dismissed, greets his new ayah with the words: 'If I do wrong, send me to my father. If you strike me, I will try to kill you. I do not wish my ayah to play with me. Go and eat rice!'

Meanwhile at Southsea, in marked contrast to his own degradation, Rudyard was to witness the early and triumphant apotheosis of his small sister, Trix. Aunty Rosa had long wanted a daughter, and the pretty golden-haired little girl soon became a favourite, accorded every privilege, from a bed in Aunty Rosa's room to the free run of her kitchen. More invidious still, Aunty Rosa took the view that on every question Trix was always in the right, and Ruddy as invariably in the wrong. No revolution could have been more absolute: and it is scarcely surprising to find, in the circumstances, that the fortunate Trix learned to read long before her brother, and that, much admired, she was already reading out a verse of the Psalms at family prayers, while Rudyard, confirmed butt of the household, found himself unable, however brisk the blows, to compound any but the simplest of words.

When we consider the type of frustration, at the hands of women, that was the lot of Kipling at Southsea, it is clear enough why, many years later, when, once again, his own masculinity was baffled and annulled by the opposition of a woman, he chose for the initial phase of conflict the desolate scenery and association of that unlovely seaside town. For in his adult relationship with the girl he calls Maisie, in *The Light that Failed*, Kipling was early to recognize that, disastrously, and by another door, he had re-entered none other than the House of Desolation.[1]

Maisie, in the opening chapter of the novel, is an orphan who shares with Dick Heldar the rigours of Aunty Rosa's household in Campbell Road. She is presented to us at the stage which Trix had reached, when she had begun to chafe against the limitations of being 'only a girl': to envy, passionately, the freedom of the 'unduly

[1] In his biography Professor Carrington reveals that Maisie, one Florence Garrard, was in fact a girl whom Kipling first met as a boarder in Mrs Holloway's house at Southsea.

favoured' boys: a freedom denied to her, however ardent her desire to compete and to excel. The note of aggression, of competitiveness, is sounded at the outset; and it verges, rapidly, on the lethal, for Dick and Maisie are discovered, with illicitly purchased cartridges, at pistol-practice on the sea-shore with a second-hand revolver. Vividly, love and hostility flicker between the adolescent couple: and Dick has only just emerged from that phase in which he took a sadistic joy in teasing a companion who, shackled by the conditions of her sex, was unable, effectively, to retaliate. It is in an atmosphere so charged that, when it is her turn to handle the pistol, Maisie narrowly misses killing her friend and tormentor. Half stunned, the sting of the powder still on his cheek: 'You nearly blinded me,' the boy exclaims. The theme of blindness is emphasized a second time, after he has declared his love for her, and they have exchanged kisses. 'A gust of the growing wind drove the girl's long black hair across his face . . . and for a moment he was in the dark, – a darkness that stung.'

Ten years elapse before Dick and Maisie meet again: accidentally, in London. The element of competitiveness, submerged in the pleasure of an unexpected reunion, reappears almost at once. For Dick, it turns out, is an artist; and despite the fact that in the old days at Southsea he had loudly derided her attempts at drawing, Maisie, too, has persisted in making art her career. But as this point Dick scores again, and heavily. For whereas Maisie after years of dogged work has won no recognition whatsoever, the public and the critics alike have been electrified, of late, by the brilliance of Dick Heldar's portraits of the British soldier at work and at play.

Poor Dick's moment of 'fine, rank, vulgar triumph' is, however, short-lived. Maisie dislikes his pictures, which, she says, 'smell of tobacco and blood'. She is interested in his success only in so far as she can discover the means to emulate it. Little else matters to her. Sensing only too well his attitude to what he contemptuously calls 'Woman's Art', she sees Dick's professed love for her as a trap, designed, expressly, to ensnare and to frustrate her. Vainly, throughout the book, Dick argues and pleads with her: an argument, unconcluded, that was to spill over into the novel that followed in close succession upon *The Light that Failed*. This book, *The Naulahka*, was written in collaboration with Wolcott Balestier: but in those final chapters, which, as circumstances attest, are attributable to Kipling alone, the wrangling continues; and goaded by Nick Tarvin's insistence that she shall give up her career in order to become his wife, Kate Sheriff pleads her own and Maisie's case simultaneously:

'Suppose I ask you to give up the centre and meaning of *your* life? Suppose I ask you to give up *your* work? And suppose I offered in exchange – marriage! No, no.' She shook her head. 'Marriage is good; but what man would pay that price for it?'

Although the sober and obstinate Kate – 'Our little maid that hath no breasts' – is described in a verse-heading as 'An alien in the courts of Love', it is nowhere suggested that her flight from marriage is due to an aversion to the physical intimacy therein involved. The case of Maisie, however, as Dick Heldar finds to his cost, is at once more complex and more intractable. For if Dick, in his turn, is less unscrupulous than Nick Tarvin, he is also less robust. 'We've both nice little wills of our own, and one or

Childhood

1 Rudyard Kipling at around the time of his sixth birthday, when he first went to live in the 'House of Desolation' at Southsea

2 *Opposite* Kipling's mother, Mrs J. L. Kipling,
formerly Alice Macdonald

3 Amateur theatricals in India: Alice Kipling on the
extreme right

4 Rudyard Kipling on his mother's knee, 1866

5 *Opposite* John Lockwood Kipling (1837–1911)

6 *Right* 'A wood-carver': drawing by John Lockwood Kipling, Simla 1870

7 *Below* The Mayo School of Art, Lahore, at the turn of the century: a metal-working class

8 *Opposite top* The Kiplings' house at Lahore

9 *Opposite bottom* The Durbar Room at Osborne House, Osborne, Isle of Wight

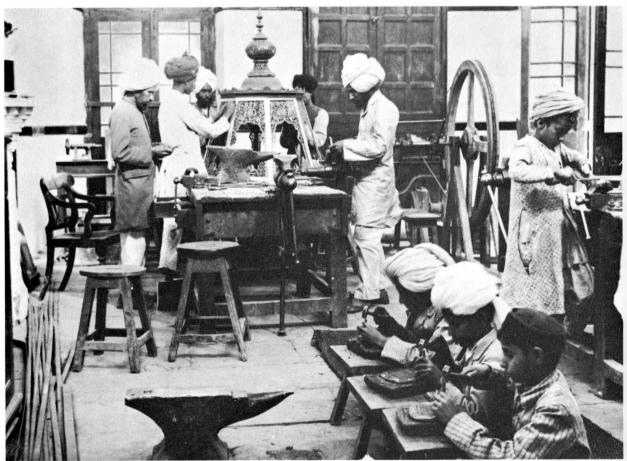

10 John Lockwood Kipling's book-plate, done by himself

EX LIBRIS

FUMUS GLORIA MUNDI

J·L·K

JOHN LOCKWOOD KIPLING

11 Lorne Lodge, Southsea, where Kipling lived 1871–7. 'A new small house smelling of aridity and emptiness . . .' (*Something of Myself*)

other of us has to be broken,' he tells Maisie at the outset. It is not Maisie who is
destroyed. Very early, by her unremitting preoccupation with her work, by the invin-
cible coldness of her character, she succeeds in reducing Dick to a condition in
which the erstwhile confident young braggart turns on her silently the 'look of a
beaten hound waiting for the word to crawl to his mistress's feet'. The degradation
is total: deprived of all initiative in the relationship, Dick is allotted the feminine and
subservient rôle that he accepts with a meekness strange in a man seasoned by camp
and battlefield, by the variegated life of a dozen foreign ports, but not so incomprehensible, perhaps, in this (surely) atypical war correspondent, who at the approach of
a regiment of the Guards cannot refrain from crying out in ecstasy, 'Oh, my men! –
my beautiful men!'

Since *The Light that Failed* contains so faithful an account of the circumstances,
personal and professional, of Kipling's life in the London of 1890, there is no reason
to doubt that Maisie, too, is a life-like portrait. If the Victorian reviewers complained,
however, that she was not convincing, it was because such women were not yet a fully
established type, either in life or in literature. When *Jude the Obscure* was first published in Germany, Thomas Hardy received a letter from a prominent critic in that
country. Sue Bridehead, the critic wrote,

was the first delineation in fiction of . . . the woman of the feminist movement – the slight,
pale 'bachelor' girl – the intellectualised, emancipated bundle of nerves that modern conditions were producing, mainly in cities as yet; who does not recognise the necessity for most
of her sex to follow marriage as a profession . . .

In one respect, the critic was wrong: Sue was not the first. Maisie had preceded her
by at least four years: and although Sue Bridehead, the work of Hardy's maturity, is
an infinitely subtler and more complex portrait than the sketch so rapidly and angrily
roughed out by a boy in his twenties, there is, nevertheless, a marked affinity between
the two women. Physically, they are as alike as sisters: equally small and slight, with
the same dark hair and thin, vivid lips. Both have been tomboys in youth; both, in
later life, have taken up some form of art as an occupation. The major affinity, however, lies at a deeper level of experience. Like Sue Bridehead, Maisie has an uncon-
querable aversion to the conditions of sexual love. Once, and once only, does the adult
Dick succeed in kissing the woman he has loved for so long. The reaction is a violent
one: Maisie is both furious and terrified: months later, at the mere recollection of the
episode, she fiercely brushes her mouth against the sleeve of her nightgown, as if to
erase even the memory of so intolerable a contact. The implications of that gesture are
fully and tragically realized in the scene in which Sue leaps from her bedroom window,
rather than accept, once more, what is to her the torture of a husband's embrace.

The story of Dick Heldar, it will be found, has a close affinity with that of the
young Christminster graduate who falls in love with Sue Bridehead. For fifteen
months, Sue shares the young man's room, his income, his books, his possessions;
refusing all the while, with 'the elusiveness of her curious double nature', to be his
mistress: with the result that, exhausted by an 'epicene tenderness' which, in effect,

takes all and concedes nothing, the young man sickens and dies: as Jude, in his turn, will perish when his destiny is finally linked with one 'so uncarnate as to seem at times impossible as a human wife to any average man'. This incapacity, Maisie shares; and it is not unfitting, perhaps, that in presenting her, Kipling – at once her creator and her victim – has seen fit to divest her of all attributes save one: the baleful power of *La Belle Dame Sans Merci* to blight the human virtue of the mortal she aimlessly ensnares.

By the time this stage is reached, the light, reduced, of late, to an uneven flicker, has failed altogether. Dick is now blind; the effect of a sword-cut in the Sudan, the eye-specialist tells him, unaware that Maisie, as a lethal force, has antedated that campaign by as many as ten good years. For it is made abundantly plain at the outset that the power-cut which gives the book its title is the handiwork of Maisie alone: that it is her antagonism, her usurpation, at every juncture, of the dominant rôle, which have reduced an over-confident, over-successful young man to darkness and to impotence: a condition which leaves this minor Samson no other solution than to grope his way back to the battlefield, where, aspiring, like an aphrodisiac, the smell of gunpowder and slaughter, he achieves a self-sought death at the hands of his friend, the enemy.

As for Maisie (in a final scene, she has taken advantage of Dick's blindness to slip away and leave him for good) she is disposed of in a single sentence. Curtly, 'And that is the end of Maisie,' wrote Rudyard Kipling. Not quite. A belated echo of *The Light that Failed* theme was to make itself heard twenty years later, and from an unexpected quarter. The children's book, *Rewards and Fairies*, published in 1910, contains a story called 'The Knife and the Naked Chalk'. It is a Promethean tale of a primitive Briton, who desires a new and potent weapon, the Magic Knife perfected by a neighbouring tribe. In exchange for the knife, the Priestess of the tribe exacts from him a major sacrifice: with an iron knife heated in the flame she puts out his right eye. Thus maimed, but armed with the Magic Knife, he returns to his own tribe. Regarding him now as a God, men shrink from his shadow, and the maiden he loves takes advantage of his part-blindness to slip away and leave him to his fate. Maimed and deserted, he falls into the darkness of delirium. He is tended by his mother.

When my spirit came back I heard her whisper in my ear, 'Whether you live or die, or are made different, I am your Mother.' That was good – better even than the going away of the sickness. Though I was ashamed to have fallen down, yet I was very glad. She was glad too. Neither of us wished to lose the other. There is only one Mother for the one son.

Rudyard Kipling, as we know, suffered a serious breakdown in consequence to the strain and frustration of those early months in London. The above passage may profitably be compared with the dedication that adorns the first English edition of *The Light that Failed*. There are three verses. The last of these runs:

> If I were damned of body and soul,
> I know whose prayers would make me whole,
> *Mother o' mine, O mother o' mine!*

Janet Adam Smith
BOY OF LETTERS

IN January 1878 Cormell Price helped William Morris and Edward Burne-Jones organize the Workmen's Neutrality Demonstrations at Islington and Exeter Hall, to protest against Disraeli's policy of intervention in the Russo-Turkish war. The war-party was cock-a-hoop with 'We don't want to fight but by Jingo if we do'; the peace-party retaliated with a song written by Morris to the tune of 'The Hardy Norseman's Home of Yore'. The Islington meeting was noisy, and Morris reported that, 'it quite refused to cheer the Empress Brown'.

That same month Rudyard Kipling, a spectacled boy of twelve who had enjoyed six years of heaven with his parents in India, and survived six of hell with foster-parents in Southsea, arrived at the United Services College of which Cormell Price was headmaster – indeed, travelled down with Price from London a day or two after the anti-war meetings, The anti-imperialist, anti-jingo friend of the Pre-Raphaelites took in the boy who was to become the darling of the jingoes and imperialists. Boy and master were, and remained, the best of friends.

This is the first odd thing about Kipling's schooldays.

United Services Proprietary College Ltd was a public school on the cheap. It was founded in 1874 by a group of retired Army officers with sons destined for the Services, who could not afford the fees at existing schools. At Westward Ho! on Bideford Bay – a bathing resort (named after Kingsley's novel) which had never caught on – they 'found a real bargain' as Stalky's original later put it: a row of twelve lodging houses, five storeys high. They added on a gymnasium, which also served for chapel and assembly hall, and that was that. No ancient buildings, no old pieties, no sweetness and light: all was raw, functional and bracing. Two hundred boys were needed to keep the place solvent, so to the sons of Army officers, who made up about three-quarters of the school, were added a number of tough boys who had been thrown out of other schools. To run the place, the founders chose Cormell Price, head of the modern side of Haileybury; to them his chief recommendation was his outstanding success as a coach for the Army Entrance examination. For this was the function of Westward Ho!: not to turn out Christian gentlemen, or muscular Christians, but to get the boys through the competitive examination which, since 1871, had become the gateway to a commission – and to get them through direct from school, and cut out the expense of a London crammer, who might charge up to £300 a year.* The Army Class was allowed to smoke (out of doors) not through any liberal notions, but because at this stage the school was in direct competition with the crammers' shops, where smoking was common form.

So Cormell Price was appointed, and Price (with the job lot of staff that he had collected) got his boys into the Army; but what an odd fish to be so successful a recruiting officer! Burne-Jones had been a friend from their schooldays at King Edward's, Birmingham; William Morris, from Oxford. 'Dearest Crom', wrote Morris from Avranches, in the long vacation of 1855, telling Price all about Chartres,

* I have not been able to discover the fees at the foundation of United Services College: but it seems likely that they were slightly lower than those at Haileybury, which in 1874 were £24.10.0 a term.

Dreux, Evreux and Rouen, and signing 'most loving, Topsy'. Price, with Swinburne, was recruited by Morris and Rossetti to help in the redecoration of the Oxford Union; with Morris, Rossetti, R. W. Dixon and Burne-Jones, he contributed to *The Oxford and Cambridge Magazine* of 1856. After Oxford he studied medicine in London, then, deciding he would never make a doctor, went off to Russia for three years as tutor in the Orloff-Davidoff family, bringing home a great love of Russia and her literature. He kept up his old friendships: Morris and Burne-Jones stayed with him at Broadway – 'at Crom Price's Tower among the winds and the clouds' – and in 1880 he was one of the party of special friends who rowed with Morris from Kelmscott House in Hammersmith to Kelmscott Manor at Lechlade. It was through these friendships that he came to have Kipling as a pupil. Mrs Kipling was a sister of Georgina Burne-Jones; 'Uncle Crom' was a family friend. In sending their son to Westward Ho! the Kiplings were choosing the headmaster rather than the school.

Westward Ho! had been going for four years when Kipling arrived. What he was like in this setting is mainly to be gathered from the memories of his two school friends Dunsterville (*Stalky's Reminiscences*, 1928) and Beresford (*Schooldays with Kipling*, 1936), and to a lesser degree from his own (*Something of Myself*, 1937). There is also his short, early article of 1893, 'An English School'. As Dunsterville warns, 'the memories of old gentlemen over sixty are not to be entirely trusted'; but a clear impression come through, of a boy who was as assured of becoming a writer as his contemporaries were of becoming soldiers.

The school was bleak enough: 'Even by the standards of those days it was primitive in its appointments, and our food would now raise a mutiny on Dartmoor. I remember no time, after home-tips had been spent, when we would not eat dry bread, if we could steal it from the trays in the basement for tea.' But it was healthy, no epidemics were remembered, and both Kipling and Dunsterville emphasize that it was 'a notably "clean" school'. Kipling later attributed this to the open curtainless dormitories, through which masters (and draughts) constantly found their way, and to Price's policy of 'sending us to bed dead tired' – tiredness due not only to games, but to strenuous bathing off the Pebble Ridge, runs and paperchases and a good deal of noisy ragging, to which the headmaster turned a blind eye.

Cleanness did not rule out bullying. When Dunsterville went to the school in 1875 at the age of ten (his father was one of the founders) 'bullying was rampant. One amusement for older boys was to hold the little ones out of the top-storey windows by their ankles.' Because of it, Kipling's first year 'was not pleasant'. Not only boys bullied: there was a dreadful chaplain, Campbell, whose face Dunsterville could never recall 'without an expression of ferocity in it, nor his hand without a cane in it'. When he preached a soppy farewell sermon, many of his former victims were touched, if not to forgiveness, at least to let bygones be bygones. Not Kipling: 'Two years' bullying is not paid for with half-an-hour's blubbering in a pulpit.'

Within this unpromising framework Kipling made his own life and went his own way. His short sight and spectacles – 'Gigger', for 'Giglamps', was his school name –

9

let him off games: he had much free time, and he read greedily. From the start he made no bones about his tastes and his intentions: 'a wild desire to embrace English literature as a whole and French as far as possible'. Fresh from *Tom Jones* and *Atalanta in Calydon*, he simply could not understand other boys' tastes for *Jack Harkaway*, or *Ned Kelly, the Ironclad Bushranger*: 'it really got on his nerves'. He did not brag of Uncle Topsy who told him saga-tales, or of having met Browning, but he made it plain that there was a world where men wrote books and painted pictures and that this was where he already half-belonged – and not the world of school. In this attitude he was supported by Beresford, a detached and mature Irish boy, whose quiet insolence infuriated masters. When the two of them collected Dunsterville as a third to share a study, Kipling had his secure base: two friends who let him be himself, and write his poems in his Russia-leather, gilt-edged, cream-laid manuscript books, without mockery or intrusion. Beresford and Dunsterville were in the First XV, but they knew better than to play their matches over again in the study.

Within that study the gods were literature and art. As man of letters, Kipling propagated his enthusiasms: for Chaucer, the Elizabethans, Dryden, Browning, Poe, Whitman, Edwin Arnold's *Light of Asia*. As aesthete, he ordered the redecoration of the study: stencilled dadoes of Greek honeysuckle and key patterns, olive-green and grey-blue paint, Japanese fans, glass pictures, odd bits of china picked up in Bideford – 'we all drank our cocoa out of old Worcester or Rockingham or Crown Derby'. (They all hoped to pick up treasures in junk-shops; but, as Beresford wryly noted later, the treasures were under their noses, in the waste-paper basket crammed with Kipling's rough drafts.) When Kipling hung out a banner made of an umbrella decorated with sunflowers and lilies, 'we felt we were giving the Coll. some of the romance of Venice'. The other aesthetic study was the Head's, in the middle house of the row, with its Pre-Raphaelite reproductions and Rossetti drawings of Janey Morris.

Kipling imposed his values on his two friends, and the three of them, so Beresford considered, imposed something of their outlook on the school as a whole:

At Westward Ho! during the Gigger regime games and athletics were not placed above brains in the estimation of many of the boys. It was necessary indeed to be a little apologetic about sports and repetitions of *mens sana in corpore sano*, or whatever it is, and to be constantly aware that in the large world outside the school, there were very different standards operative from those of the football field or the cricket pitch.

He thought that the bullying of smaller boys greatly diminished, as a result of Kipling's attitude: what a silly and childish occupation for boys who would soon be men!

The three boys accepted the authority that made sense in terms of their future – for instance, masters who made them work hard to get through the Army exam – but had little use for the authority that was only relevant to the limited world of school. They broke rules and bounds to suit themselves, and were very ingenious in not being found out. Kipling managed to appear fairly law-abiding, said Beresford, because it would be most undignified for a man of letters to be whacked by boy prefects or chivvied about by retired army sergeants. But he made it plain to the prefects and games captains – who decorated *their* studies with football caps and team photographs – what he thought of them and their toys.

Ridicule, satire and mimicry were his weapons, as they were in his dealings with the masters. Chief of these antagonists was Mr Crofts, a BNC man who had twice won the Diamond Sculls and whom Price had recruited as a first-class Latin coach. He too knew the use of ridicule and satire. Beresford recounts a major confrontation after Kipling had called Whitman the greatest living poet – but such attacks seem not to have hurt Kipling deeply: they were pinpricks compared to the moral and physical tortures of the Southsea years. And they could be relished for their vocabulary and style, for what they could add to Kipling's own armoury of words and ripostes. The running engagement between master and boy was really a mock battle, and Kipling kept on good terms with Crofts after he left school, sending him copies of his poems from India. 'He taught me to loathe Horace for two years; to forget him for twenty, and then to love him for the rest of my days.' During the two years of loathing, Crofts set Kipling an imposition for a shocking Horace translation; Kipling retaliated with a version of *Donec eram tibi* in Devonshire dialect. Crofts knew it was no future officer he was squashing: he hurled *Men and Women* at Kipling's head, with sarcastic words about 'Gigadibs, the literary man', but expected Kipling to keep the book and let him use his library, where the boy found 'all the poets from Chaucer to Matthew Arnold'.

Gentler encouragement came from the chaplain, Willes (the sadistic Campbell's successor), who treated Kipling in his last terms as the man-of-the-world he felt himself to be: they would talk late over pipes and whisky, and 'our bard would turn up in the dormitory about midnight, a little squiffy'. The Head too kept a very kindly eye on his friends' son. He revived the school *Chronicle* for Kipling's benefit, giving the embryo writer a chance to practise his different styles in public and, like Crofts, let him have the run of his library: the discoveries which the boy made there included Hakluyt and Peacock, Pushkin and Lermontov (in French translations).

By the school in general, Kipling was accepted as their bard, whose job it was to write the verses describing the year's events which everybody sang to the tune of *Vive la Compagnie* at the end of the annual theatricals. By boys and masters – even the master who prophesied he would die in a garret as a scurrilous journalist – he was accepted as the school's man of letters. So, original and eccentric as he was – even in his looks, with his pebble glasses and his early black moustache – Kipling was never an outsider. Nor was he really at odds with the prevailing ethos of the school. The place was purposeful, as he was, though to a different end; and there was little sentiment or tradition to offend, though some masters had tried to import a bit from other schools. Boys were there to be got into the Army, and there was no need to work them up about it. Cormell Price distrusted patriotic emotion as much as he did religious – 'agnosticism rather hung about him'. The boys were following their fathers into jobs; they were not encouraged to dream of dying gloriously for their country. A debate on the merits of the Army and the Navy was soon reduced to a discussion of which service had the best food.

His face firmly set towards literature, Kipling showed no particular interest in his friends' military futures. He told Beresford that war was no subject for poetry. The verses he wrote for the school to see were squibs, limericks, parodies. The poems he wrote for himself and sent to his parents (who printed them in Lahore in 1881, without his knowledge) were about love, nature, death, despair. But in his last year at school he startled his two friends with an uncharacteristic set of verses: a loyal Ode, written on the occasion of an attempt to assassinate Queen Victoria in March 1882, and entitled 'Ave Imperatrix'. It was published in the *Chronicle*, and purported to speak for the school. Beresford (though Dunsterville later disagreed) was sure that Kipling's tongue was in his cheek and that one of his motives was to annoy Crofts, no admirer of the Empress. What Kipling kept dark at the time is that, even to the title, it was an echo of a poem by Oscar Wilde, published the year before (and perhaps discovered by Kipling in Cormell Price's study?):

> The brazen-throated clarion blows
> Across the Pathan's reedy fen,
> And the high steeps of Indian snows
> Shake to the tread of armed men . . .
>
> Such greeting as should come from those
> Whose fathers faced the Sepoy hordes,
> Or served you in the Russian snows
> And dying, left their sons their swords.

Which is Kipling? Which Wilde? And was Wilde's tongue too in his cheek?

'You must not be too hopeful of his sticking to any programme but literature,' Cormell Price wrote to Kipling's parents in November 1881. Six months later he was able to tell their son that a place had been found for him on the *Civil and Military Gazette* in Lahore. Not yet seventeen, Kipling stepped straight from school to a man's job. The headmaster who was so successful at packing his boys into Sandhurst and Woolwich played his part too in setting the boy of letters on his way.

Kipling left school in 1882, *Stalky & Co.* was published in 1899: seventeen years, during which he had done his 'seven years hard' on the *Gazette* and the *Pioneer*, observed Mrs Hauksbee and the Gadsbys, fraternized with soldiers three, frequented club, mess-room, and the corridors of power in Simla, and become knowing about India as at school he had been knowing about literature and art. Seventeen years during which – on the strength of this knowingness – he had rocketed to fame, become a voice to be heard; and had changed, or modified, his allegiance. Less pompously than Curzon, but no less firmly, he came to believe that the work of running India 'had been placed by the inscrutable decree of Providence upon the shoulders of the British race'.

This shift in allegiance is neatly charted in a story Kipling wrote in 1890, 'A Conference of the Powers': a confrontation between the established writer Eustace

Cleever and three young subalterns on leave, which takes place in the narrator's London flat. Cleever, who is full of civilian misconceptions as to what the Army actually *does* – 'the whole idea of warfare seems so foreign and unnatural, so essentially vulgar' – listens to the young men's matter-of-fact and underplayed accounts of their doings in India and beyond. 'I haven't seen much,' says one apologetically, 'only Burmese jungle.' ' "And dead men, and war, and power, and responsibility," said Cleever, under his breath.' The young men, who tremendously admire a book of his, carry him off for an evening on the town – at the Empire! He comes back to tell the narrator that it is they, not he, who have been really living. 'Whereby I understood that Eustace Cleever, decorator and colourman in words, was blaspheming his own Art, and would be sorry for this in the morning.' The 'I' of the tale doesn't in the least decry Art; what he – and Kipling – is saying is that the artist should sometimes come out of his comfortable and mutually admiring coterie and look at the men of action on whom his comfort and peace depends. The Sons of Mary should make some effort to understand and interpret the Sons of Martha. By the time he wrote the Stalky stories, Kipling's commitment to literature was no less than it had been at school: but he was now practising his art for a purpose beyond art.

In 1893, for an American paper, *Youth's Companion*, Kipling wrote an account of United Services College, 'An English School'. In it he defended the functional approach to education:

Some of the masters, particularly on the classical side, vowed that Army examinations were making education no more than mark-hunting; but there are a great many kinds of education, and I think the Head knew it, for he taught us hosts of things that we never found out we knew till afterwards. And surely it must be better to turn out men who do real work than men who write about what they think about what other people have done or ought to do.

A scholar may, as the Latin masters said, get more pleasure out of his life than an Army officer, but only little children believe that a man's life is given him to decorate with pretty little things, as though it were a girl's room or a picture screen.

(Did he have the Aesthetes and Decadents in mind? Or even to some extent the Pre-Raphaelites on whom he had been nurtured? I don't think he ever made an open attack on them.) Other aspects of life in Westward Ho! described in the American article were the way rough characters – 'those with whom Cheltenham could do nothing, whom Sherborne found too tough, and whom even Marlborough had politely asked to leave' – were turned into men; the scorn those future soldiers had for anything, like a cadet corps, that smacked of 'playing at soldiers'; the splendours and triumphs of the First XV; the visits of old boys, who would sleep in their old dormitories and tell tales of their new Army life. Above all, in this article, he praised the Headmaster: approachable, understanding, a marvellous trainer and handler of boys to fit them for 'the big race that led into the English Army'. The article ends with some tales of the boys' later exploits in India and Burma – 'it is curious to notice how little the character of the man differs from that of the boy of sixteen or seventeen' – and with five verses of 'Ave Imperatrix', though Kipling does not say that he wrote it. By this time there is no question of tongue-in-cheek, or getting a rise out of anti-imperialist Crofts. Whatever the original motive, Kipling now meant every word of it.

In July 1894, Kipling was back at Westward Ho!, speaking for the Old Boys at Cormell Price's last prizegiving: 'Ours is not a tradition of mere bricks and mortar – of ancient buildings and mediaeval endowments – but rather of direct and individual obligation to the care, tenderness, sympathy, wisdom, insight, and justice of one man – Mr Price.' He talked of the school's reputation, recently confirmed by the late Commander-in-Chief in India, Lord Roberts, for turning out 'a good, trustworthy and efficient type of officer', and went on: 'Indeed our aims are not high! It is not much that we set before us! All that the College – all that Mr Price – has ever aimed at was to make men able to make and keep empires.'

Three years after publishing 'An English School' the idea came to him 'of beginning some tracts or parables on the education of the young. These, for reasons honestly beyond my control, turned themselves into a series of tales called *Stalky & Co.*' Kipling had great faith in the power of the fable to convey a precept: and *Stalky* is as full of precepts as *Tom Brown* or *Eric*, though they are more subtly disposed. Twenty-six years after its publication he wrote in a copy of the book: 'This is not intended to be merely a humorous book, but it is an Education, a work of the greatest value.'

It was education of a very specialized sort: 'to make men able to make and keep empires' – in practice, the India of which Victoria was Empress. (Kipling's boys don't go into the Guards or the Household Cavalry.) What qualities were needed for the situations in which these boys would find themselves: hunting down Pathan raiders; making roads through hostile country; negotiating with a tribal chief; surviving a hard winter in a hill-fort with the passes blocked? How could a school best inculcate and nourish such qualities? To such questions, Kipling provides, in *Stalky*, unorthodox answers.

Nine-tenths of *Stalky* come from the real world of Kipling's boyhood: the twelve bleak houses, the Pebble Ridge, the hide-outs in the furze for quiet pipes and reading, the lighthearted breaking of bounds, the ragging, the lying, the mockery of 'high-minded, pure-souled boys', the scoring-off masters. Games are played down – even more than in life, where Dunsterville and Beresford were both in the first XV. The public-school spirit is mocked – when King starts preaching it in the Head's absence, the boys retaliate by playing marbles, a board-school game! Literature and art are still important to the boys – there must be more literary allusions in *Stalky* than in any other school story. The place is not glamourized: 'We aren't a public school. We're a limited liability company paying four per cent.' What stands out – when one comes back to the stories after discovering all one can about the reality – is the purposefulness of Stalky's world. Kipling as craftsman shaped the raw material of his and his friends' exploits to make good stories ('Unless they please, they are not heard at all' he says of those who write fables); Kipling the teacher shaped them further in a certain direction. Every story is an object-lesson: how to bluff your way out of a tight corner; how to score off a too-confident enemy; how to turn the enemy's strength against himself; how to deal with a bully; how to save your skin. And the lessons will be as relevant in Chitral or Waziristan as among the fields and classrooms of the Coll. This is the burden of 'Slaves of the Lamp, Part II', where Stalky, ten years after school, gets out of a tight corner among the Pathans by using the same tactics with which he once scored against the master King. The boys' campaigns have begun at school, with King, and Prout, and Foxy the drill-sergeant standing in for the real enemies of the future. Sometimes the boys are the rebel tribes, outwitting authority; sometimes, as in 'The Moral Reformers' they are authority, bringing the barbarians to heel.

Whatever rules they break, whatever petty tyrant they mock, they never question the fundamental reason of their being at this particular school: 'We've got to get into the Army or – get out, haven't we? . . . All the rest's flumdiddle. Can't you see?' They are aware of their futures, in an unexcited way. News comes of the death in action of a boy who left a few terms ago: 'How many does that make to us?' Old boys come back on leave with played-down stories of skirmish and rescue: 'There's nothing to tell.' The reader too is jerked into the future with a sudden parenthesis. 'Yet he did not know that Wade minor would be a bimbashi of the Egyptian Army ere his thirtieth year.' ' "What about marchin' in public?" said Hogan, not foreseeing that three years later he should die in the Burmese sunlight outside Minhla Fort.'

The boys never query the end they are destined for – never even wonder why 'the Army examiners gave thousands of marks for Latin' – any more than Kipling queried the British presence in India. The point of the story 'The Flag of their Country' is not just that they despise the patriotic rhetoric of the 'jelly-bellied flag-flapper' MP; it's that they don't need it. They are already dedicated men.

Over all the turbulent scene, godlike, presides the Head. He is breaking his charges in for their future roles (Kipling was very fond of the image of training colts); he knows how much latitude to give, where to bring them up short, caning 'with flagrant injustice' to mark the limits he will tolerate (even though their clever tactics have kept them on the right side of the law) and to accustom them to the notion that the world is not a just place. He prefers the trespasses of the ingenious and enterprising to the 'costive and unaccommodating virtue' of the exemplary prefect. He knows where to encourage, where to ignore. He is in perfect control.

Much in the character of 'Prooshian Bates, the downy bird', is recognizably Cormell Price: approachable, unpompous, chary of emotion, not given to preaching. But the real headmaster of Beresford's and Dunsterville's memoirs seems a much more harassed and less masterful character than this 'nursing mother of jingoes' (Beresford), just as the real school seems a much more casual and ramshackle place than the College of fiction. Dunsterville considered that Cormell Price had been given 'an almost hopeless task': with an unmanageable lot of masters, no say in the selection of boys, no traditions, and no money, his energies were absorbed in keeping the place going at all. What probably did most to save the real College was Price's success in beating the Army examiners. Kipling elevated his headmaster when he put him into fiction, but he did him one 'flagrant injustice'. The mild Cormell Price used the cane sparingly; *Stalky's* Head is a tremendous swisher and thwacker.

No more than real Price or fictional Bates did Kipling like straight preaching; for all that, *Stalky* is pervaded by a very firm ethos. Independence, ingenuity, resourcefulness, disregard for red tape and petty authority, ability to scrape a way out of trouble – these are the virtues held up for admiration, along with some other more orthodox, such as loyalty (particularly to the small group) and a duty to help the oppressed which does not preclude a savage relish in kicking the oppressor. Boys with these virtues have real authority, and influence for good and evil, far beyond the authority and influence of prefects, 'the giddy palladiums of public schools'. But – and here is one of the odd things about *Stalky* – how many boys do consistently demonstrate these virtues? Three – out of two hundred! Stalky's and his friends' imaginative unorthodoxy is set off by the slow-witted orthodoxy of the 'high-minded pure-souled boys', the prefects and games captains whose ideals the three ridicule and whose authority they flout. Yet Kipling wanted to show *all* the boys as potential officers of initiative and resource. 'There's nobody like Stalky,' says Dick Four, in the second 'Slaves of the Lamp' story, after recounting Stalky's exploits among the Pathans (which include making puns in Pushtu and topping off an argument with a smutty story); but Beetle, now the narrator, won't have this: 'India's full of Stalkies – Cheltenham and Marlborough and Haileybury chaps – that we don't know anything about.' Here I think Kipling the fabulist was making a belated stand against Kipling the story-teller (we remember his words about the 'parables in the education of the young' that turned 'for reasons honestly beyond my control' into the Stalky stories). The story-teller implies that there was only one Stalky – and Co.; the fabulist wants us to understand that they were turned out in numbers at 'The School Before its Time' (as he called it in his autobiography) and the other public schools most like it. The story-teller seems often the nearer to the truth of Kipling's own lived experience at Westward Ho!

The *Stalky* ethos was raw, practical, and unsentimental, and it shocked a good many patriots and loyal Old Boys, who preferred the more refined outlook of that other writer of empire, Henry Newbolt. Newbolt too saw the road that led from school to the frontier, but he saw it more conventionally, more sentimentally, and with far less knowledge of what the frontier actually was like. In poems like 'Clifton Chapel', 'Vitaï Lampada', 'He Fell Among Thieves', he presents his boys as strengthened for their service by the pieties of chapel, college, ancient manor, village church – and playing fields.

> The sand of the desert is sodden red, –
>   Red with the wreck of a square that broke; –
> The Gatling's jammed and the Colonel dead,
>   And the regiment blind with dust and smoke
> The river of death has brimmed his banks,
>   And England's far, and Honour a name,

But the voice of a schoolboy rallies the ranks:
'Play up! Play up! and play the game!'

Newbolt's soldier who fell among Afghan thieves spends the last night of his life thinking about his school, his college, and his old country home. Stalky, one feels, would have used his night to talk his way out of trouble, with Afghan puns and smutty stories. Newbolt celebrates the solitary hero, honourable and brave, making a gallant gesture in a desperate (and conventionally conceived) situation – for England's sake. Kipling celebrates the ingenious and crafty hero, working with others in a vividly realized situation – to do his job. Newbolt's poetical heroes tend to die, nobly; Kipling's prose ones to survive, craftily. Kipling's were more use to the Empire. 'Thanks to me,' as Mulvaney says after a frontier skirmish, 'there was no casualties an' no glory.'

I have not been concerned in this essay to make a critique of *Stalky*, or to offer a value judgement; only to show how Kipling reshaped his school experiences, and to what end. He dedicated these fables of Empire to Cormell Price, the anti-imperialist of 1878. It was a long way from the meeting at Islington that refused to cheer the Empress Brown.

A. W. Baldwin
JOHN LOCKWOOD KIPLING

'My father was a great man,' wrote Rudyard Kipling to a friend, after the funeral of John Lockwood Kipling.

The family was of Yorkshire farming stock. At Pickering, on 6 July 1837, a first son was born to Frances Lockwood, daughter of a Cleveland architect and wife of the Reverend Joseph Kipling, a young Wesleyan minister. One name only was given to the child: John. It was John himself who, when he grew up, added a second: Lockwood. In the space of the next ten years another son, Joseph, and four daughters, Jane, Ann, Hannah and Ruth were born, some of whom lived to an embarrassingly poor old age. Young Joseph, after an exemplary career at school, became a dressmaker in Malton. All the family except John chose to abide in Yorkshire. Both parents died at Skipton; he in 1862, she in 1886.

It was in the high noon of Wesley's great creation, which had brought comfort to so many of the hopelessly poor, that the boys received a sound education in Latin, French, mathematics and scripture at Woodhouse Grove, the Northern Connexional School, nobly built facing the moorland hills near Bradford.

There seems nothing to be discovered about John's adolescent years, and all too little about his young manhood, but attendance at some technical or art school is likely to have followed Woodhouse Grove, which he left at the age of fourteen. What is certain, in view of his later reputation in India, is that he must have put in an heroic amount of reading and enquiring on his own account. He won a national scholarship, which enabled him to begin designing and modelling under Philip Cunliffe Owen at the earliest art schools and museum in South Kensington. It is known that some years later he took a job as an artist in pottery at Burslem, in Staffordshire. There, where the Wedgwood Memorial Institute displays on its façade some of his early work, he was employed by Pinder, Bourne & Co., soon to be absorbed by the growing firm of Doulton, then at Lambeth. His drawings at that period were almost always marked with the initials J.K. There was never an L for Lockwood.

He returned to South Kensington in the summer of 1863 to play a valuable part as an architectural sculptor in the development of the new buildings which were inspired by the Prince Consort and are now known as the Victoria and Albert Museum. How valuable that part was may be judged from the fact that there is today, high up on the face of a wall of the inner courtyard, a frieze, designed by Godfrey Sykes in 1910, representing seven of the chief officials and artists concerned. Among these eminent Albertians stands twenty-seven-year-old John Kipling, looking, with his bald head and beard, no less venerable than they.

But we must direct our attention to the Potteries, for it is the marital consequence of his sojourn there that strikes the imagination of posterity. This is how the cards came out.

The Reverend Frederic William Macdonald began his first circuit at Burslem at the age of twenty in 1862. It was not so much the fact that both his and John Kipling's fathers were Wesleyan ministers, as that they had literary and other tastes in common, which drew these two clever young men together. Visits to Macdonald by his attractive sisters from Wolverhampton led to their introduction to Kipling. Alice, the eldest, especially touched his heart; and at a Pinder family picnic beside Lake Rudyard, a few miles north of Burslem, the moment of revelation occurred. Both agreed afterwards that the catalyst was a passage from a not yet well-known poet, Robert Browning, in reference to a gaunt old horse nearby: lines quoted by John and promptly continued by Alice.

Soon after this event leading to their engagement in the summer of 1863 John travelled down, by way of Wolverhampton, for presentation to the Macdonald parents to take up his job at South Kensington. It was not for nearly two years that marriage was deemed prudent, and this was made easier by his appointment as Professor of Architectural Sculpture at an art school newly endowed in Bombay by a rich Indian gentleman: an appointment terminable at pleasure after three years' trial.

The wedding took place at Saint Mary Abbot's old church, Kensington, on 18 March. In the register John described himself as an 'artist' and 'of full age'. Alice, by the way, was the elder by about three months. He signed his name that day 'John Lockwood Kipling', with an elaborate twirl of the J such as he used sometimes to execute, rather in the style of ornamental iron-work; and, according to Alice's sister, who was a witness, the ring was as thick as a costermonger's.

After the wedding-breakfast, just across the street at 41 Kensington Square, the house of another of Alice's sisters, Georgiana Burne Jones, John hurried off to fetch his luggage from his rooms at 35 Pelham Street. He lost a key and left his money behind before the couple got away to the railway station in a hansom-cab, bound for Skipton and then Wolverhampton. From there John returned to London for a few days' business, missed his train back, and was rejoined by Alice on 4 April in good time for them both to embark on the 12th at Southampton in the *Ripon*. Punctuality was one art that John never mastered.

Hitherto in this account one has had to rely for facts upon a very few private and public notes and documents; but from 1865 onward some of John's picturesque letters still exist, although everything written to his son and his son's family will almost certainly have been destroyed – as seemed to them best; and from 1875 there is a further source in a manuscript of one who became a close friend of all those Macdonald sisters: Miss Editha Plowden, whose brother, for whom she was keeping house during some of the Indian period, occupied a judicial post in Lahore.

Some of the earliest words posted to England from John's pen were to his twenty-year-old sister-in-law, Louisa, written on the back page of a letter from Alice. He portrayed a Bombay scene in the earliest days of his new life, before he had become familiar with the divers Indian races or any of their tongues: 'I stood in the thick of a dense native crowd watching the gas lighted the other night and grieved deeply that I could not understand the buzzing conversation round me. "Fire-box" was perpetually repeated & I made out that the gasometer was regarded as a big box full of fire that sent out flames along the pipes. I have another seriatim question to ask . . .' which was about 'godmothering' the coming baby.

Bombay, however it may have looked to the newcomers, John described long afterwards as 'a blazing beauty of a city . . . I never see it but to renew my conviction that it is the finest city in the world in so far as beauty is concerned' – a bold verdict indeed for one noted for his moderation. In that city the modelling professor from Yorkshire 'laid the artistic foundations with splendid thoroughness of the largest and most comprehensive School of Arts and Crafts in India – one of the largest in the world'. Those are the words of a writer in *The Kipling Journal* sixty years later. John made no attempt to foist English art upon the native, but with his wise culture he fostered the local pottery, weaving, carving and all kinds of fabrication and depiction. Both he and his wife threw themselves into the life of the country and, with sound health to back them, brought well-balanced minds to meet all situations.

J. H. Rivett-Carnac, in his *Many Memories*, observed that the Kiplings' knowledge of all things Indian was superior to that of many senior officials, and that they could both 'see persons and events from the humorous side and were the most excellent company'. Moreover, whether or not it was known to their neighbours, both having as Alice put it, 'a twist for scribbling', they took to writing: tales and articles for the Punjab press, for which John was one of the local correspondents, and for such English magazines as would accept their offerings.

Their son, Rudyard, was born in Bombay at the end of December 1865; Alice, known as Trix, was born in Burne Jones's house at Fulham in June 1868; and there came in April 1870, a second son, named John, who died immediately.

In 1875, John was appointed Principal of the new Mayo School of Art and Curator of the Museum at Lahore. Again he had to build from practically nothing, and do it in an area which, as that great servant of India, Sir Walter Lawrence, said, would 'try the temper of angels'.

John proceeded on the same lines as at Bombay, with a few pupils in a shabby one-storeyed house of large rooms, training and working, until he was able to bequeath, eighteen years later, a flourishing school in splendid buildings of his own design. Throughout this time his routine work was varied by organizing sections of exhibitions all over the world, and by the normal recurrence of leave either in England or at Himalayan mountain resorts.

Early in the following year he fell sick with fever, which turned into typhoid, the scourge of Lahore. Nothing but Alice's unresting devotion saved his life. Had he died, she would certainly have returned to live in England, with consequences to Anglo-Indian literature that may be imagined. His strength not very long restored, John found that he had to play a small but significant part in the preparations for the Durbar to be held at Delhi on New Year's Day, 1877, for the purpose of proclaiming the Queen Empress of India. It had been discovered that he knew something of heraldry, and he was required at short notice to devise and manufacture silk banners for about seventy native princes and a few others including the Viceroy. John and Alice managed to get them done in time. Having in his career seen enough in official quarters of praise and blame unjustly assigned, he professed astonishment at being rewarded with five hundred rupees and a silver medal, counting himself lucky, he said, 'to have escaped a wigging'. Joking apart, the money came in very useful when, shortly afterwards, Alice had to return to England to succour her two small children parentless in Southsea.

In 1882 Rudyard and, in the next year, Trix came out to make their home in their parents' house. Happiness and confidence throve among the four, and literary production more than doubled. They all joined in the publication of *Quartette*, being *The Christmas Annual of the Civil & Military Gazette by Four Anglo-Indian Writers*: prose and verse.

A lifetime's finished work by John Kipling in a variety of arts and crafts, many shared or anonymous, has not left much for the present generation to evaluate. Accuracy was the keynote of his art. Sketches, paintings in sepia, illustrations for books, work in gesso, metal and wood, designs for pottery and other materials, were invented, created, enjoyed, and passed into the artistic deadland of forgotten works. What can be most easily seen today are his illustrations to the two *Jungle Books* and *Kim*. Not so easily found are books on Indian subjects such as *Across the Border or Pathan and Biloch*, by Edward Oliver, and those by Flora Annie Steel, some of which he illustrated.

He designed and worked upon, or supervised, at least two great rooms in the Indian style in England (as well as one at Barnes Court in Simla). The first was in the Duke of Connaught's house at Bagshot Park. The other was the Durbar Room at Osborne House, which Queen Victoria desired John Kipling to create for her. He, being busy enough with his normal work, deputed one Ram Singh to have both of these jobs executed, himself keeping a careful eye on their design and performance, both by correspondence and, whenever in England, in person. On its completion, however, the Queen noted to her secretary that she wished Ram Singh to get all the praise. Whether John on this occasion expected a wigging one does not know.

As to literature, his skill in the use of words was impressive, although no one is likely to accept the son's opinion that the father's was the finer pen. He wrote in his spare time during most of his working life. No verses are to be found; but there is evidence of marked literary style in his admirable *Beast and Man in India*, illustrated by himself, as well as of his learning and his modesty, his tolerance to mankind and his tenderness to beastkind. A magazine romance in a Mediterranean setting, one copy of which is certainly extant, is occasionally interesting where the author betrays his own tastes and prejudices. Its title is *Inezilla*.

He was on the whole a temperate critic; and it is as a critic, and as a critic of critics, in the following instance of his son's latest book, *Kim*, that his temperature may be taken. John had played some part in the story's composition, as he had in earlier works, and had done the illustrations. Readers may remember in the preface to *Life's Handicap* '. . . These tales have been collected from all places and all sorts of people . . . and a few, the very best, my father gave me.' Here is part of a letter about *Kim* written by John in October 1901, to Mr Cope Cornford:

I thought the notices on the whole were pretty good – very good indeed. You shouldn't pump (hot) water unawares upon a gracious public full of nerves – and *Kim* is in some respects pretty considerable a douche – so Indian, so remote, and in appearance so uncaring for the ordinary reader. The kind of reviewer who finds fault because it is what it sets out to be and not a carefully constructed drama with a plot and a finale as the Daily Chronicle man – is pretty futile. But I thought there were some honest attempts to see eye to eye with the writer – which is one attitude a fair reviewer adopts.

Before making an attempt to explore his personality, something should be said of his physical appearance. An article from *The Kipling Journal* of many years ago says that a Mr Dhurandar of Bombay remembers him as 'a tall man of grave appearance and kindly manner'. We must not be misled. He stood, in fact, about five feet three. The kindly manner, indeed an air of benevolence, certainly corresponds with most accounts of him. His own bookplate shows, in relief, a seated profile figure, the left hand supporting an open volume, the right hand the bowl of a briar pipe, while wreaths of smoke swirl about him, not obscuring the words FUMUS GLORIA MUNDI, boldly blocked amidst the puffs; the self-portrait is of a bald Socratic head and features, with pince-nez on the nose.

Miss Plowden has described him in the evenings at Lahore, reading aloud with his beautiful enunciation; reading also French books, which he used to enjoy translating fluently into English as he went along. When making some observation, she says, he had a habit of half closing the lids of his fine grey eyes, leaning his head back and thrusting out his bearded chin.

From aspect, now, to character. The words of Sir Walter Lawrence, in his book *The India We Served*, explain what many felt about John Kipling. Lawrence writes that he was living in the Punjab Club 'next to the room of one of the sweetest characters I have ever known ... When I think of the lines: "His little, nameless, unremembered acts of kindness and of love", I think of wise and gentle John Lockwood Kipling.' Such was his selflessness that his countless acts of all kinds, little or great, were often unremembered.

Neither he nor Alice, both children of ministers and loving fathers, were churchgoers, nor do they leave behind any traces of belief in church dogma. Some attitudes of their parents' congregations had early set their teeth on edge. In John's case there is no lack of evidence of this distaste in his *obiter dicta* and *scripta*, although he always acknowledged the splendid grounding in the Methodist educational system; as well he might. Prudery and sanctimoniousness were his especial poisons.

Two passages in books will serve to indicate family aversion from this religious attitude, one in John's novelette, the other in a tale of Rudyard's from *Life's Handicap*. Chapel experience had cut deep: directly into the father, vicariously into the son. This, from *Inezilla*, must be autobiographical:

... I have knelt with my brow pressed against the back of a rush-bottomed chair in ritualistic Churches in England ... I have bowed my head in baize-lined pews of Dissent; I have knelt at the amateur prayer-meetings of those evangelical ladies and gentlemen who propose to 'unite in prayer' as godless people propose to 'have a little music' or a hand at whist ... I have marvelled at the ravings of methodist ranters round weeping and snuffling victims at the 'penitent bench' ...

The other from *On Greenhow Hill*, a piece of bitter reminiscence from the Yorkshire mouth of Private Learoyd, readers may care to find for themselves. In brief, John

Learoyd and John Kipling had had enough of it. Nevertheless, it must not be assumed that Alice and John were atheists, for most certainly they were not.

Differences of temperament and of circumstance might have prevented the Reverend Fred Macdonald from enjoying much more than a relative regard for his heretical brother-in-law; yet what he writes in *As a Tale that is Told* of the impression that John made upon him is worth attention. Fred warms to 'his gentleness of spirit, his unselfish affection and general lovableness'; but he is also sensible of his rare mental qualities.

His power of acquiring and retaining knowledge was extraordinary. His memory seemed to let nothing slip from its grasp . . . His curiosity, in the nobler sense of the term, was alive and active in almost every field of knowledge. All things interested him. He seemed to know something about everything, as well as everything about some things. He was widely read, and what he read he remembered and had at his disposal . . . He made no show of his knowledge, or oppressed one with it . . . Sometimes with a gentle scepticism he would abate the confidence of those who were too sure of what they knew, or would supplement what he had modestly advanced in a way that showed he had more at his disposal if it were called for.

How successful a father he was need not be discussed, for his son has testified to it again and again. How successful a husband is not so well known, and is more delicate to prove. Miss Plowden's record is practically the only authority on that subject. Though young enough to be their daughter, she had been on terms of close friendship with the Kiplings for half a lifetime.

The coming together of John and Alice had kindled the one constant flame. Alice was said to have become engaged to be married to three or four suitors, and her devout and affectionate father had told her that she was a flirt. The Plowden notes continue: 'John rather enjoyed in later life contemplating his former flames . . . The two were so peculiarly suited . . . their remarkable abilities had been trained in so many directions, their interests were so varied, they could not have been bored if they had tried.' Far apart, as they sometimes had to be, they were desolate.

In 1877, the morning after Alice's departure for England to arrange their children's schooling, John looked 'as though he had cried all night. His voice seemed to have fallen half a tone, and he spoke with a languor that made my heart ache. His office walls were lined with casts from the antique, and, looking at the Venus torso, he said listlessly: "I think I will take her home to live with me." '

John's task in India came to an end in 1893. At the age of fifty-six he and Alice came back to England to set up their first and last Western home, necessarily in more modest state, at the Gables, Tisbury, in Wiltshire, to be close to their friends the Percy Wyndhams, who lived in a large house called Clouds.

Sometimes they felt hungry for the socialities of far Lahore; but on the whole they were busy and serene as ever, so long as their health was good. Rudyard and his American wife spent the first summer or two at Arundell House in the village. Much joyful work in writing and illustrating was done together by father and son in John's garden studio which had been constructed for him. Trix, in an unhealthy mental state, was often with them. Many visits were paid and friends received. John even stayed with the younger Kiplings in South Africa and the United States. Mother-in-law and daughter-in-law were never at ease together. There is no evidence of John's feelings on the relationship. And all the time at Tisbury, as may be supposed, they interested themselves in neighbourly matters.

From Alice's letters to her sister, Louisa Baldwin, one gets the impression that John's health and spirits were not always of the best. Much depended upon how his work was turning out. Yet her last letter, three months before her death and five before his, brought cheering news: '. . . John has finished his Indian types very successfully, and his work is much appreciated . . . He is really very well & *how* he has enjoyed his drawings!'

A few of John's letters to Miss Plowden in the late 1890s and early 1900s are somewhat woebegone: 'I am rather in the dumps just now with liver and nervous depression . . . At this moment if the angel Gabriel appeared I should assure him he couldn't blow his trumpet fit for a Christian to hear.' But after 1903 they brighten, and he is as keenly optimistic as ever; for instance, giving advice on some design of hers: 'I think your study excellent, but for this purpose I should think a more summary kind of treatment with no drawing to speak of would have been as good. Burne Jones used to do what he called Luini Kids with his finger on window panes that were delicious in this fashion – so do the Japs just slices of curves . . . There be millions of cupidities in the Art Library & all over the V. & A. Mus.'

December 1906: 'Hear from Lahore that the Sch: of Art is booming along at a great rate. More numbers, more money (and for the Museum) and all my pet schemes being carried out. They want my portrait to hang up as their Venerable Founder – they don't use those words – sacred to that strong old John Wesley, but similar like.' And that letter is signed with quite an arabesque capital J for the J. L. Kipling.

Extracts from 1907 and 1908 end the series: 'I am shaken to pieces by a persistent cough – really a tobacco cough – which I *could* cure in a week to some extent by giving up smoking – which I haven't the pluck to do.'

And: 'Came here lately a . . . Miss Charlton, a maiden lady of a certain age who for the better preservation of her purse (& virtue) lives at a sort of convent in Kensington Square in which abode of Godliness she gathers all the scandal she can find . . . She was a bore of the first water & a cross-examining bore which I find the worst of all. And she could tell you exactly who was meant in Rud's Simla stories, – and multifold twopenny petty piffle of that kind, which seems a pity, for she has brains . . .

'I wish I had anything cheerful to say of myself but during the last six months I have plunged five years full into old age and decrepitude, with a good deal of perfectly useless, unwarrantable, wicked & therefore uncontrollable discontent.'

Alice died of heart failure, after a few days' sickness on 23 November 1910. John's heart, long since unsound, had little strength to continue without hers. It failed him at Clouds on 26 January 1911; and he was buried beside his wife in Tisbury churchyard.

Was he a great man? Well, it was from him that his son derived his universal curiosity, his prodigious memory, his exacting diligence, his inflexible standards, and much else of like quality. If it is too much to say that John Kipling was a great man, it is not enough to say only that he was the father of a genius.

Nirad C. Chaudhuri

THE FINEST STORY ABOUT INDIA–IN ENGLISH

IF I were to leave it to the reader to name the book, there might be some passing hesitation, a hasty review of alternative claims, but I do not think that in the end the answer would be anything but *Kim*. I would go further and say that in *Kim* its author wrote not only the finest novel in the English language with an Indian theme, but also one of the greatest of English novels in spite of the theme. This rider is necessary, because the association of anything in English literature with India suggests a qualified excellence, an achievement which is to be judged by its special standards, or even a work which in form and content has in it more than a shade of the second-rate. But *Kim* is great by any standards that ever obtained in any age of English literature.

This will come as a surprise from a Bengali, Kipling's *bête noire*, who heartily returned the compliment, and I shall add shock to surprise by confessing that I had not read *Kim* till about three years ago. The only work by Kipling which I had read before was *The Jungle Book*. I read it first when I was only ten years old, and I have never ceased reading it. It is now as much a part of me as are the Arabian Nights, Grimm's Fairy Tales, and Aesop's Fables, or for that matter the Ramayana and the Mahabharata. But I never had the courage or inclination to pass on to Kipling's other books, for I had heard of his 'imperialism' and contempt for Bengalis. I thought I should be hurt by an aggressive display of Anglo-Saxon pride, and while British rule lasted I should have been, because the contempt was both real and outspoken. Anyone curious to sample its expression might as well read a story called 'The Head of the District'.

But the disappearance of British rule has emancipated some, if not all, of us from the political inhibition against Kipling. His dislike for Indians who had received a Western education was both irresponsible and indiscreet, and in the light of what has followed almost foolish. His countrymen are now making such handsome amends for it that we can afford not only to overlook it, but even to refer back to it as a corrective to the new adulation which is perhaps doing us more harm than the old contumely ever did. The contempt made us rise at times to the artistic level of Shylock considered as the representative of a persecuted race, the admiration is making us behave rather like the Rev. William Collins.

There was no originality in Kipling's rudeness to us, but only a repetition, in the forthright Kiplingian manner, of what was being said in every mess and club. His political fads were explicit, and he was never sheepish about them. But his politics were the characteristic politics of the *epigoni*, when the epic age of British world politics was already past, and the British people had ceased to bring about great mutations in the history of the world.

It is curious to note that when Clive was in India and Wolfe in Canada, with the Elder Pitt at their back in Whitehall, English literary men were engaged in writing *Tom Jones* or *A Sentimental Journey*. When England was saving herself by her exertions and Europe by her example, English literature got *Pride and Prejudice* and *Emma*. At a later epoch when Englishmen were still capable of perishing on the road to Jellalabad, bivouacking on the field of Ferozshah while the fate of British India

At Westward Ho!

12 Masters and pupils at Westward Ho!: Kipling, Beresford ('M'Turk'), Dunsterville ('Stalky'), M. H. Pugh ('Prout'), the Headmaster, William Crofts ('King'). Contemporary sketches by G. C. Beresford

17 *Above left* The Rev. J. C. Campbell, chaplain during Kipling's first years at Westward Ho!, distinguished, according to Beresford, by his 'unhesitating hostility to the human species in boy form'

18 *Above right* Sergeant Schofield, drill-instructor at Westward Ho! ('Foxy' in *Stalky & Co.*)

19 Cormell Price, alias 'Uncle Crom', alias the Head

20 M'Turk (G. C. Beresford) in later life

21 Stalky (Major-General L. L. Dunsterville) in later life

trembled in the balance, or winning battles and dying of cholera around Delhi and Lucknow, they wrote *The Pickwick Papers*. After the settling down of British domestic politics, the Roundhead and the Cavalier, the Covenanter and the Jacobite had gone abroad, where they were doing what they were expected to do. In those times English politics had no need to invade literature. The age of imperialism, Conservative and Liberal, had to arrive to make that necessary. The result was an adulteration of each by the other.

But Kipling's politics, which even now are something of a hurdle in the way of giving him a secure place in English literature, and which certainly brought him under a cloud during the last years of his life, are no essential ingredient of his writings. Kipling the writer is always able to rise above Kipling the political man. His imagination soared above his political opinions as Tolstoy's presentation of human character transcended his pet military and historical theories in *War and Peace*. Of course, quite a large number of his themes are drawn from what might legitimately be called political life, but these have been personalized and transformed into equally legitimate artistic themes. It is the easiest thing to wash out the free acid of Kiplingian politics from his finished goods.

Coming to particulars, *Kim* would never have been a great book if it had to depend for its validity and appeal on the spy story, and we really are not called upon to judge it as an exposition in fiction of the Anglo-Russian rivalry in Asia. Kipling's attitude to war and diplomacy had a streak of naïveté and even claptrap in it, which made Lord Cromer, in whom high politics ran in the blood, once call him, if I remember rightly, a cheeky beggar.

The spy story in *Kim* is nothing more than the diplomatic conceit of an age of peace, in which people enjoyed all kinds of scares, including war scares, and even invented them, in order to have an excuse for letting off some jingoistic steam, to ring a change on the boredom of living in piping times of peace. India in the last decades of the nineteenth century was full of all sorts of fanciful misgivings about Russian intrigues and the machinations of the Rajas and Maharajas, which the clever darkly hinted at and the simple credulously believed in. There is an echo of this even in one of Tagore's stories in Bengali.

But in *Kim* this political mode, which Kipling seems to have taken more seriously than it deserved to be, is only a peg to hang a wholly different story, the real story of the book. I wonder if, in spite of their great love for it, Englishmen have quite understood what *Kim* is about. It has often been read piecemeal, as every great story can be, for its details, evocative either of the Himalayas or of the Indo-Gangetic plain. These are so interesting and gripping that the reader hardly feels the need for a larger unifying theme, and does not take the trouble to look for it.

No very great harm is done if *Tom Jones* or *The Pickwick Papers* are read in this fashion, because the larger unity can be supplied by the English reader from his inward consciousness of the world in which the episodes are happening. The setting is all-pervasive, like the sea on which the waves are rolling, or the atmosphere in which

22 *Opposite* Kipling in 1882, shortly before returning to India

separate features are seen in a landscape. But, in the very nature of things, English readers cannot feel the underlying bond of *Kim*, because the story belongs to a far-away and unfamiliar world. So, unless told about it, most of them are likely to be left with a sense of having been tantalized by a half-told story.

I doubt, however, even if Kipling himself was conscious of the design I am going to attribute to him. He was an intuitionist, and I do not think he ever felt the need for intellectualizing his artistic motivation. His imagination worked at white heat, and it worked without analytic reasoning at many levels and on very diverse themes.

There was, for example, the life lived by his countrymen and countrywomen in India, in which work on the plains was counter-balanced by love on the hills. Dealing with the latter, Kipling had an outlet for his ambition to write like Maupassant, and he partly fulfilled it. But this aspect of Anglo-Indian life was so small in scale and so trivial in quality, and the impact on Kipling of other and starker themes was so strong, that his treatment of sex with a P & O luggage label on it never passed from comedy to tragedy. So he escaped the madhouse, and remained in a sense a Maupassant manqué.

Soldiering and administration in India raised him to a higher and more humane level. No one else has brought home more powerfully the grandeur and misery of the dual rôle of the British people in India. But even here Kipling's importance is likely to be more historical than artistic, in spite of the fact that in many stories he achieved the timeless within the framework of what now appears to be time-barred. His greatness in this field lies rather in the creation of individualized national and historical types than true individuals. In this Kipling plays the Racine to Wode-house's Molière.

There is also a Kipling who is not above dealing in literary bric-à-brac from the East, under the influence of the romanticism which I believe is a product of the impact of the Arabian Nights, bowdlerized of course, on the youthful imagination of Occi-dentals. This Kipling, as indeed all Western fanciers of things oriental, is prone to falsify the theme of Eastern love. The story, 'Without Benefit of Clergy', is a typical instance of this falsification. Mr Somerset Maugham has praised this story highly, but I am afraid I do not share his enthusiasm. In its intention the story seems to me to be a wholly undeserved idealization of an Anglo-Muhammadan liaison, and in its execu-tion a piece of decided sentimentality, which if it does not ring wholly false does not ring true either. This weakness makes Kipling romanticize even the bazaar prostitute of India, against whom the military authorities used to warn Thomas Atkins with the utmost realism. We orientals who know oriental love for what it is, are partly amused and partly scandalized by Western attempts to sugar it. Lastly, Kipling was not also completely immune to the abracadabra of Hindu necromancy.

But it is none of these things which constitute the greatness of *Kim*, although even these are suggested here and there in the book. It is the product of Kipling's vision of a much bigger India, a vision whose profundity we Indians would be hard put to it to match even in an Indian language, not to speak of English. He had arrived at a true and moving sense of that India which is almost timeless, and had come to love it.

This India pervades all his books in greater or lesser degree and constitutes the foundation on which he weaves his contrapuntal patterns. In certain books this foundation is virtually the real theme, and so it is in *Kim*. But the book is specially important in this that through it Kipling projects not only his vision of the basic India he knew so well, but also his feeling for the core and the most significant part of this basic India. In order to see what it is, some *a priori* consideration of the Indian scene and Indian life as material for imaginative writing is called for.

On account of its vastness and variety India is treacherous ground for all foreign writers. The English novelist who feels that the material at home has been worn more or less threadbare and comes to India in search of the new and the exotic sees apparently promising subjects everywhere. He meets the odd and the amusing, the pitiful and the pathetic at every turn. There is not a single mile-long stretch, if he walks all the way from Apollo Bunder to Mount Everest, which will not yield enough material to fill many notebooks. The unwary writer is usually caught by the first gin-trap in his path, and writes with awful seriousness or self-conscious art about things on which those who know India will not waste a tear or throw away a smile.

English writers of today are misled even by the conditions of imaginative writing at home. The big themes of English life have apparently been exhausted, and the grand style worked to the full. So what remains for the author out for originality is to skim the odd and the accidental in subject matter, and try the clever or the over-sophisticated manner in treatment. Their example seduces even Indian writers dealing with their own country. Some of them indulge in grotesque Joycean antics when they might have been Homeric. In stark contrast to the literary situation in England, in India it is the big theme and the simple treatment which have remained unexploited – if Kipling is excepted.

It is time to return to them. Great novels can be written about the geography of India alone, assimilating the human beings to the flora and the fauna. There are, for instance, the Himalayas, or if one wants to breathe in a less rarefied air, the wooded hills of the Vindhyas, full of green and dark mystery. Kipling wrote about both, and long before him our greatest Sanskrit poets had done so. Kalidasa's imagination was haunted by the Himalayas, and in one marmoreal phrase he compared their eternal snows to the piled up laughter of Siva. Bhavabhuti, who is only next to Kalidasa, wrote about a part of the Vindhya region: 'Here are the Prasravana Hills, with their soft blue made softer still by the ever-drizzling clouds, their caverns echoing the babbling Godavari, their woods a solid mass of azure, made up of tangled foliage.' This passage, written in the eighth century, matches Kipling's evocation of the gurgling Waingunga and the home territory of the Seeonee pack.

There is also the vast Indo-Gangetic plain, which is green and dun by turns, conforming to the oscillations of peace and anarchy in India. In the green phases men bend over furrows and sheaves, women crowd round the wells, bullock carts creak leisurely along, fat monkeys watch the doings of their distant kinsfolk from the branches of Neem and Sisam, whose tender shoots they pick and munch unhurriedly.

Hardly any form of the power that is keeping the peace is seen anywhere. Occasionally, there is intrusion of power of another kind. A lazy tiger or a bounder of a leopard raids the village byre, but even they are too easy-going to kill more than is necessary to maintain their feline existence and prestige.

So far, cyclically, this phase has alternated with a dun phase, in which the great plain turns khaki. Cavalrymen gallop across it with sloped lances, raising clouds of dust to mark their trail. Man's ferocity outruns his strength. The populace cower in half-ruined villages and thinning scrub, and hyenas carry off children. From their branches the monkeys no longer bear testimony to peace, they stare into the dust haze, shiver and chatter for fear of they-know-not-what hunger-fury that might be lurking in the unseen.

Kipling was equally at home in our plains, hills, and mountains, and like all great novelists he remains firmly ecological. There are in *Kim* not only entrancing descriptions of the Himalayas but a picture of the green phase on the great plain that is uncanny in its combination of romance and actuality. We Indians shall never cease to be grateful to Kipling for having shown the many faces of our country in all their beauty, power, and truth.

As regards the human material the best choice in India is always the simplest choice, namely, the people and their religion. I do not say this because they are obvious. Though ubiquitous, they can be very unobtrusive. The common people of India have through the ages become so adapted to the environment, that they have been absorbed by it. They live like badgers or prairie dogs in their earth, and their religion is as deeply entrenched. This religion is so sure of itself that it does not care about self-assertion, which enables the present ruling class, too Anglicized by half, not only to proclaim the secular state, but even to believe in its existence.

But to those who have an eye for the permanent and a feeling for the elemental, the people and their religion furnish material of a tractable kind. In order to deal with it the Western writer does not need that specialized knowledge and sensibility, to acquire which he has inevitably to de-Westernize himself and turn from a creative artist to a propagandist. Many Europeans have paid this price in trying to explore the higher reaches of Hinduism.

Kipling's artistic and spiritual instincts led him to these elemental and inexhaustible themes, although he may not have been wholly original in his choice, for in this as in many other things he was controlled by the general bias of British rule in India towards the commonalty. But whether completely original or not he stands supreme among Western writers for his treatment of the biggest reality in India, which is made up of the life of people and religion in the twin setting of the mountains and the plain. These four are the main and real characters in *Kim*.

But there is something more as well. The people and religion, the mountains and the plain not only constitute the major features of the physical and moral entity called India, they are also related to one another very intimately. The geography of India exhibits a curious paradox. In northern India there is no intermingling of hill and

32

plain, and in passing from the one to the other a man passes from one world to another. For hundreds of miles the ground does not show any rise at all, and abruptly it soars to snowy heights. At the same time there is an unbreakable articulation between the Himalayas and the Indo-Gangetic plain.

Even Kalidasa, who was ignorant of the true geography of the Himalayas, felt it. He described the Himalayas as a Divine Soul which, dipping in the eastern and western oceans, formed the measuring rod of the earth as known to him. However figuratively expressed, the notion corresponded to a reality in Indian geography, for the entire Indo-Gangetic plain has a northward and snow-ward orientation, and without the Himalayas it would hang loose, to be eroded by winds until the primeval seas which it had filled up came in again.

This unique pattern of separateness and combination is repeated in the relationship between life in the world and religion in India. On the one hand, a Hindu's existence in the temporal order is isolated from his aspirations in the spiritual, while he is in the world he is also of the world, and if he yearns after the spiritual he has to abandon worldly life altogether, even forgetting his name and station in it. In Hinduism the two lives never mingle. This will be disbelieved in the West on account of the widely held notion that spirituality pervades and dominates every aspect of Indian life. This is a fundamental, though natural, mistake. For what really intermingles with worldly life in Hindu society is not religion in the Western sense, but the supernatural in the service of man. Nature's relentless enmity to man in the tropics destroys his self-confidence and leads him to seek the intervention of occult powers, whom he tries to persuade, wheedle, or coerce by means of worship, offerings, and spells, to override natural laws. It is the ever-present spectacle of gods yoked to worldly ends which makes Western observers think that they are seeing an all-pervasive spirituality.

On the other hand, the world is not self-sufficient, not only because even with the supernatural interwoven with it no true spiritual satisfaction can be had out of it, but also because even with the help of the gods the greater majority of men cannot wrest out of the cruel struggle for existence anything beyond a bare survival. So pride of life cannot grow and there is an ever-present sense of mockery in living. Thus, worldly existence hangs in the air like the Indo-Gangetic plain, robbed of all significance, unless it can be given anchorage in true spirituality, which the Hindu imagination has always placed in the Himalayas, the abode of beatitude and salvation. The result is an articulation between worldly life and religion, and the affiliation of this articulation to the geographical articulation between the mountains and the plain, and all the four are fused to make up the highest unity in India.

Kipling took over this unity, with its fourfold articulation, as the foundation of *Kim*, and superimposed the adventitious themes. He had every right to do so. For, once a writer has grasped the fundamental unity, he is free to put anything on it, and it does not matter whether it is the Anglo-Russian rivalry of the nineteenth century or the five-year planning of today. The overpowering background will reduce everything set against it to its right proportions, and the Indian engineers will march across it as fleetingly as the Mavericks.

But to attribute such a design to Kipling is to turn the blunt Anglo-Saxon that he was into a mountebank of the esoteric. I should certainly have been guilty of this offence if I had suggested that Kipling's larger theme, so far as it conforms to my interpretation, was a deliberate affair. It was not, because Kipling wrote his books by living in his subjects, steeping himself in their atmosphere until the interaction of his own being with the surroundings produced a definite quality of the imagination. No great writer ever looks for a subject, collects detail for it, or lays on local colour. He has to experience the particular and the local colour before he has even a feel of the subject. So he builds up his books by an elimination of all details besides those which will force their way in, and not by sprinkling them on the theme from his notebook. Kipling is not that tiresome creature, the notebook novelist of India.

Next, there was the intrinsic quality of his personality. He hit upon the greatest themes in India through his sincere primitiveness, in which there was no archaistic pose. Many Latins have made a fetish of Hindu spirituality, but as soon as they move out of their native logic they slip into a rigmarole which is worse than a Hindu's rigmarole about his own religion. Kipling's perception of Hinduism is the product of a convincing yet mysterious primitiveness. Perhaps it is a northern mystery, to which we who live in the tropics have no key:

> O tell her, Swallow, thou that knowest each
> That bright and fierce and fickle is the South,
> And dark and true and tender is the North.

Kipling had in him more than a touch of the heathenism of the German forests, and he made his way into Hinduism through the long-forgotten common heritage of all the peoples who speak the Indo-European languages. Living in India, he had also become half a *butparast*, idol-worshipper, and it was out of his *butparasti*, idolatry, that he created the amazing *panchayat* or conclave of the gods in the story of 'The Bridge-builders'.

But his heathenism was lighted up by the mysticism of northern Christianity. Kipling was something of a denier of the world, who could scoff at success and failure as equal imposture. But his abnegation had nothing in it of the self-mortification of the Hindu Sadhu, whom the ancient Greeks called gymnosophist, or of the anchorites of Syria and the Thebaid. He was able to raise Hindu asceticism, as in the story of Purun Bhagat, above its bed of spikes, and in the quest of the Lama in *Kim* made the negative renunciation of Buddhism the same as the positive faith of Thomas à Kempis.

The Lama, however, raises a difficulty which must be put out of the way. For it may be asked: Why did Kipling, if it was his purpose to illustrate India spiritually, choose a Tibetan and a Buddhist as its exponent? In reply, the point might be made that Buddhism was also one form of Hindu spirituality. But I think, with Kipling, the reason for the choice was different. In the first place, like a good artist, he stood on the firm ground of personal experience. His interest in Buddhism was roused by the Gandhara sculptures in the Lahore museum, of which his father was the curator. It is

34

fashionable now to call this Hellenistic expression of Indian art decadent and even debased. But if it inspired this beautiful quest, we Indians at all events should not be ungrateful to these stones.

But I think there was also a second reason. Hindu spirituality, even at its most unworldly and serene, has a suggestion of power and action, a kind of super-magical motivation which is not consistent with perfect beatitude and mystic quietism. Although ostensibly aiming at the breaking of the cycle of Karma and rebirth, it is found to be entangled in it. So a Hindu's spirituality and his existence in the world are in a subtle way in touch with each other. In his spiritual activities he is like a dynamo, generating electricity, in his worldly life a motor that expends it.

It is very difficult for a non-Hindu to see this latent nexus. It escaped even Kipling. In 'Purun Bhagat', when describing the saint Purun's attempt to save the villagers and the animals from the landslide, he wrote: 'He was no longer the holy man, but Sir Purun Dass, KCIE, Prime Minister of no small State, a man accustomed to command, going out to save life.' This is wrong, for the man of action at a crisis and the holy man are the same – the distinction is non-existent in Hinduism, for in the ultimate analysis its spirituality is the Old Guard of the cosmos, held in reserve. But although incapable of realizing all this consciously, Kipling must have felt that his purpose would not be served by this kind of spiritual greatness. So he created his Lama, mixing Christianity with Buddhism.[1]

Last of all, he saved the book from all suggestion of pedantry and humbug by putting it in the most English of all English forms of fiction, a serio-comic saga. The English genius is unmatched in the capacity to make the commonplace significant by transforming it into a fantasy or extravaganza. Kipling's achievement is on the same lines – he has made the serious irresistible by lightening its burden.

This is not the place to analyse in detail Kipling's treatment of his themes, but it might be pointed out that he conforms to the Hindu view by making the Lama an instrument of power in the eyes of his worldly admirers, but is un-Hindu in making him come back to the plains for the final Enlightenment. This is Christian in spirit.

Michael Edwardes
'OH TO MEET AN ARMY MAN'
Kipling and the Soldiers

RICHARD LE GALLIENNE got it almost right in 1900. Kipling, he wrote, was a 'war correspondent in love with soldiers'. It was intended as critical condemnation, a liberal dismissal of the 'heartless vulgarity' of a writer who had the effrontery to laud military imperialism to a people who generally despised soldiers and were indifferent to empire. All the same, though limited, it was a shrewd judgement. Kipling certainly loved soldiers – but not blindly. The trumpet and drum were among the chosen instruments but some very queer tunes were played upon them. The 'war correspondence', too, breaking with tradition, revealed the fear and the terror as well as the epical, the incompetence as well as the heroism. In Kipling, British soldiers break and run away from the enemy – the kind of behaviour usually reserved for foreigners and natives. Kipling's turn-of-the-century critics (and later ones, too) found it impossible to reconcile his honesty with his glorification of the military virtues. A high priest who allowed such a large element of imperfection in the Chosen could be nothing other than a cynical *poseur*.

But they were wrong in thinking Kipling to be as sophisticated as they hoped they were themselves. His honesty was not subordinate to artifice, but conditioned by special experience – that of growing up, intellectually, in the closed society of the British in India. That world, with all its faults, he saw as the simulacrum of the best of all possible worlds, the world of action contained within a simple framework of rules and duties. Within a few weeks of his return to London from India in 1889 he was homesick for it, and expressed his longing in verses sent to the newspaper that had first employed him, the *Civil and Military Gazette* of Lahore. After sneering at the conceits of metropolitan intellectuals, stuck in their ivory towers, he concluded:

> It's Oh to meet an Army man,
>   Set up, and trimmed and taut,
> Who does not spout hashed libraries
>   Or think the next man's thought,
> And walks as though he owned himself,
>   And hogs his bristles short.

It is significant that in these verses there is no nostalgia for India as a place – only for a breed of man Kipling had known, and known intimately, there. Kipling had no wish to return to India. As a writer it was too small for him. In fact, he only made one other short visit in 1891. The India of his seven years' stay – the India of Lahore and Allahabad, of Simla, of the mess, and the barrack room – remained for him an immensely detailed but static portrait. From this unchanging data bank Kipling was to draw the anecdote, the colour, and the philosophy of action which gave both authenticity and didactic purpose to stories and verses about soldiers.

What did Kipling actually know about war and soldiers in India? Nothing at first-hand about war, for his stay in India saw a period of unusual peace in that principal area of British-Indian military activity, the North-West Frontier. But there were plenty of soldiers to talk to. Working on the *Civil and Military Gazette* in Lahore, the capital of the Punjab – a province which then included the frontier areas – Kipling delighted in listening to 'shop'. At the mess table he would hear, as Bobby Wicks in 'Only a Subaltern' heard, 'legends told him of battles fought at long odds, without fear as without support . . . of friendships deep as the sea and steady as the fighting line; of honour won by hard roads for honour's sake; and of instant and unquestioning devotion to the Regiment – the Regiment that claims the lives of all and lives for ever'.

Then there would be the tales of experiences dragged out from the reticence characteristic of gentlemen at 'ghostly dinners . . . with Subalterns in charge of the Infantry Detachment at Fort Lahore, where, all among marble-inlaid empty apartments of dead Queens, or under the domes of old tombs, meals began with the regulation thirty grains of quinine in the sherry, and ended – as Allah pleased!'

When Kipling arrived in India in 1882, the talk was of the Second Afghan War which had ended two years before. During his stay in India, Upper Burma was annexed (1886) and the long period of 'pacification' begun.

But if there were few wars, there was always military activity. The Punjab was soldiers' country. The province had been part of British India for only thirty years and was still, to a large extent, policed by the army. In the Frontier areas, the majority of the civil administrators were army officers. Behind all, loomed the Punjab 'tradition' of swift and decisive action. From this most untypical part of British India, Kipling acquired his admiration for the 'military virtues'.

In fact, they were very apparent. British rule in the Punjab had been founded by that formidable duumvirate, the brothers John and Henry Lawrence. Henry had been killed in the besieged Residency at Lucknow during the Mutiny of 1857, requesting that his grave should bear the inscription: 'Here lies Henry Lawrence who tried to do his duty.' John had lived on to become Viceroy, and had died in 1879. Memories of both were strong in the Punjab. Henry had established the tradition with his young subalterns. 'What days they were,' one of them recalled. 'How Henry Lawrence would send us off to great distances; Edwardes to Bannu, Nicholson to Peshawar, Abbot to Hazara, Lumsden to somewhere else . . . giving us a tract of country as big as half of England, and giving us no more helpful directions than these: "Settle the country; make the people happy; and take care there are no rows!" '[1]

What names to impress one so young as Kipling, who could talk in the mess to experienced men with tales to tell almost as heroic as those of the founders of the Punjab, and yet were scarcely older than himself. The Punjab had been, and still was, young man's country, young officer's country. The proof of the work was all around to see. In the whole of British India there was no part in which the British had impressed themselves so much upon the life of the people. The land had been transformed by the most sophisticated of irrigation schemes; forest had been planted; roads and railways built. A prosperous wheat-growing country of sturdy peasants – and it was all the work of young men, building on the work of young men.

In the beginning, it had been the young officer who had done everything – someone, perhaps, like Herbert Edwardes of Bannu (now named, in his memory, Edwardesabad). In three months in 1848, Lieutenant Edwardes had pacified a valley of wild

[1] E. Edwardes, *Memoirs of the Life and Letters of Major-General Sir Herbert Edwardes* (1886).

tribesmen, founded a new town, and begun a military and commercial road thirty feet broad and twenty-five miles long 'through a formerly roadless valley' which – Edwardes wrote two years later in his very popular work, *A Year on the Punjab Frontier* –

has since been completed . . . and is now, under the protection of ordinary police, travelled by the merchant and traveller in ease and security: tracts of country from which the fertilising mountain streams were diverted by feuds, have been brought back to cultivation by the protection of a strong government; others lying waste because disputed, had been adjudicated, apportioned, occupied and sown once more . . . a people who had worn arms as we wear clothes, and used them as we use knives and forks, had ceased to carry arms at all: and though they quarrelled still, learned to bring their differences to the war of the civil court instead of the sharp issue of the sword.

Thirty years later, of course, there were engineers and forestry officers, civil administrators and judges to serve and consolidate the conquest, but for Kipling these were really only the lay members of some military order whose paladins remained the bright, heroic subalterns, little changed from those of an earlier era. Did not these young men guard the empire's frontiers against Pathans and, beyond them, Russians? In Burma, they outwitted unsavoury bandits who were foolish enough to resist the boons of the *pax Britannica*. And when Indians of differing religions insisted on killing each other, so that the army had to be called out to aid the civil power, there 'was joy in the hearts of all the subalterns' and the Queen's Peace was duly kept intact.

Even his contemporaries found Kipling's subalterns a bit hard to take. Later critics found them incredible – but then they assumed that, as the background of empire was unacceptable to them, the portraits which occupied the foreground must necessarily be false. They were not, and there is ample documentary evidence to prove that Kipling drew upon an actuality that, on more than one occasion, exceeded his own expression of it.

The code of the subaltern was quite simple – self-denial, law, order, and obedience, blessed with the adventurous ardour and audacity of youth. It was a stoic code which cheerfully accepted hardship and even the prospect of an unheroic death:

> A scrimmage in a Border station –
> A canter down some dark defile –
> Two thousand pounds of education
> Drops to a ten-rupee *jezail* –
> The Crammer's boast, the Squadron's pride
> Shot like a rabbit in a ride!

Kipling was not alone in seeing in the military virtues the essence of empire. The army in India had its philosopher as well as its poet. Sir James Fitzjames Stephen, Law Member of the government of India from 1869 until 1872, conceived British power in India as a vast bridge over which the Indian people were passing from darkness into light. The twin piers of that bridge were military force and justice, which he defined as 'a firm and constant determination on the part of the English to promote impartially and by all lawful means what they regard as the lasting good of the natives of India'. Without force, justice was a 'weak aspiration after an unattainable end'. But, Stephen was convinced, 'so long as the masterful will, the stout heart, the active brain, the calm nerves and the strong body which make up military force are directed to the object I have defined as constituting justice', there was nothing to fear.

To both Stephen and Kipling, the Queen's Peace was a living thing. Stephen even went so far as to liken it to the universal peace announced at the time of Christ's nativity. Under its benevolent sway, a revolution took place just as surely as a lake was formed by damming a river. But there were always threats to peace, and not only from the general anarchy of the world outside its range. Purpose could be eroded by indifference as surely as by a failure of nerve. Kipling's soldier stories and verses were, in part, a tribute to those whose behaviour he so admired, but they were primarily directed towards the dwellers in the civilized comforts of London who had no idea of what the Empire was really about, nor of how easily it could be lost. Discipline and devotion were the characteristics Kipling believed he saw in the militaristic society of his little corner of the Indian empire, and it was a message he wished to pass on:

> Keep ye the Law – be swift in all obedience –
> Clear the land of evil, drive the road and bridge the ford.
> Make ye sure to each his own
> That he reap where he hath sown;
> By the peace among Our peoples let men know we serve the Lord!

Unfortunately, in spite of the support of such political philosophers as Fitzjames Stephen, the view that a military empire sustained and expanded by a dedicated group of young men was somehow *morally good* held few attractions for the British at home. In general, the Victorian middle and upper classes considered Army officers a necessary evil and Other Ranks as the scum of the earth. The Navy was a different matter; not only was there a long tradition of sentiment for Jolly Tars and Hearts of Oak, but the belief of a nation of shopkeepers that the Navy kept the lanes of commerce clear. No one considered the Empire really *profitable*. Its petty wars always cost a lot of hard-earned cash, and the only tangible return was a few million more objectionable natives. If Kipling had stuck to the simple colours of the recruiting sergeant, to the gaudy picture of youth with sword in hand, trumpets blaring, and the flag on high, all might have been ignored. But he did not. Instead, he insisted that his military community was an ideal to be admired and emulated. As for the intellectuals, they could never forgive Kipling for his portrayal of a community which despised thinkers and glorified men who did things out of obedience and duty.

Kipling compounded his crime by exploring, for the first time in English literature, the real life of another essential part of the military community, the private soldier. It was an exploration made with bitter honesty. The British soldier of song and ballad was the British Grenadier, who might compare more than favourably with Alexander and Hercules while fighting, but was considered dirty and immoral when he was not:

> Then it's Tommy this, an' Tommy that,
> an' 'Tommy, 'ow's yer soul?'

41

But it's 'Thin red line of 'eroes' when the
drums begin to roll . . .

Kipling's bitterness was again directed against those who made 'mock o' uniforms that
guard you while you sleep' and refused to recognize that the ordinary soldier followed
the same rules and observed the same duties as the subalterns, though in a somewhat
different manner – that in fact they were an inseparable component of the ideal.

But Kipling's intense sense of responsibility would not permit him to deform
reality. His honesty compelled him to show Things As They Are. Again he drew upon
his Indian experience. Industrious commentators have tried to penetrate the living
source of such characters as Mulvaney, Ortheris, and Learoyd, to tack Kipling's
stories and verses to a documentary last. There may, indeed, have been one, but it is
of no great importance. Kipling listened and looked. He made the acquaintance of
soldiers stationed at the military cantonment at Mian Mir, just outside Lahore, men
from the Northumberland Fusiliers, and the East Surreys, that 'London recruited
confederacy of skilful dog-stealers, some of them my good and loyal friends'. He heard
their stories of action and observed their life in barracks and camp.

The life of this mercenary army in India was not an easy one. It is almost impossible
for men armoured by inoculations and soothed by air-conditioning to imagine what
hell a soldier's life could be, and usually was, in late nineteenth-century India.
Barracks were in general not healthy places, either mentally or physically. There had,
it was true, been some change in conditions since Florence Nightingale had commented twenty years earlier that 'When asked about Drains, the Army in India was
like the London woman who replied: "No, thank God, we have none of them foul,
stinking things here"!', but little had been done to leaven the boredom of a soldier's
day, which she had described as

> Bed till daybreak,
> drill for an hour,
> breakfast served to him by native servants,
> bed,
> dinner served to him by native servants,
> drink,
> tea – and *da capo*.

Out of this corrosive boredom burst 'hot weather shootings' and their sequel, the
terrible panoply of a military execution, the 'Dead March' playing, the regiment in
hollow square, the coffin waiting by the scaffold.

In the hot weather, too, out of the miasma of horse-piss and stinking drains the
regiment would flee before the pursuing cholera.

> Since August when it started, it's been stickin' to our tail,
> Though they've had us out by marches an' they've 'ad us back by rail;
> But it runs as fast as troop trains, and we cannot get away,
> An' the sick-list to the colonel makes ten more today.

No wonder T. Atkins drank and whored – and was attacked for it by interfering do-gooders. Among these could be numbered Lord Roberts, then commander-in-chief in India, with whom Kipling rode 'up Simla Mall . . . on his usual explosive red Arab, while he asked me what the men thought about their accommodation, entertainment rooms and the like'. Roberts obviously did not listen carefully, because he supported the Army Temperance Association although it was clear to Kipling that beer was not alcohol but a prophylactic medicine. As for whoring, the campaign against the Contagious Diseases Act in Britain had led to the closing down of regimental brothels in India. This 'official virtue' cost the army 'nine thousand expensive white men a year laid up from venereal disease'. Actually, the Army was more astute than Kipling gave it credit for. Within a few years the old system was back again, though less blatantly. But Kipling chose to take this concern with public morality as another attack on the men he so admired, men whose burden, he believed, was greater by far than their sins.

His dislike of interference from the ignorant in the capital of the empire was shared by powerful men in India. The British in India had never really accepted the domi-nance of the metropolitan executive and parliament. Before the opening of the Red Sea telegraph in 1870, the government of India had been almost independent, taking decisions and getting ratification – however reluctantly – months later. Even after the linking of Britain and India by telegraph wires, it had resisted executive control. The trouble with India was that, unlike Canada or Australia, it was not a colony of British settlement but a caravanserai of transients. The only settlers were planters, of indigo, of tea and coffee, a tiny minority essentially commercial and, in Kipling's terms, exploitive.

There had been a number of suggestions for more determined colonization. In one of his soldier stories, 'His Private Honour', Kipling presents, perhaps only half seriously, one of these – a project for a new India based upon a territorial army 'of specially paid men enlisted for twelve years' service in Her Majesty's Indian posses-sions, with the option of extending on medical certificates for another five and the certainty of a pension at the end'. This would have been an army such as 'the world had never seen', making India its home and allowing its members to marry 'within reason'. As India had its Hills, and in them a suitable climate for colonizers, Kipling suggested that Kashmir should be bought back 'from the drunken imbecile who was turning it into a hell', and then the time-expired men 'would breed us white soldiers, and perhaps a second fighting line of Eurasians'.

The edges of the dream spread wider 'to an independent India hiring warships from the mother-country, guarding Aden on the one side and Singapore on the other . . . a colonised, manufacturing India, with a permanent surplus and her own flag'. But even this vision could not have satisfied every hope. It was not only the ignorant at home who let down Kipling's stoic subalterns and wayward but dedicated soldiers. Senior commanders not infrequently mismanaged their small wars, leaving the men who actually did the fighting vulnerable to the fears and failures of real human beings. British soldiers did, on occasion, break and run before the enemy.

> I 'eard the knives be'ind me, but I dursn't face my man,
> Nor I don't know where I went to, 'cause I didn't 'alt to see,

43

> Till I 'eard a beggar squealin' out for quarter as 'e ran,
> An' I thought I knew the voice an' – it was me!

Of course, the men rallied, and of course they won. History, the special history of Kipling's experience, confirmed it.

Kipling was, and remains, the only literary source we have for the mercenary army of the late nineteenth century, and his picture is by no means misleading. But were his individual portraits true to life? Robert Graves, writing in 1923, suggested that Kipling-reading officers accepted the picture and moulded their men in its image, so that between 1887 and 1914 most soldiers grew more and more to be 'Kipling's Own'. At least one of Kipling's archetypal subalterns, Sir George Younghusband, supported this in his memoirs (1917). 'I myself,' he wrote, 'had served for many years with soldiers, but had never heard the words or expressions that Rudyard Kipling's soldiers used. Many a time did I ask my brother Officers whether they had heard them. No, never. But sure enough, a few years after, the soldiers thought, and talked, and expressed themselves exactly like Rudyard Kipling had taught them in his stories . . . Rudyard Kipling made the modern soldier.'

Life imitating art? Perhaps. But life dealt badly with the ideal the art expressed. The twentieth century, with its ever-widening horizons, pushed the Punjab tradition into the most parochial of history's pigeonholes. The South African war and, more decisively, the First World War, made clear the utter wastefulness of death, that ultimate in individual sacrifice. Duty, obedience – for what? Kipling saw clearly the coming of Armageddon. The South African war jolted him out of the cosiness of small Frontier wars against natives into the harsh world of potential threat from equals. The 'lesser breeds without the Law' of that dire warning, *Recessional*, are not Afghan tribesmen but Germans.

Kipling did not immediately abandon the ideal. He certainly saw the threats to it more clearly. Criticism of incompetent leadership at the top becomes shriller:

> The General got 'is decorations thick
> (The men that backed 'is lies could not complain),
> The Staff 'ad D.S.Os till we was sick,
> An' the soldier – 'ad the work to do again.

But a change had taken place. From the aggressive imperialism of his Indian experience, Kipling turned to the demands of defence. He was among the early advocates of compulsory national service, an enlargement of the military community through which there would be a concentration of the military virtues into some kind of ultimate weapon of defence. Conscription had to wait upon the demands of the First World War for replacements for that generation which, though it did not think much of Kipling's soldiers, cheerfully embraced his patriotism and died in the Flanders mud.

The postwar world, a world in which all the foundations had been shaken and many destroyed, confirmed the pessimism that had slowly engulfed Kipling after the revelations of the South African war. All that remained was a tiny fragment of history, encapsulated by a moralist who was also a great artist.

Philip Mason
KIPLING AND THE CIVILIANS

WHEN I was about twelve years old, I wrote some verses in adulation of Rudyard Kipling of which, fortunately, only two lines survive. They began:

Shakespeare was all very well in his way,
Milton was not at all bad . . .

But by the time I was nineteen, his name was an offence to me. Now I can read him again with admiration for his skill as a story-teller and for his power of calling up scents and sounds; of admiration, too, for his brilliance in condensing humdrum experience into excitement and turning trivialities into drama. But in almost all his earlier stories I shudder, at least once, and sometimes much more than once, at his *awfulness*, by which I mean the showmanship, the blatancy, the knowing nudge which says: 'See how clever I am.' And sometimes I resent the slickness with which he can jerk tears from my eyes. He makes men lose their tempers, says his biographer Charles Carrington; they either hate him or love him or sometimes both.

Any attempt to sketch the world of Kipling, even a part of it, must take account of the fascination and repulsion which he inspired. I believe myself that it is partly due to his own inability – at least in his early days – to choose one from the many different facets of his personality and stick to it with any consistency. He is uncertain about himself. He cannot make up his mind what club he wants to join. He will suddenly peer out from behind the mask of the moment wearing another mask, because he wants you to understand that really he is not the person he was just pretending to be.

There were good reasons for this in his childhood and school life and they continued in his early manhood. He was suddenly transferred from a loving home, not to mention an affectionate and indulgent circle of Indian servants, to a harsh world where there was very little love or admiration. This kind of shock has indeed occurred at about that age in varying degrees to countless English boys of the professional and middle classes. Extroverts who are good at games and passable at Latin, Maths and Greek quickly win the esteem of other boys and of masters and put the crisis behind them; from now on, they belong to the new world of school. Others have to find some kind of mask which enables them to defend themselves well enough against a society they feel to be alien – and they slip away when they can to worlds of fantasy.

Kipling was one of these. He never quite belonged to the world of school, and the experience of not quite belonging which he expressed in *Stalky & Co.* was common enough. At thirteen I knew inarticulately that it was something I understood, and I rejoiced when the bad boys of Number Five study (who never reached the Sixth) scored off their silly old housemaster and the clever young prefects of their last term. So did thousands of others. But someone whose reaction, even as a boy, was hostile told me: 'I felt he was a sneak schoolmaster who pretended to be on the side of the boys but wasn't really.'

This I think puts a finger on one of the essential ambivalences which lie at the root of Kipling's character. He is not really against school. The Headmaster was wise if the Housemaster was silly. No one can seriously doubt that he wished he too could have played in the Old Boys' match 'magnificent in black jersey, white knickers and black stockings'. But he couldn't. He was left outside. So he poured scorn on those who said ' "Yes, sir," and "Oh, sir," an' "No, sir," an' "Please, sir," '; but was he really a rebel? Stories about bee-hives and steam-engines and the parts of a ship shout again and again that what he really admired was the harmonious whole in which all the parts worked together without one dissonant note.

But this inconsistent man could never quite leave it at that. He had not himself fitted into the smooth machine of school, so he had to picture a world in which the outsider triumphed. And he never could quite persuade himself that he fitted in to other worlds after he left school. At Simla, a cub reporter for the *Civil and Military Gazette* would not be the kind of young man whom ambitious mammas with marriageable daughters asked to dinner before a dance.

> He wrote for divers papers which, as everybody knows,
> Is worse than serving in a shop or scaring off the crows.

Simla was more caste-ridden than anywhere else even in Anglo-India, and it was not enough to have an artist father – also a freak – who had been petted by Lord Dufferin. Nor was he for a long time an accepted member of a permanent community anywhere else. He lived for some years in rural Vermont but eventually decided that he did not want to be American. When he settled down in England, he wrote to a friend: '. . . we discovered England, which we had never done before . . . England . . . is the most marvellous of all foreign countries that I have ever been in. It is made up of trees and green fields and mud and the gentry, and at last I'm one of the gentry . . .' This of course was half a joke, but with 'the county' in Sussex – as earlier with the Army and later with the Navy – he was always eager to show that he was *practically* one of the initiate – but not quite. Suddenly he will flash in the reader's face some fragment of esoteric knowledge which hints that he *is* a full member of some other fraternity. He understands – he keeps saying – how soldiers and masters of foxhounds and naval officers feel; they accept him as one of themselves – but then he must twitch aside his outer garment and show us his knowledge of freemasonry or gypsy folklore or seventeenth-century herbiaries.

The uncertainty as to whether he is a rebel or part of the establishment – the eagerness to belong to a gang but determination that you shouldn't think it his *only* gang – was bound to colour the way Kipling looked at official Anglo-India. He is one with it when it is assailed from outside, by Pagett MP or less dangerous tourists, who 'call us "colonists", and dine in a flannel-shirt and tweeds, under that delusion . . .' He is behind it when it builds bridges, displays its power, and works efficiently, like a machine. 'They obey' – he makes an Indian officer explain to an Afghan chief, 'Mule, horse, elephant or bullock, he obeys his driver, and the driver his sergeant, and the sergeant his lieutenant, and the lieutenant his captain, and the captain his major, and the major his colonel, and the colonel his brigadier commanding three regiments, and the brigadier his general, who obeys the Viceroy, who is the servant of the Empress.

Thus it is done!' And, in another story, 'the Deputy is above the Assistant, the Commissioner above the Deputy, the Lieutenant-Governor above the Commissioner and the Viceroy above all four. . . .'

But this smooth subordination of the individual is again the outer shell and there is another inside. It is with the man who doesn't get to the top and take the limelight that the boy from Number Five study can identify himself. And so there is special admiration for the man behind the scenes who makes the machine work by some ingenious trick, who can make one enemy attack another, like Stalky, or who can cross the frontier into the native world which no one else understands, like Strickland. Mulvaney, the old soldier who lost his stripes because he couldn't resist one good drunk a month, in two separate stories steps in to command a company because the officer who has just arrived from England is too young and ignorant.

When Kipling is carving the outer crust of his empire-building scene, his engineers, forest officers, policemen and deputy commissioners work tirelessly, racked by fever and a remorseful nostalgia for all they left behind, shouldering other men's burdens, asking no reward but the satisfaction of duty well done. But they are all very much alike. Consider Finlayson, of the Bridge-builders. 'For three years he had endured heat and cold, disappointment, discomfort, danger and disease, with responsibility almost too heavy for one pair of shoulders . . .' And now, on the eve of success: 'There stood his bridge before him in the sunlight . . . – his bridge, raw and ugly as original sin, but *pukka* – permanent – to endure when all memory of the builder . . . had perished.' But Finlayson never says anything that could not have been said by Mottram, Spurstow, Hummil or Lowndes, the four men who sat playing whist in the story called 'At the End of the Passage'. The opening scene of this story, incidentally, shows Kipling at his best, painting with exact economy of line, the boredom, loneliness and heat which is driving one of the four to madness and death. But the four men, none the less, are no more than members of the station club, working sahibs, cut from the pages of a mail order catalogue, parts of the machine. Even Trejago and Holden, who cross the boundary and each of whom lives with an Indian woman, would be indistinguishable if it were not that Holden is in love and Trejago merely amuses himself. And his Roman working sahibs – Valens and Pertinax – are cut from the same catalogue.

The working sahib, the lonely District Officer, may be a lay figure, but Kipling approves of him. 'Pettit, the Deputy Commissioner, covered with dust and sweat, but calm and gently smiling, cantered up the clean-swept street in rear of the main body of the rioters.' He was on the job, doing his duty for the Empress, and so in the same class as 'Pot' Mullins, Captain of the Games at Westward Ho! But in general it was inevitable that Kipling should display an occasional spurt of irritated hostility against civilians, in the narrow sense in which the term was used in Anglo-India, meaning the Indian Civil Service. How could he avoid it? They *were* the establishment and had got where they were by being in the Sixth and going to universities. Far too many of them were like Aurelian McGoggin, who was 'over-engined for his beam'. 'He was clever – brilliantly clever – but his cleverness worked the wrong **way** . . .' There was also Anthony Barr-Saggott. 'Departmentally, he was one of the best men the Government of India owned. Socially, he was like unto a blandishing gorilla.' And there was Saumarez, 'a strange man, with few merits so far as men could see, though he was popular with women and carried enough conceit to stock a Viceroy's Council and leave a little over for the Commander-in-Chief's Staff'. Pinecoffin, poor boy, who was hounded by Nafferton so remorselessly on the subject of *Pig*, was another young civilian who does not emerge very well from his trials. He 'whimpered' under punishment and 'blustered feebly', like those clever young prefects at Westward Ho!

This was inevitable, in the light of Kipling's mixture of irritation with the establishment and admiration for what it did. On the whole, the civilians ranged in his gallery are treated rather better than might have been expected. There is even a favourable picture of one senior civilian, a 'Jubilee Knight', Jimmy Hawkins, described as 'a good chap, even though he is a thrice-born civilian'. But like the other working sahibs, he does not come alive as a person. And it is of interest that Kipling never set himself to understand the basic techniques of a district officer's work. It was, after all, his most constant recipe for a story to master the work of a specialist and the jargon in which he expressed it, and then to work his plot in this material. But though he applies this ploy to marine engineering, naval tactics, gunnery, wireless and much else, there is no story which deals with the bread-and-butter of ordinary district administration. 'The Head of the District' sounds as though it should, but the district is on the North-West Frontier, where the task of the Deputy Commissioner is to keep the tribes beyond the administrative frontier in some kind of order. This demanded a delicate balance between reward and punishment, between one section of the tribe and another; it meant reducing, by bluff and persuasion, the use of actual force to a minimum. But this was in many ways different from the job of an ordinary district officer, who had no tribesmen. He needed some of the same quality; he had to prevent riots between Hindu, Sikh and Muslim, perhaps between Sunni and Shia, to keep bribery and extortion within reasonable limits, to see that the police were neither tyrannous nor idle. This part Kipling understood, and also the benevolent hobbies that good district officers cherished – the avenues of trees, the tanks for storing rainwater, the hospitals for women.

> 'Why is my district death-rate low?'
>   Said Binks of Hezabad.
> 'Wells, drains and sewage outfalls are
>   My own peculiar fad.'

But this was the tip of the iceberg. The solid bulk of district work below the surface was the network of maps and records in which every crop in every field was registered. This was the basis of the ownership and cultivation of land, of rent paid by tenants, of revenue paid to the government, of the rights a man could leave to his son. Kipling approached it only once, in the very slight story called 'Tods' Amendment'. But while this story does show that he realized how important land tenure was for the villager, he never turns it into one of his full-dress stories – as he does building bridges or dealing with famine. An unpromising subject, perhaps, but not more so, surely, than ships' engines.

But 'The Head of the District' is worth another look. Orde is dying, of fever and overwork. His thoughts are for his wife and the district, especially for the fighting-men of a frontier clan, the Khusru Kheyl, who have come to love him. His wife is on the other side of the Indus, which has risen till it is 'five miles of raving muddy water'. She cannot cross and he dies without seeing her, after a last speech to the chief of the Khusru Kheyl, who 'chokes audibly', and to his faithful assistant Tallantyre. It is hard to summarize without sounding novelettish and it is saved from the novelet-tish, not by character, for the two men are working sahibs, cut from the illustrated catalogue, but by detail, the coughing horse, the camp-fire, the cold, the sound of the river. Tallantyre knows the district and will stay on but he is not senior enough to have permanent charge. Then the 'Very Greatest of All the Viceroys' decides to appoint a Bengali. His arrival is the signal for an immediate rising of the Khusru Kheyl, who have to be suppressed with some loss of life; the Bengali runs away, calling everyone to witness that he has not officially taken charge, and Tallantyre, who puts things right, takes the blame. There is a final characteristic grim pun; the Khusru Kheyl bring Tallantyre, as token of submission, what they believe is the head of the fleeing Deputy Commissioner, though it is in fact his brother's.

Now while it is true that the earliest Indian members of the Indian Civil Service were Bengalis, I am confident that none of them were posted to the Punjab, which when this story was written administered the Frontier. The story originated, I sus-pect, in a smoking-room conversation: 'The next thing they'll do . . .', it must have begun. But it contains several familiar ingredients in a Kipling recipe – cardboard characters, a melodramatic plot, convincing detail; the man in the background who unselfishly bears the blame; the folly of uninformed liberalism.

It would be easy – indeed, justifiable – to label this story 'racist', but it is my main theme that Kipling is a chameleon who takes different colours with different back-grounds. And he was not always in the smoking-room. Hurry Chunder Mookherjee, the Bengali in *Kim*, is a more sympathetic figure than any Englishman in the book. Indeed, I find myself usually more at home with the early Kipling when he is writing about Indians or historical figures or the jungle animals. He is less self-conscious than when dealing with the English because he has no need to convince us about where he fits in himself; he is clearly the outsider. And here he is content to be the outsider and to record what he sees. When he does this he is at his best.

Kipling's later essays in science fiction suggest that his political ideal was a board of impersonal technocrats. Yet he hated the Secretariat, the Supreme Government and, in general, the impersonal 'They' at the head of things. Thus there is a fundamental inconsistency in his view of the Raj. He was in fact much more inconsistent than most people give him credit for being. But there is a deeper criticism than this of his whole work. Work – discipline – self-effacement – yes, but what is it all *for*? After his son was killed in 1915, a more coherent view begins to emerge – but that, as he would have said himself, is another story.

James Morris
HILL STATIONS

For a writer of visual sensibilities, nothing could be much more stimulating than the first sight of a north India hill station, seen from horse-back, tonga or Chevrolet as the road from the plains turns its last laborious bend out of the deodars. Tightly compressed upon its ridge, there stands the little town demurely. Behind it the stupendous Himalayas rise; away to the south the foothills tumble in terrace and fold towards the plains; and if the light behind one's back is harsh, in front everything is moist and green, or clothed in snow like a Christmas recollection.

The setting is theatrical, yet instantly one's mind is drawn to the modest centre of the stage – for your hill station is really scarcely more than a village, and is ludicrously dwarfed by the scale of things. It is not a very beautiful artifact, taken structure by structure, but it has the startling impact of an intruder. It is defiantly out of place. Where there should be an eaved white temple with prayer flags, there rises instead a Gothic church, with a steeple and a weathercock, and the white blobs of tombstones in the yard behind. Where one might expect the palace of Mir or Maharajah, a hotel in the Eastbourne manner stands, wicker chairs upon its lawn, awnings above its windows. There are military-looking buildings here and there, and genteel Balmoral villas disposed among shrubberies, and along the top of the ridge, a bandstand at one end and what looks from a distance like a superannuated Midlands town hall at the other, there runs a wide paved esplanade, with benches to admire the Himalayan prospect from, and a fountain in a garden.

In decreasing consequence down the ridge to the south, the rest of the town falls obsequiously: lesser hotels, pensions and villas, a smoky jumble of bazaars, the splodge of an open-air market, a car park at the bottom where the taxis and rickshaws wait, until the last rickety huts and shacks peter out on the open hillside. It is a figurative kind of town – posh and foreign on the summit, half-caste halfway down, utterly indigenous in the lowest layer: and it has a functional symmetry and compactness, because the station is built on a narrow eminence, for health's sake, and cannot easily expand.

Yet it is not the shape of it that is exciting, but the suggestion it gives of concentrated force. For all its Cheltenham trappings, it looks a fierce, perhaps a vicious kind of place. It is all in movement. Even from a distance one can see the urgent jostle of its bazaars, the scramble of its buses and lorries, the bright crowds of tourists strolling arm in arm along the Mall, or clattering hilariously about on mountain ponies. The air is full of fizz; hoots, shouts and even bugles sound; sometimes the sun flashes brilliantly off a window, or a troop of monkeys scrambles over a tin roof.

This insignificant and in some ways preposterous little settlement is a monument of absolute power. It is the belvedere of an alien ruling race, from whose terraces, as from some celestial gazebo, they could look down from the cool heights to the sweltering expanses, far below, of their unimaginable empire. As such the Indian hill station was crucible to the art of the one literary genius of Anglo-India. With its combination of exoticism, high spirits, ridiculousness, intense social activity, historical meaning and great political power, it afforded the young Rudyard Kipling as exact a milieu as

23 *Opposite* 'But some say, and among these be the Ghurkas, who watched on the hillside, that the battle was won by Jakin and Lew . . .' 'The Drums of the Fore and Aft', an incident from the Afghan wars described by Kipling in *Wee Willie Winkie*, and painted by E. Matthew Hale

The Indian Journalist: Early Triumphs

24 *Left* Kipling à la carte: Menu-card by J. L. Kipling for his son's twenty-fifth birthday in London

25 *Below left* The Indian Journalist

26 *Below right* Publishing office of the *Pioneer*, Allahabad, where Kipling worked 1887–9

27 *Right* Kipling worked on the staff of the *Civil and Military Gazette* from 1882 to 1887: *Departmental Ditties* and most of the *Plain Tales from the Hills* first appeared in the paper

28 *Below* The *Pioneer*, unlike the *Civil and Military Gazette*, had an all-India readership

29 *Above* Simla: the Mall and Town Hall

30 *Left* Simla: the Lower Bazaar. 'A man who knows his way there can defy all the police of India's summer capital' (*Kim*)

31 *Opposite top* The Viceroy, military style: Lord Dufferin (of whom Kipling approved) and staff, 1885

32 *Opposite bottom left* An Anglo-Indian Christmas, Madras, 1870

33 *Opposite bottom right* The Viceroy, civilian style: Lord Ripon (of whom Kipling disapproved) and staff, 1883

34 *Top left Quartette* was the Kiplings' family
magazine, which they persuaded the *Civil and Military
Gazette* to issue as a Christmas annual

35 *Top centre* Ortheris, Mulvaney and Learoyd make
their debut

36 *Top right* The first *Wee Willie Winkie*

37 *Above* Zam-Zammah, the 'great green-bronze
piece' outside the Museum at Lahore (see *Kim*,
Chapter I)

38 *Opposite top* A return visit to Lahore, 1891

39 *Opposite bottom left* With the Channel Squadron:
Kipling 'carried at a canter round the quarterdeck'
after giving a reading on board HMS *Majestic*, 1898

40 *Opposite bottom right* 'Oblige me by referring to the
Files . . .' Kipling in an Indian newspaper office
(drawing by A. S. Boyd)

Mr Rudyard Kipling
assists at a flower Stall

41 Villiers Street, which, at
the time Kipling lived there in
1890–1, was 'primitive and
passionate in its habits and
population' (*Something of
Myself*)

42 Wolcott Balestier: 'poor
dear big-spirited
only-by-death quenchable
Wolcott' (Henry James)

America

43 Kipling in Main Street, Brattleboro, 1893

44 'Naulakha', Kipling's house in Vermont (named in memory of Wolcott Balestier)

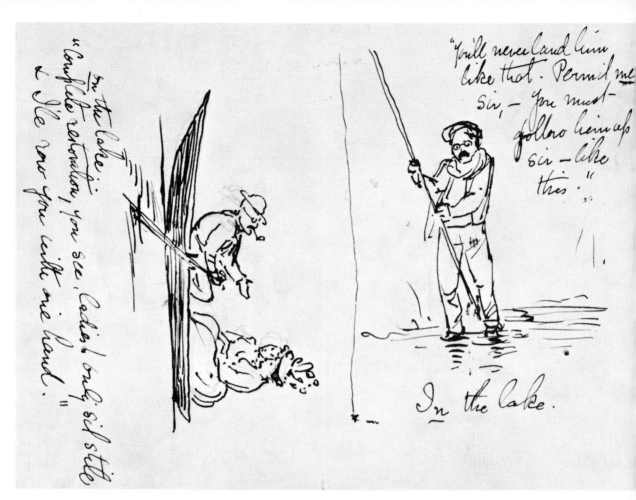

45 Kipling during his convalescence at Lakewood,
New Jersey, 1899: sketches by John Lockwood
Kipling

46 *Right* Mrs Rudyard Kipling in 'Naulakha'

47 *Top left* Beatty Balestier, Kipling's brother-in-law, on his farm near Brattleboro, Vermont, in the 1890s

48 *Top right* Mrs Rudyard Kipling at the reins, Brattleboro, *c.* 1895

49 *Above* James Conland, the Kiplings' family doctor in Vermont. 'The best friend I made in New England' (*Something of Myself*): the American edition of *Captains Courageous* is dedicated to him

50 *Right* 'The daughter that was all to him . . .': Josephine Kipling and nurse, *c.* 1895

WILDEN
JANUARY 15 1879

Mock Turtle Soup.
Turbot with Lobster Sauce.
Oyster Patés.
Stewed Kidneys.
Boiled Turkey - Tongue with
Oyster Sauce.
Roast Haunch of Mutton.
Pheasants à la Gitana.
Roast Hare.
Plum Pudding.
Mince   Pies.
Jellies   Cheesecakes
&c.   &c.

"A gentleman in kharki."

THE JUNGLE BOOK — RUDYARD KIPLING

MANY CARGOES — W.W.JACOBS

Chekhov found in the mouldering Russian provinces, or Conrad on his merchant ships.

Hill stations were never thought of by the Mogul princes, who preferred more languid delights of lake or palace: though they are now favourite holiday places for middle-class Indians, they were specifically the device of the British, who pined always for brisker recreations of the north. They were perhaps the only truly original socio-architectural product of the British overseas empire – which was not by and large a building empire, such as those of Rome or Spain, but relied for glory, in its pragmatic way, upon intangibles. Until Lutyens and Baker built New Delhi, in the fat autumn of empire, there was almost no group of buildings, let alone a whole town, that posterity could class as British Imperial. The cities of the white possessions were merely transplants, and in the East the British seldom tried to impose a style upon the country, but were content with cross-bred alien and native, Gothic with Mogul, classical with Hindu.

The hill stations were an exception. Most of them were in the north, in the wild and remote foothills of the Himalayas, and there the British were able to start from scratch. Until the arrival of their military surveyors and engineers, there was generally nothing substantial on the spot at all. The three most celebrated stations, Darjeeling, Mussoorie and Simla, all came into existence soon after the extension of the imperial frontier to the Himalayas, when only scattered tribes of hill people lived up there: they were originally intended as sanatoria, only gradually acquiring, as news of their advantages reached the scorched plains, status as pleasure resorts too. Mussoorie and Simla were settled in the 1820s, Darjeeling in the 1830s, and they became the classic archetypes of many lesser stations. All three have much in common, and will probably for ever remain the truest monuments of the Anglo-Indian life-style.

They might have been made for the short story writer. Their compactness lent themselves to the form. Darjeeling, for example, which is the least ugly of the three, and the most splendidly set, is visually a neatly-hatched compression of planes. The horizontals are their buildings in their tiers; the verticals are the tall thin trees which stand everywhere like cypresses in Italy, and are matched by the tower of St Andrew's at the top; the diagonals are the slopes of the hills themselves, which frame the town, and by intersecting behind it accentuate the meshed and intricate texture of the scene. The hill stations were mostly built by military engineers, the ablest specialists of Victoria's armies, and if their individual buildings are generally undistinguished and sometimes repellent, their civic patterns are rather handsome. Bath, itself the echo of an earlier empire, was young when these little towns were born, and probably we see, in their simple but elegant plans, innocent derivations of Lansdowne and Great Pulteney.

Kipling doubtless visited most of the stations at one time or another – his parents rang the changes for their summer retreats, and Murree and Dalhousie were both close to their home in Lahore. Simla, though, the grandest of them all, was the one he chiefly wrote about. In Simla he saw for the first time his Great Ones assembled in work and pleasure (and old India hands maintained he was permanently embittered by their aloofness). In Simla he first glimpsed the 'fast life' of Anglo-India (and

51 *Above left* Menu-card by J. L. Kipling for a Conservative dinner
party at Alfred Baldwin's house in Worcestershire
52 *Above right* A gentleman in khaki ordered South . . . Song-sheet of
'The Absent-Minded Beggar' (1899)
53 *Left* Biscuit tin, 1910

incited Maud Diver herself to restore the honour of Anglo-Indian womanhood). In Simla he found Mrs Hauksbee, and knowing no better at twenty-three, dedicated his first book to her as 'the wittiest woman in India'.

Perhaps she was, but probably not. At Simla especially, the summer capital of the Indian Empire, everything was falsely intensified. 'The scene was grand,' wrote an anonymous commentator in the 1850s, 'and the effect upon the mind almost over-powering: but soon this feeling of exultation subsided into an extreme exhilaration of animal spirits, as involuntary as though one had swallowed a tolerable dose of laugh-ing gas, and recklessly bid defiance to the grovelling cares of the world below.' The sense of detachment, or relief from the terrible heat of the lowlands, coupled with the marvellous stimulant of the altitude, gave life an electric vivacity up there, and made nearly everybody live more dangerously.

For an observer of conduct the hill stations were like gold-fish bowls. Here was a particular segment of fairly ordinary humanity briefly thrown together, hugger-mugger, in a very extraordinary situation. Its participants were members of a minus-cule ruling élite, a few thousand to rule many millions, and this in itself heightened their self-absorption, and made them live almost in caricature, or allegory. Though they stuck inflexibly to the values of their distant homeland, they were planted in the middle of an immense alien population, most of whose ways and purposes seemed to them altogether inexplicable. And to cap it all they were, like characters in some symbolic drama, removed to a high hill-top hundreds of miles from anywhere, isolated in a town about the size of Lyme Regis, say, in which they found a kind of inter-bred upper-crust, and exposed for a few weeks in the year to the undistracted observation of each other.

Jane Austen, given similar opportunities at Simla or Darjeeling, would have en-joyed herself wonderfully, but would have found the material, I think, too rich a mixture. Somerset Maugham and Graham Greene, Kipling's successors in this imperial genre, might have found it too spirited for their cynic vision. But for Kipling in his twenties, the hill station was perfect. It was like a short-story course in some college of literature: the characters, authentic but exaggerated, categorized for the student by rank, employment, race and class of lodging; the situation clearly disposed, in a limited choice of locale and opportunity; the plots, one would imagine, often ready-made; and the whole enclosed in the natural dramatic unity of the setting.

Unity of time, too, for most of the Europeans were only in the hills for short visits, and everything had the quality of immediacy. In the hills it was always holiday and life was lived in a round of balls, races, picnics, excursions, sketching parties, drinks at the Club, tea on the Mall, amateur dramatics, art exhibitions and gossip. For once in British India there were almost as many women as men; the average age was very young; the gaiety was infectious; it was no wonder that flirtation flourished, and young men who spent the rest of the year cooped up in dismal cantonments, or alone with a few more bachelors in awful backwaters of the Raj, let themselves go in the hills, and ornamented many an otherwise plainer tale.

Village life is always intense, and these were inflamed villages: Simla in the 1890s had a population of about 30,000, but probably not more than 3,500 were Europeans. Intrigue of course was rife, rivalry could be unforgiving, affairs flamed and died:

> Amen! here ends the comedy
> Where it began in all good will,
> Since Love and Leave together flee
> As driven mist on Jakko Hill!

These were tennis-club passions, shallow and transient, for it was essentially a bourgeois society that frequented the hill stations. Kipling realized this all too clearly, and Lady Curzon, when she moved with her husband into the Vice-Regal Lodge at Simla, recognized it wanly from the start. 'We shall make up our minds,' she resolved nevertheless, 'not to be fastidious.'

Perhaps the milieu would have been *too* shallow, even for the apprentice Kipling, if it had not been for the presence of power. Simla's froth and felinity might have been enough for a Saki, but Kipling's instinct went beyond. Despite its absurdities Simla really was, for several months of every year, one of the most powerful places on earth. From his half-timbered villa Peterhof, the Queen's Viceroy, with all his attendant generals and administrators, his plumed aides, his advisers, his vast corps of clerks and communicators, his ladies and his bodyguards, ruled the affairs of a legendary empire. His writ was absolute over a hundred million souls. The armies at his disposal were the greatest in Asia, and the presence of his authority, away up there in that silly hill village, decreed the political balance of the world.

So if the social glitter of the hills was specious, the pretension preposterous and the scandal mostly commonplace, the power represented by that Anglo-Indian assembly was very real. The 'Simla set', whose presence so awed junior officers of government, and no doubt visiting reporters too, was a power-élite: the most fascinating thing about that most astonishing of capitals was its intimate juxtaposition of the provincial and the metropolitan, the trivial and the immeasurable – Tods' Amendment, in fact. Kipling himself, aged twenty, immortalized this paradox in *Departmental Ditties* –

> They fight
> Until the Middle Classes take them back,
> One of ten millions plus a C.S.I.

– and it is implicit to his stories too. Somewhere behind the flirtatious subalterns and the flighty memsahibs, beyond the range of Strickland or even Mrs H., we sense the movement of grander intrigues and nobler affairs. Simla was full of consequence, half-concealed behind the frivolity, from the Viceroy guarded by his scimitared Sikhs to the myriad agents and conspirators who haunted the town. Kipling loved the hierarchy of order, transmitted from aristocratic pro-consuls through all the grades of human responsibility to the furthest corners of the empire, and Simla offered a paradigm of the process – standing there in the Mall, one could almost see Authority itself, a nearly tangible abstraction, winging down the tonga road from Peterhof to the plains.

It is sometimes said that Kipling was naïve in his reactions to the hill stations – that he mistook suburban snobbery for social importance, infidelity where there was only badinage or harmless dalliance. I do not find it so. His stories seem to me exactly to catch the cheap surface excitement of the hill stations, and the power that lay below. Of course he over-coloured his Simla, and his contemporaries in India reacted violently to his innuendoes of social vice and lesser administrative corruption. But as an artist, rather than a reporter, with uncanny precocity he saw it all true. He recognized the hill stations as forcing-houses of the human condition, where everything was heightened: and so, alone among all the Englishmen who ever walked on Jakko or looked from Tiger Hill across to Everest, he removed them from the context of the Raj, and gave them a more universal sovereignty.

Colin MacInnes

KIPLING AND THE
MUSIC HALLS

POETS may dream of a universal audience for whom their lines, however intricate and profound, are instantly accessible: of listeners who, whether educated or illiterate, can grasp the essence of their meaning, and sense the beauty of their words. Such was the audience, we may imagine, of Shakespeare's plays: a composite of scholars who perhaps understood most, and of groundlings who at any rate grasped something; and in the works of the Elizabethan poets we may feel that popular, demotic art was not yet totally estranged from the fine art of the academies.

Throughout the seventeenth and eighteenth centuries, with the rise of a literate middle class divorced from the culture of its humbler origins, the gap between pop and fine art widened: popular balladry diminished and was less esteemed, while illiteracy, and decline of the direct speech in the theatre, made fine art inaccessible to the multitudes. Poets, perforce, addressed themselves to the educated, and this even when they knew something of popular poetry; while some, like Robert Burns, tried uneasily to speak both to an uncouth and a polite audience. Thus, while one may imagine an alert yokel making something even out of Ben Jonson's scholarly productions, one can scarcely visualize his descendant making much of Alexander Pope's. Nor could one so easily conceive of the greatest poet of the later age being a man from outside the universities, as Shakespeare was in an earlier, and more cohesive, era.

By the nineteenth century, the gap had become a chasm. The accelerating pace of industrialization destroyed most of the older rural culture, while that of the urban middle classes became preponderant, and set the tone. Even Wordsworth's attempts, in revulsion against eighteenth-century artificialities, to simplify the language, resulted in poems intended for the literate. Swinburne's deep interest in the older ballads, and his deft pastiches of them, arose from the nostalgia of a scholar, and not from an instinctive creative spirit. Brave attempts were made by artists of social conscience, like Ruskin and William Morris, to 'bring art to the poor' by lectures, cheap editions and the like; and Tennyson, when his hard-cover volumes had sold in thousands, brought out shilling paperbacks intended for the masses. But in reality, artistic contact between the literate and unread had shrunk to almost nothing; as had, indeed, social contact of any kind.

At the end of the Victorian era, then, demotic poetry had almost vanished, though vestiges survived in rural areas untouched by industrial upheaval, and in such sea shanties as were still sung. At the same time there had arisen, in the huge late Victorian cities, a commercialized pop poetry that had none of the beauty of the old country songs, and yet was demotic in the sense that these verses were written by, and for, the people. The chief form these new pop poems took was that of songs sung in the music halls; of which there were, in the High Victorian era, some thousands in the country, for which tens of thousands of songs were written, and which were performed by hundreds of men and women singers as famous, in their day, as pop stars are in ours.

Considered by serious poetic standards, and even those proper to popular poetry, no great claims can be made for the music-hall songs. One test of this is that, bereft of their usually delightful tunes, the words themselves, isolated in cold print, seem often feeble; whereas in an authentic ballad, though a great song is always a combination of the arts of word and music, the lines can stand comfortably alone. The music-hall lyrics are apt, epigrammatic, witty, and technically, extremely deft; yet they are so often flawed either, when treating of the emotions, by sentimentality, or when of ideas, by an excessive jocosity. All the same, the mass of these songs does provide a lively, and in many ways revealing, portrait of the preoccupations, and the prejudices, of working-class life in late Victorian and Edwardian England.

At the time they were first projected, these songs were little known to educated people. One reason was class stratification, both social and artistic: the middle classes simply did not believe the workers had any culture of their own at all – though a good case can be made, I think, for the best of the music-hall songs being of higher artistic merit than the works of lesser 'serious' poets: between the productions of Alfred Austin, for example, and of Felix McGlennon, say, or Edgar Bateman of the Halls, I would not hesitate whom to crown with laurels. Another reason for this ignorance was that the Halls themselves were far from reputable. Today, dukes visit discothèques, and for the more timid, TV, radio and recordings bring pop songs into the safety of the home; but even in the 'naughty nineties', only bohemians and mavericks – and of these, only the males – ventured into the Alhambra, the Tivoli or the Old Mo.

Of these maverick explorers of the music-hall sub-culture, it is certain Rudyard Kipling was one. On his second return from India, after his *Civil and Military Gazette* days in Lahore, he lived in Villiers street, opposite Gatti's-under-the-Arches, with the Tivoli, another illustrious Hall, just round the corner in the Strand; and it is inconceivable that his restless curiosity did not carry him inside. In addition, since this was his *Barrack Room Ballads* period, his interest in demotic speech and habits was consuming; and remembering that Kipling's knowledge of the working classes was that of a social anthropologist, not a participant in any direct sense, what better place to study his low life raw material than in the relative safety and anonymity of the Halls? But the link between Kipling and the Halls would seem to go rather further than this: it would seem likely there are parallels, and even cross-fertilizations, between his art and theirs.

Considering that Kipling is, at his best, a major poet, and that even the most effective music-hall bards are highly minor ones, this may, at first, seem an impertinent suggestion; but not if one remembers the remarkable diversity, both of theme and style, of Kipling's verse. Thus, if one compares, say, 'Harp Song of the Dane Women', with its splendid poignancy and gravity, with the tinkling rumbustiousness of 'The Song of the Banjo', it is almost as if the poet speaks with two entirely different voices. Or how can the author of a sublime patriotic hymn like 'Recessional', be also he who penned the nasty lines of 'Loot'? Well, he was; and often when Kipling becomes brash, bumptious, and even outright vulgar, he stands close to the spirit of the Halls.

Then as to style, when it comes to the 'popular' poems, in which he writes what purports to be proletarian speech, there are lines that are almost interchangeable with those of music-hall ditties. Thus, who wrote which?

Who's it to be? 'Er or me?
Don't be afraid to say!

True love! New love!
Best take 'em for a new love . . .

This is all the more so, when one realizes that some (though not all) of the music-hall
lyricists were not working class at all but men who, like Kipling, were imitating, not
feeling, popular speech; though in their case any lack of authenticity would automatic-
ally be corrected by the singers who were, almost without exception, from the people.
Kipling, of course, even at his worst, is better than the music-hall bards: he's too
gifted not to be; and in fact, when he is writing horribly, it is his very artistry in doing
so that makes his fall from grace all the more repellent. I think it would be going too
far to suggest that Kipling, in his 'popular' poems, was actually influenced by the
Halls – although he might have been, to some extent, just as he was by any popular
speech he heard. But technically, he was away ahead of the music-hall artists, and
from his conversation with the troops in India, he seems to have learned all he wanted
to of pop speech (as he understood it) long before he came back to England. Nevertheless, the *mood* of the Halls may have affected him: for they were just as blatantly
chauvinistic as he was in his less endearing moods, and their songs certainly echoed
his when it came to themes of patriotic fervour, especially at the time of the Boer War.

As to the influence of Kipling *on* the Halls, this is unquestionable – indeed, Leo
Dryden, an immensely popular star of the turn of the century, was known, because of
his 'imperial' ditties, as 'The Kipling of the Halls'. Kipling may thus be one of the
first great poets for centuries whose work became known, on a large scale, to those
who could scarcely read, or did not do so at all. Perhaps some of the works of earlier
masters of great popularity, such as Scott and Tennyson, did eventually pass from the
printed page to direct verbal communication by recitation; but in Kipling's case, we
know this happened on a considerable scale – largely because pop performances by-
passed the necessity for the printed word. Thus, some of Kipling's more blatant
poems – such as 'If', 'Gunga Din', or 'Mandalay' – were 'delivered', often set to
music, on the Halls; also at 'smokers' in social clubs – semi-private performances in
what were, in effect, mini-music halls.

There is, of course, no real analogy with the glories of direct communication in the
Elizabethan theatre. For quite apart from any comparison of the talents of Kipling
and of the Elizabethan poets, it was not even Kipling's best work that was sung or
recited at the Halls. Nevertheless, there was some sort of a breakthrough here in that
almost total separation between educated and pop culture. It is easier to imagine,
realistically, both the Lord Mayor and his coachman enjoying Kipling's verse, than
it is (to take a poet of possibly equivalent stature) their fathers both liking Browning's
in an earlier age.

There is another sense in which Kipling may be felt to be a pioneer. Music hall has
evolved, since its final decay some fifty years ago, and through many permutations,
into modern variety and pop song. And I think there is no question that in the best

contemporary lyrics and material for variety, there is an element that may legitimately be called poetic. So that in England today, there is little doubt that younger poets are interested in pop poetry to a far greater degree than were most of their poetic ancestors in Kipling's time.

It may thus be that the rigid divisions between fine and pop culture are to some extent softening. This is not, of course, to suggest that our culture is so integrated that anything like an Elizabethan situation would be possible; nor is there now anything like the harmonious and diffused popular culture which we may suppose existed in those days. Pop poetry, indeed, begins now not around the maypole but, almost as soon as it is created, in the recording studio; while scholarly verse, whether good or less so, remains, on the whole, the interest of an erudite minority. Yet some reciprocal influence, as between fine art and pop, exists already, and will probably expand; and it would seem that the appreciation of Kipling's verse in the Halls, which heralded this development, was one of the many curious achievements of this most curious man.

Leon Edel

A YOUNG MAN FROM
THE PROVINCES

Rudyard Kipling and Wolcott Balestier

CHARLES WOLCOTT BALESTIER, an enterprising young man – he was then twenty-seven – genial, versatile, accommodating, arrived in London in December 1888 to serve as agent for a New York publisher. In the three ensuing years he made a distinctive place for himself in a courageous and business-like attempt to overcome the pirating of English writers in America, obtaining at the same time a 'stable' of famous authors for his firm. There was a touch of genius in this proceeding: and then he was not afraid to beard British literary lions in their dens. He arrived in London without knowing a single Englishman and he died – quite suddenly of typhoid at the end of the three years – leaving behind him a wider circle of friends there (so said Edmund Gosse) 'than, probably, any other living American'. Balestier's compatriot, Henry James, said, 'it never occurred to him that there was not a way round an obstacle', and he referred to his 'Napoleonic propensities'. Rudyard Kipling, who knew him best, remained silent, nursing a profound grief. He spoke years later of Balestier's having died 'so suddenly and so far away: we had so much to say to each other; and now I have got to wait so long before I can say it'. Indeed on the subject of his dead friend, he was never able to say what he wanted. Balestier is not mentioned in Kipling's fragmentary autobiography, although many less important acquaintances are.

A darkening photograph shows the features of this American who touched so swiftly and so deeply such eminent lives. Within its dimness we discern a high forehead; the hair is neatly parted and combed-down; we glimpse an oversize and floppy ear (Gosse called his ears 'sensitive') and a prominent nose, the line of which is continued in a long pencil Balestier is holding to his mouth as if he were chewing on it while pondering a sentence. Looking out of the shadows are large uncertain eyes. The figure slouches uncomfortably, awkwardly, with its right elbow on the table, the left hand pressed with great emphasis on the left thigh. Frozen in time and chiaroscuro, the long, lean, slouching shape suggests little of the 'charisma' and the nervous energy with which Balestier addressed himself to enterprise, charm, conquest. We must turn again to the words of Gosse, who had his living image – 'a carefully-dressed young-old man' and again 'an elderly youth'. His mouth, said Gosse, was mobile and whimsical; he carried himself in a stooping way as in the photograph; his physique seemed ill-matched to the vigour he demonstrated, 'the protean variety and charm of intellectual vitality'. On this all the witnesses agree. Henry James said he had an exotic and curious influence on those around him, and he added that he possessed a peculiar genius. *Exotic, curious, peculiar* – these special words in James's lexicon point to Balestier's flexible spirit, a gift of artless enthusiasm, an ability to put himself in the place of those he encountered – in a word a young man, extrovert and self-assured. There remained always something boyish about him, in his exuberance, his elasticity, his manner of reaching for reality in the midst of day-dreams.

The way in which he established himself in London suggests his curious American romanticism. He selected his rooms, which served also as his office, not in the Strand, nor in Bloomsbury. Nothing would do but chambers in Dean's Yard, right beside Westminster Abbey. The bells chimed; the shouts of Westminster School boys,

playing association football, mingled with the chimes. It was ancient, it was picturesque, it was literature; it was a young American's dream of London and of England,
and a way of combining the picturesque with the commercial. Arthur Waugh (future
father of novelists) has told in his memoirs how Balestier recruited and trained him to
handle proofs and authors. Balestier had smelled the advent of international copyright, which would end the pirating of English works in America. With his sound
business-sense he urged writers to let him have their works before they were published in England so that they could appear promptly in America in legitimate form.
To this end he signed contracts and paid royalties. English writers understandably
greeted this bearer of bounty from overseas with open arms, especially since he
brought a largeness of spirit, good humour, and a kind of elderly fatherliness, housed
in his young frame, that made him a recipient of confidences. Moreover he was tactful
and discreet. 'He was not merely one of our conquerors,' said Gosse (who in reality
thought Balestier in some ways a rather pushing fellow) 'but the most successful of
them all.'

Another young man from the provinces, from India, who had known England in
boyhood, arrived in the capital eight or nine months after Balestier. It would never
have occurred to Rudyard Kipling to seek rooms beside the Thames, under the
towers of the Abbey. He had been accustomed from childhood to the sound of distant
temple bells; and to the spectacle of teeming multitudes. He liked to be in the midst
of things, and in his rooms in the Strand, in Embankment Chambers (in Villiers
Street) he could hear the rumble of the Charing Cross trains. He would always like
trains, machines, vastness. He liked the life that swarmed around him. His windows
looked into the entrance of a music hall; strange characters, all manner of females in
particular, drifted in and out. An aroma of sausage from the sausage maker's just
below his rooms, mingled with other odours as he sat and wrote. Kipling would
always be masculine-gregarious. He liked soldierly fellows. But there was something
aloof in him, for his unhappy childhood had sown seeds of distrust, and distanced
him from humans, especially women.

It was Edmund Gosse who advised Balestier to read Kipling, the genius of the hour
from India. 'Rudyard Kipling?' retorted Balestier with simulated indifference. 'Is it
a man or a woman? What's its real name?' Gosse was somewhat ruffled. 'You won't
be allowed to go on asking such questions,' he said and he predicted Kipling would be
one of the greatest writers of the day. 'Pooh, pooh,' said Balestier, sustaining his pose,
'now you are shouting.' But when Gosse came to Dean's Yard three days later he noted
that a pile of the blue pamphlets in which Kipling had been published in India was
lying on Balestier's desk.

We know that when Balestier hunted out Kipling the latter was in no mood for
American overtures. Americans were pirates. Moreover Balestier pushed him hard.
Arthur Waugh has described how he was sent to Villiers Street to ask for a certain
work of Kipling's not yet completed. He remembered the dark room and the bard
from India sitting on a bed with sheets of manuscript surrounding him. 'Extraordi-
narily importunate person this Mr Balestier,' muttered Kipling to Waugh. 'Tell him

The Book of a Hundred Mornings is all over my bed and may never get finished. Tell him to inquire again in six months.'

But Waugh remembered 'my chief's importunity was to be satisfied in less time than that'. Presently, of all the authors who came and went in the house beside the Abbey, there was none more frequent – or more welcomed – than the author of 'The Ballad of East and West'.

Charles Wolcott Balestier was born in Rochester, New York, in 1861. His family was from New England, but there had been Huguenot ancestors who owned plantations in Martinique. Wolcott grew up surrounded by an admiring mother and two devoted sisters; the father seems to have died when his son was quite young. Balestier met the world with the assurance that he was the beloved male object in his family; there was no faltering of identity, no misgiving about his capacities. He attended Cornell; he wrote sketches for the *Atlantic*, and was patted on the back by William Dean Howells. For a while he was a reporter and a library assistant in New York, and then, at ease with the world, he set out to explore the American west. He camped in mining towns in Colorado, he made his way southward to Mexico. Frail in health, he seems nevertheless to have found enough energy to be ceaselessly active. Returning to New York in his mid-twenties, he joined the publishing firm of John Lovell, and in due course, as we have seen, was dispatched to London to carry out his plans for more amicable – and lucrative – relations between American publishers and English writers. What he carried with him also was a vision of the American heartland and of the railway, then making its way across the continent.

As the expanse of America was in Balestier's mind, so the expanse of India was in the mind of Kipling: his inward vision harboured a sense of the spacious colonial life, servants, people, animals, ancient rites and the great tracts of desert, although his boyhood had been less fortunate than Balestier's, and he harboured always melancholy and distrust, where Balestier reached out to people, objects, experiences. Both on the other hand shared in common a love for the male world of the Victorians. Woman's place in that era was distinctly in the home. This was an unchallenged fact. The barroom, soldiering, the sea – the pistol, the galloping horse – West or East – both knew this kind of camaraderie intimately, in the actual and in fancy. Kipling had lately written his famous ballad in which West and East were never supposed to meet, but one must not overlook the lines in which he made such a meeting possible:

> . . . there is neither East nor West, Border, nor Breed, nor Birth
> When two strong men stand face to face, though they come from the
> ends of the earth.

In retrospect we can read this as a prophecy of his friendship with Wolcott Balestier. 'No man,' says Kipling's biographer, Charles Carrington, 'ever exercised so dominating an influence over Rudyard Kipling as did Wolcott Balestier during the months of their intimacy.'

66

The record of this friendship must be deduced from scraps of information. We know that it was brief, less than a year, but the friendship had a strange and powerful intensity. After their first aloof meetings, Balestier's winning ways, his assurance, his four years of seniority, established him as counsellor and comrade in the eyes of the young man from India. Moreover Balestier's mother and sisters, who had come to England to bask in their son's success, and take care of him, made Kipling feel thoroughly at home. Once the publisher had organized his affairs, and established his good faith, he was able to take London in an easier stride; he found a small cottage retreat on the Isle of Wight, on the south shore, where his sister Caroline was often hostess. Henry James remembered a couple of August days there, a drive with Balestier to Freshwater over the great downs, a lunch in the open and 'a rambling lazy lounge on the high cliffs'. Balestier loved this temporary refuge where the great autumn windstorms ministered to his sense of romance and drama. Kipling was with him more often than James. Not only had the two become bosom friends, but they were working together. 'I have been seeing even more of Kipling with whom I am writing a story in collaboration,' Balestier announced to the benignant Howells. Henry James remembered that 'an intimate personal alliance with Mr Rudyard Kipling had led to his working in concert with that extraordinary genius, a lesson precious, doubtless, and wasted, like so many of his irrepressible young experiments – wasted, I mean, in the sense of its being a morning without a morrow'.

That Kipling, so powerful in his craft, should accept as collaborator an amateur, even though in some ways a skilful journalist, may seem curious if we judge the collaboration with professional eyes. But such collaboration – unless it relates to hackwork – is usually an act of friendship, a partnership of the spirit, an act of love. There was also its practical side. Balestier had convinced Kipling that what the author of 'The Ballad of East and West' needed to do was to write – with him – a novel of East and West. He knew the American plains and the infant towns; he knew the men of the frontier; what more charming than to transplant a full-blooded American into exotic Anglo-India. Henry James might move Americans of the eastern seaboard into the titled houses of England, but what a reach one might give the 'international' novel to have an American on horseback involved with the magic and intrigue of the East. So there they were, whether in Dean's Yard or in the cottage on the Isle of Wight: Wolcott at one of those early big clumsy typewriters, Kipling pacing the floor, 'each composing, suggesting, or criticising in turn, and the mind of each stimulating the other to its best work'.

The story announced to Howells was the novel *The Naulahka* and some years later Kipling included it in his collected works, as if Balestier's part of it belonged in the corpus of his own writings. It was a tribute to this magical moment, to memories that haunted him for a lifetime. If Balestier had neither the verbal endowment nor the required imagination, he had his own concretions of experience and he made the collaboration work. Reading the American's clumsily-written newspaperish tales, we sense a Kiplingesque temperament which does not possess Kipling's literary power. In another incarnation the two probably would not have bothered with something as effete as literature; they might have been a couple of happy cowboys, 'pals' of the plains, so great was their love of movement and courage and the sense of mastery of ground and sky from a galloping horse. They might also have been railwaymen feeling the power of their engine as they ran – say – the No. 14 over the range on one day and brought back the No. 3 the next. They would have played with real trains with the same delight and attention that boys play with models. Every signal, every stop, every sidetrack, every hint of danger would have been an adventure – not least the conquest of space and time.

The Naulahka makes strange reading today. It embodies all the qualities of what we have come to call the 'western'. Its general burden is that woman's world is marriage and domesticity and that men belong wherever high adventure is to be lived. The opening scenes, written by Balestier, set in an American town which awaits the coming of the railroad, consist of a long-drawn-out argument between the town's leading politician and the girl he wants to marry. She wants to be a missionary nurse in India; she is a very 'manly' woman. The American hero has no alternative but to follow her. The two Americans, male and female, thus arrive in the world of Rudyard Kipling – and here that master of the Anglo-Indian scene takes over. Among the rash commitments of the hero, is the promise of a bribe to a woman who can influence a railroad president to bring the railroad to his western town: he is certain he can bring back a rare temple necklace, the 'Naulahka'. The American gallops his way through the best-written parts of the story – Kipling's parts – in India. He is the hero of a thousand deaths. Bullets always miss him; his own aim is deadly. Daggers are thrown; there are plots of poison and kidnap. He is the future Owen Wister cowboy dressed in Kipling's prose with the sensual qualities of the Indian landscape and Indian heat and smells and long night-rides rendered for us with the vividness of a modern movie, long before the coming of the cinema. There they were, the two collaborators, like a couple of literary Teddy Roosevelts, 'from the ends of the earth', sharing day-dreams and entering one another's fantasies, fantasies of masculine prowess, with the glee of boys just out of school. In that sense, Balestier was Kipling's 'double'. Kipling looked up to him, as if his four years' seniority gave him particular authority. Balestier in turn looked up to Kipling, because he was a literary genius. All this we can discern in the fruit of their collaboration. Late in 1891, their tale done and beginning to appear in the magazines, Kipling set out on a long trip to re-immerse himself in his India. He parted from Balestier in the full confidence they would meet again. Balestier was busy then with a new dream of empire. He and Heinemann would form the firm of 'Heinemann and Balestier', they would publish continental editions. Baron Tauchnitz, who had had the field to himself, would be challenged.

In the interest of the new firm Balestier journeyed to Dresden in November of 1891. Almost immediately Heinemann received a message from the American Consul reporting that his partner had come down with typhoid. Mrs Balestier, Caroline and Josephine, went to the bedside of the son and brother. He lingered for three weeks. Henry James and William Heinemann set out early in December, but it was no longer to attend the living. Alice James, the novelist's sister, recorded in her diary,

68

'The young Balestier, the effective and the indispensable, dead! swept away like a cobweb, of which gossamer substance he seem to have been himself compounded, simply spirit and energy, with the slightest of fleshly wrappings.'

It was a dismal moment – the mourning women, the alien cemetery in Dresden, the baroque German funeral equipage – and it all seemed strange and macabre to Henry James, with his thoughts of the 'yesterday-much-living-boy'. The services were read by a local chaplain. James handed to Balestier's younger sister a pot of English flowers he had brought across the channel: Mrs Gosse had given him this bit of English earth and fragrance and the sister let it fall into the foreign grave. As James came away, the older sister, Caroline, beckoned to him to ride with her in her carriage. They were alone in it; she wanted to talk to him. 'Poor little concentrated Carrie' sat and talked in the big black and silver coach, with its black and silver footmen perched behind, dressed in her deep mourning. James found her 'remarkable in her force, acuteness, capacity and courage – and in the intense – almost manly – nature of her emotion. She is a worthy sister of poor dear big-spirited, only-by-death-quenchable Wolcott.' James would always remember 'her little vivid, clear-talking, clear-*seeing* black robed image'. And he added, in a letter to Gosse, 'she can do and face, and more than face and do, for all three of them, anything and everything that they will have to meet now'. He never revealed what she said to him, but an enigmatic sentence to Gosse suggests that she may have hinted at the possibility of a marriage to Rudyard Kipling. 'One thing, I believe the poor girl would *not* meet – but God grant (and the complexity of "genius" grant), that she may not have to meet it – as there is reason to suppose that she will. What this tribulation is – or would be, rather, I can indicate better when I see you.' We may believe this was James's way of saying he could not believe in such a marriage and that he hoped it might be averted. One can believe the only 'tribulation' Caroline might have had at this moment would have been a negative word from the celebrated story-teller to whom she had sent a cable bearing the terrible news.

Kipling received word of Balestier's death in Lahore, to which he had just returned. We have no record of his grief, but we know that it was long and it was profound. He left promptly for London and made the journey – difficult as it was then – in a fortnight. Henry James wrote a long tribute; Gosse memorialized Wolcott; other authors in London paid elegant praise. Kipling remained silent, he who could be so articulate. What indeed could he say that would measure his grief? It is clear, however, and so his biographer assumes, that Wolcott's death determined him to marry Caroline. There had been some courtship during the previous year; but there also were rumours that its course had not been smooth. Kipling was not at his ease with women. Moreover Kipling's mother opposed the match. She had from the first had an intuition that '*that* woman is going to marry our Rudyard'. Another plain-spoken Kipling relative called Caroline Balestier 'a good man spoiled'. But perhaps this 'manliness' enabled her to become a kind of permanent 'stand-in' for her dead brother in Kipling's life: it was almost as if the extinguished friendship could be revived, within the intimacy of marriage, a permanent anodyne for grief. At any rate, Henry James, performing his rôle with becoming gravity, played the father and gave Caroline Balestier in marriage to Rudyard Kipling at All Souls, Langham Place, on 18 January 1892, scarcely five weeks after Wolcott's burial in Dresden. The bride was in mourning; Mrs Balestier and the younger daughter were home with influenza. Heinemann, James, the Gosses, one of Kipling's Poynter relatives, made up the congregation at this strange nuptial over which hung so profound a shadow. Henry James said he couldn't understand Kipling's marrying Caroline; it was 'an odd little marriage'. A few days later the newly-married couple sailed for America.

Was it Wolcott's personal magic that gave to this particular friendship such depths and intensities? Who can say? Years later, Henry James, brooding on this, and writing every year in remembrance to Mrs Balestier (on the anniversary of his Dresden pilgrimage), wondered what 'Wolcott would have made of some of Rudyard's actualities – and what complications *that* friendship might have had to reckon with: but the mystery swallows up the question'. As we review our meagre records, the memorials, the gossip, the newspaper paragraphs, we discern above all that the two men were singularly matched. It had been a meeting of Anglo-American West with Anglo-Indian East: the two 'strong' men could enter into each other's lives and dreams and had a common sense of grandeur. Both had found themselves in the thick human scene of London at the very dawn of the 1890s. Both could share the memories of their lives on continents. Balestier had large plans of business empires and wealth, great coalitions of art and prosperity. Kipling had a night-dream – recorded late in life – that somehow matches. He was leading an enormous force of cavalry mounted on red horses with new leather saddles under the glare of a green moon across steppes 'so vast that they revealed the circle of the earth'. Kipling's imagination, we can see, was no less Napoleonic than Balestier's. They invented adventures as they invented difficulties to challenge their courage and their manliness. Kipling would say that what he liked in Americans was not only their 'English instincts' but the fact that they were trained 'from youth to believe that nothing was impossible'. Balestier was Kipling's kind of American.

He was more. Behind a façade of exaggerated masculinity and cowboy swagger, was their attachment in an age when the world of men was well-defined. Over drinks, in bars or in their clubs, men could exchange intimate feelings and stories, know, possess, a profound sense of brotherhood and union. It was the love of man for man, the hearty kind that swaps tall tales and could use language prohibited then in the drawing room. Between Balestier and Kipling it was a case of camaraderie and of love, almost at first sight. Platonic, quite clearly. Both would have been terrified at any other suggestion.

Louis Cornell
THE AMERICAN VENTURE

IN the spring of 1889 a young journalist decided to leave India and see the world. The Allahabad *Pioneer* wished to pay him for travel sketches; the charming Mrs Hill and her pleasant husband, eastward bound on a visit to her home in Pennsylvania, offered themselves as travelling companions; new lands beckoned. In March the three friends watched India disappear astern, and two months later Rudyard Kipling first set foot on the soil of the United States.

Already in 1889 Kipling had more than a casual tourist's interest in America: above all English writers of his generation, he was steeped in American literature. Many years before, as quite a young child, he had discovered Emerson's poems; in school he imitated the metre of 'Hiawatha' and defended Whitman against the sarcasm of Mr Crofts; later, in India, he began his career as a story-teller with pastiches of the tales of Poe. With the older American writers he was on terms of easy familiarity. But in 1865, the year of Kipling's birth, Lee had surrendered at Appomattox and a new America was born. The gentilities of transcendental Boston were swept away in an international flood of enthusiasm for a new American literature based on the humour of the backwoods and the western frontier. The Yankee wit of Artemus Ward first caught the London public in the sixties. Then came C. G. Leland's Hans Breitmann, whose German-American dialect verses Kipling found irresistible. These were the forerunners, preparing the way for Bret Harte, whose California tales took London by storm; for Joaquin Miller, startling the Pre-Raphaelites in his buckskins; for Joel Chandler Harris and his enchanting Uncle Remus stories; and for the genius who raised the humorous tradition to classic stature, Mark Twain.

Unlike the work of the great Bostonians, this was a popular literature, written by working journalists to entertain a vast new public of newspaper readers. Its impact on the English reading public was immense: throughout the seventies and eighties they rejoiced in Poker Flat and the Jumping Frog and the Tar Baby with all the abandon of Stalky, Beetle, and the 'United Idolaters'. But though the English literati were hospitable to Bret Harte and lionized Mark Twain, the literature of the time shows scarcely a trace of their influence. The aesthetes and decadents could not be expected to show much interest in Roaring Camp; the realists, following Zola's lead, were exploring the mean streets of a different kind of wilderness.

But there was one notable exception. Rudyard Kipling, fresh from the United Services College, sailed for India unencumbered by prejudices either Zolaist or aesthetic, taking his enthusiasm for Harte and Twain with him. In India he found a frontier society not totally unlike the imaginary California of his favourite writers. More important, as a working journalist he discovered that he too faced an audience more eager for amusement than subtle effects. 'Why buy Bret Harte, I asked, when I was prepared to supply home-grown fiction on the hoof?' And so he began to write as it were in the American vein. The colloquial style, the exaggeration of character and incident, the eye for local colour, the fascination with ne'er-do-wells and outcasts, the broad humour that lapses into broader farce: these are elements of the frontier convention that Kipling adopted as a matter of course. It is coincidence that the *Week's News* was serializing Harte's *Argonauts* when Kipling took over as editor. It is not an accident that the weekly continued to run three or four columns of frontier jokes, tall stories, and Negro dialect anecdotes in every issue while Kipling remained in charge.

When the editor became a roving reporter sent to 'do' America, he turned into something of a literary pilgrim as well. Arriving in San Francisco, he tried to convey his admiration for Bret Harte to an American interviewer and was disgusted to find that the American wrote off Harte as too Anglicized. He fared better on his journey north through the California hills: every landscape, every personage glimpsed by the way suggested a Harte original; his fellow-travellers shared his enthusiasm; and his Indian readers were subjected to a cascade of Bret Harte allusions. The famous tourist sights of the central United States – Yellowstone, Salt Lake City, and Chicago – were not part of Kipling's imaginative universe, and his account of them is correspondingly superficial. But when he reached Mrs Hill's home in Beaver, Pennsylvania ('Musquash on the Monongahela'), he felt he had discovered the older America of *Little Women*. The plain living and high thinking of the New England sages here combined with a freedom of social intercourse that the lonely young Anglo-Indian found altogether delightful.

The last of Kipling's American letters is the account of the traveller's interview with Mark Twain. But 'interview' is surely the wrong term: it was rather a pilgrimage; the young man came as a fellow author to pay homage to one of his masters, not as a journalist to exploit a famous public figure. It made a happy climax to the American trip. Settled in the east, Clemens seemed to represent a synthesis of all that was best in American life and letters, the gusto of his western youth now subdued to the maturity of the New England tradition. Here were the qualities Kipling loved best in American letters, combined in an American that the pilgrim could unreservedly admire.

As a conclusion to *From Sea to Sea*, the Mark Twain interview is more tactful than consistent. Through the travel letters, side by side with extravagant praise runs a strain of perplexity, irritation, even at times hostility that was to persist in most of Kipling's literary and personal dealings with America. This mixture of feelings is obvious from the start. The tone is set during the Pacific crossing when Kipling joins in conversation with a group of Americans who deplore the state of their country and attack democracy with surprising virulence. Kipling is clearly disturbed: he is not unsympathetic to the attack on democracy but is scarcely prepared to go to the lengths of the chief American spokesman; though he normally mocks American flag-waving, he is embarrassed by this equally American self-castigation. At the same time, the whole incident seems an invitation for the visitor to join in the game; it appears to establish a precedent for the kind of critical assessment of America that runs as a motif through Kipling's writings. 'I love this People,' he was to write a month or so later, 'and if any contemptuous criticism has to be done, I will do it myself.'

That his American readers didn't take kindly to the contemptuous criticism is beside the point. In fact, Kipling encountered the United States at a time when the citizens were themselves deeply perplexed as to where they stood and where they were going. Kipling's fellow passengers, though scarcely qualified as social critics, express a number of the tensions that historians have identified as characteristic of the time. Immigrants were undercutting the political power of the native Americans; westward expansion had moved too quickly, creating a new pattern of sectional rivalry; an ugly spirit of greed was driving the good men from politics. A nation that had preserved its unity through the bloodbath of the Civil War now saw that unity threatened again as expansion, immigration, and industrialization magnified rifts between region and region, class and class.

These themes recur in *From Sea to Sea* and are essential to the understanding of Kipling's other American writings; but none is as important as the theme of lawlessness. Already a keen student of power, Kipling was fascinated by the energy and versatility of the common American: 'There is nothing known to man that he will not be, and his country will sway the world with one foot as a man tilts a see-saw plank!' Yet this raw energy acknowledged no principle of order; a democracy that had made laws for itself now seemed to hold them in contempt. Gun duels were still fought on the streets of San Francisco, but this was only the most spectacular manifestation of an anarchic individualism that was dominating American life, whether in the west, where robber barons were stripping the land of her resources, or amidst the 'grotesque ferocity' of Chicago's striving millions. Accustomed to India, where every citizen had a place in Indian society or English officialdom, Kipling was unnerved by the disorderly spectacle of the western states. More to his taste were the 'peace, order, and decency' of Beaver, where he spent a month with Mrs Hill and her family. And yet, though he joined his American contemporaries in cherishing the small-town idyll, he had to recognize that 'Musquash' was no refuge from the future; already the young men were leaving the town, drawn away by the challenge of the new cities and the west.

Kipling left America in September. About a year later he undertook to write a novel in collaboration with another young journalist, Wolcott Balestier. *The Naulahka* appeared in 1892. Though inferior in quality and problematical because of Balestier's share in the writing, the book nevertheless remains interesting, if only for its expression of Kipling's mixed feelings about America. These feelings are embodied in Nick Tarvin, one of the most ambiguous of Kipling's protagonists. He represents the new man of the west; versatile, humorous, boastful, stubborn, and unscrupulous. When he cannot buy the crown jewels of Rhatore, he takes them at gunpoint. When Kate Sheriff refuses to accept him, he pursues her to the point at which his machinations bring about the destruction of the hospital she has built. In the end he gives back the Naulahka, but only because he realizes that he can't keep both the necklace and the girl.

And yet the novel does not condemn Tarvin for his lawlessness. On the contrary, he is the only character in the book who comes to life: against the pervasive lassitude of Gokral Seetarun, the drowsy salesmen, the futile missionary couple, the drugged maharajah, Tarvin's energy is thrown into spectacular relief. In this way Tarvin represents the dilemma of the American character. He is a dangerous customer, but at the same time and for that very reason an immensely attractive one. His vice of lawlessness and his merit of energy are inseparable, are but two aspects of the same whole. The paradox tantalized Kipling; but though he was to observe it at much closer quarters, he would never quite succeed in resolving it.

The first magazine instalment of *The Naulahka* was published in November 1891. By the time the last appeared in July 1892, Kipling's relations with America had become immeasurably more complicated. In the midst of their joint project, Wolcott Balestier died. His collaborator cut short a world cruise and hurried back to London, where, in a gesture mysteriously compounded of love, loyalty and solicitude, he married Wolcott's sister Caroline. Scarcely pausing in London, the young couple set sail again, bound westward now over the Atlantic trail Kipling was beginning to know so well. First stop was Brattleboro, Vermont, where the Balestiers, formerly summer visitors, had taken root as gentlemen farmers; then swiftly westward once more, north into Canada, west again by Canadian Pacific and ocean liner to Japan for a brief honeymoon among the spring flowers of Yokohama. A bank failure interrupted their holiday. Shorn of his savings, with a child on the way, Kipling brought his bride back to her family home. They settled in Brattleboro in July 1892 and remained there for four years.

The Kiplings bought land from Caroline's brother, Beatty, and began to build a house soon after their first child was born. Nevertheless, Kipling's own feelings about America, though intensified by his new commitments, remained as mixed as ever. The countryside around Brattleboro delighted him; he described his first impressions in a sketch called 'In Sight of Mount Monadnock' (1892), then returned to the same scenes in a later sketch, a brilliant piece of impressionism called 'Leaves from a Winter Note-Book' (1895). Like many a visiting American, he was attracted to the figures as well as the landscape, the dour farmers and hunters who had held on to their farms as they watched their children drift away to the cities. But already in 1892 Kipling could see beneath the surface of their picturesque lives; aided by the New England stories of Mary Eleanor Wilkins and Sarah Jewett, he could perceive the 'terrifying intimacy' of life in a country town, 'disturbed by the hatreds and troubles and jealousies that vex the minds of all but the gods'. With only the briefest experience of Brattleboro, he was able to identify the forces that would make life there intolerable for him a few years later.

The remainder of the Kiplings' wedding journey, ending with the enforced return to Vermont, provoked some further remarks about the quality of American life. New York he detested – 'The more one studied it, the more grotesquely bad it grew.' Amidst this 'shiftless outcome of squalid barbarism and reckless extravagance' flourished American lawlessness at its most repulsive, unredeemed by the energy and high spirits of the West. The Pacific journey brought brief contact with that western vigour; Kipling found it embodied in seal-hunters, explorers, developers of the boom towns; to such as these he first applied the phrase 'captains courageous'. But none of the Americans he met on that journey made as deep an impression on him as the summer visitors he encountered in Brattleboro on his return there in July. These displaced urbanites seemed to confirm what he had long suspected: the vaunted energy of the American businessman was little more than a neurotic restlessness bordering on desperation. The vigour that was civilizing the West here found too little scope, with consequences that distressed an English observer: '... out of strain is bred impatience in the shape of a young bundle of nerves, who is about as undisciplined an imp as the earth can show. Out of impatience, grown up, habituated to violent and ugly talk, ... is begotten lawlessness, encouraged by laziness and suppressed by violence when it becomes insupportable.'

That 'undisciplined imp' would take form as Harvey Cheyne four years later. Meanwhile, for all his reservations about the American character, Kipling moved into his substantial new house (it was called Naulakha in memory of Wolcott Balestier), and gave every impression of settling permanently in Brattleboro. In some respects he felt more secure, more at ease in the world than he had since he had left India. This sense of security released a flood of creative power that resulted in the stories of *The Day's Work*, the poems of *The Seven Seas*, and the richly imagined world of the two *Jungle Books*. For the first time in his life Kipling had no need to write in haste and to order.

Nevertheless, hindsight reveals that below the surface of his happiness, Kipling was not altogether at ease in Vermont. He had written of Brattleboro in 1892, 'There is so much, so very much to write, if it were worth while about that queer little town' – but he did not write about it. His only story with a Vermont setting is 'A Walking Delegate' (1894). This of course is a parable or fable: it tells us something about the hardening of Kipling's opinions concerning America, but the fact that its characters are parabolic horses, not real Vermonters, suggests even more about Kipling's imaginative estrangement from the life around him. For America still presented herself to him as a dilemma to be analysed, a puzzle rather than a scene. Her lawlessness, for example, gave rise to the speculations about the very meaning of the Law itself that inform the *Jungle Books*. Not only the Bandar-log but, much more richly and subtly, the Seeonee Pack (the 'Free People') glance at American habits and institutions; and Mowgli, growing up under the Law of the Jungle, implicitly reproaches that undisciplined imp, the American child. But for all the parabolic undercurrent of these tales, their distant setting testifies to the diffidence with which Kipling's imagination encountered the American scene.

A long visit to England in the summer of 1894 produced two relevant stories. Not precisely anti-American, 'An Error in the Fourth Dimension' and 'My Sunday at Home' show the widening rift between Kipling and his adopted countrymen. Their significance lies partly in the handling of the American protagonists, but even more in the insistence on the Englishness of the narrator. He is on his native heath, looking on while the alien Americans make fools of themselves. If any of Kipling's American public were deluding themselves that he might take out citizenship papers, if they chose to ignore the tone and message of 'A Song of the English' (1893), these stories could serve to enlighten them. Kipling's imagination was turning to the old country with a longing he had never felt before.

As the third year of the Kiplings' residence in Vermont drew to a close, domestic and international squabbles began to threaten the harmony of their lives. A visit to Washington in 1895 had given Rudyard a disturbing glimpse of Grover Cleveland's administration. Later that summer his worst suspicions seemed realized as Washington tried to magnify a Venezuelan border dispute into a war scare. Without the soothing influence of a common enemy, America and the British Empire maintained a friendliness that was at best precarious. If Kipling's occasional trumpet calls on behalf of Anglo-Saxon unity now seem a bit shrill, we must remember that they sounded above the rumblings of Anglo-American rivalry. 'So far as I was concerned,' Kipling wrote forty years later, 'I felt the atmosphere was to some extent hostile.'

Anglo-American relations worsened on the domestic level too: that summer the ever-present tension between Carrie and her brother, Beatty, erupted into a serious quarrel. Temperamental opposites, the brother and sister had been moving toward such a clash for years. Carrie was orderly and conscientious to a fault; Beatty's hard drinking and good-humoured carelessness seemed calculated – as perhaps they were – to try her patience to the limit. For Rudyard the situation carried a special irony. He could get along with Beatty splendidly as a friend and neighbour: such breezy ne'er-do-wells had sauntered through his life and his fiction from the earliest days; as long as it was only a matter of trading tall stories over a glass of whiskey, Beatty answered Kipling's deeply-felt need for masculine comradeship, for high spirits laced with imaginative profanity. But Beatty was no chance-met boon companion. Besides the family connection, he had become something like estate manager for the Balestier-Kipling houses and acreage; most of his income derived from the work he did for Carrie and Rudyard. Seldom coming up to the Kipling's high standards, he confronted the author of *The Day's Work* with a particularly harassing problem. For six years Kipling had been characterizing the American as energetic, versatile, casual, slipshod, and lawless. Now he found on his own doorstep a prize example of the type, bound to him by unbreakable ties and in a dangerous mood.

Before the storm broke, however, Kipling set to work on his most ambitious attempt to capture the essence of American life. Nearly all the materials for *Captains Courageous* were at hand in the difficult winter of 1895–6. He had already used the title once, applying it to pioneers and soldiers of fortune. He had virtually described Harvey Cheyne in his sketch of the summer visitors. At the end of that sketch he had turned away from the vacationers and found the real strength of America in her farmers, 'unhandy men to cross in their ways, set, silent, indirect in speech, and as impenetrable as that other eastern farmer who is the bedrock of another land'. Since then had come the vision of Mowgli, the child who grows up under the Law to a superhuman strength and wisdom. When Dr Conland suggested a visit to the Gloucester fishing fleet, everything seemed to come together. The discipline of the sea would provide the antidote to Harvey's slack upbringing; the 'captains courageous', now rugged fishermen, would exemplify the values of the plain folk, the good American values that were everywhere in retreat before the falsities of the Gilded Age.

In fact, the various impulses that underlie the book never really fused. The account of the fishing fleet is brilliant, for Kipling's delight in the milieu was deep and spontaneous: no matter how much he dwells on the hardships of the fisherman's life, we know that he is enjoying every minute of it. But the plan of the book required that life to be put into relation with the very different life of contemporary America, and this Kipling could not bring off. Harvey is washed from the after deck into the past, into what Kipling admitted was 'a rather beautiful localised American atmosphere that was already beginning to fade'. Eight chapters later he returns to the present. He is changed, but the world he left – for all the author's assertions – is the same. No sooner are the crewmen ashore than they fade away, leaving the stage to a regenerated Harvey who has nothing better to look forward to than life as a decent, hardworking robber baron. Feeling as he did about American life, Kipling could not invest his upbeat moral fable with any real conviction; he knew that the vanishing world of the Gloucester fleet was not going to redeem present-day America through the disciplining of her sons: *Captains Courageous* is perhaps the only one of Kipling's works that lies open to the charge of insincerity.

As American publishers outbid one another for the serial rights to Rudyard's newest book, the Kiplings' precariously-knit Brattleboro life suddenly began to unravel. The immediate cause was a noisy showdown between Rudyard and Beatty. In isolation, it would have been no more than a trivial unpleasantness. But for Kipling, who had not forgotten his brush with gun-toting desperadoes in the West, it was portentous. In a gesture that now appears suicidal, he appealed to the courts to restrain Beatty, and this delivered him into the hands of the reporters, whom he had been insulting in print for years. They in turn spread out all the details of the affair before the avid eyes of the Brattleboro neighbours, starved for gossip after four years of the Kiplings' more than English reserve. It was as if Kipling had thrown America a direct challenge to be her worst possible self: all the forces he had hated and feared since his first visit seven years before were now unleashed against him. But though his darkest conclusions about America seemed to be borne out on every side, he got no satisfaction from it. He could not very well stay in Brattleboro, and yet he hated the thought of leaving. The inevitable retreat to England was delayed till the end of that unhappy summer; the Vermont house was kept for six more years in hopes of a return; the day before the family left, Rudyard said to one of their many loyal American friends, 'There are only two places in the world where I want to live – Bombay and Brattleboro. And I can't live at either.'

Mr Edmund Wilson proposed the theory that America's rebuff drove Kipling once and for all into the arms of authority. 'He invoked the protection of the British system and at the same time prostrated himself before the power of British conquest.' There is truth in this view, but it is not the whole truth. All his life Kipling was torn between his delight in energy and his respect for order. At different stages in his career, or in particular stories and poems, one principle will be in the ascendancy, but the other can never be entirely suppressed. All his most vividly imagined figures – Mulvaney, the three schoolboys, Mowgli, and especially Kim – share a deeply ambiguous relation to authority, just as Kipling did himself: only Teshoo Lama, released from the Wheel, transcends this dialectical tug-of-war.

Kipling's fascination with energy led him to the United States in the first place; but it is clear in retrospect that he could not or would not attune his imagination to the dilemmas and contradictions of American life. Withdrawing to a sanctuary from which he could observe the Gilded Age yet remain protected from it, he tried to make an enclave for himself in the hills above Brattleboro. An assembly of the forces he dreaded conspired to drive him from his redoubt; but there is no reason to believe that he could have stayed in Brattleboro if Beatty had left him alone. Naulakha gave him a breathing space in which to recover fragments of his own and America's past: to remain there, in a seclusion increasingly hostile, would have denied his artistic commitment to record the struggle between old order and new energy that was working itself out on both sides of the Atlantic. America would find her own spokesmen in the coming times. But, as England's imperial day began to draw to its close, it was upon her darkling plains, amidst her ignorant armies, that Kipling was forced to seek the resolution of the great dialectic that moved his life.

George Shepperson
KIPLING AND THE BOER WAR

... you're *our* partic'lar author, you're our patron an' our friend,
You're the poet of the cuss-word and the swear,
You're the poet of the people where the red-mapped lands extend ...

IN these words of affectionate parody, a young British private soldier (later to become famous as Edgar Wallace) who was serving as a medical orderly in the Simonstown Hospital, South Africa, welcomed Rudyard Kipling to Cape Town in January 1898. They were lines which revealed Kipling's remarkable popularity amongst British soldiers and English-speaking peoples all over the world on the eve of the war between Great Britain and the two South African Dutch republics across the Vaal and the Orange Rivers.

To Afrikaners (Boers), however, this patriotic writer, with his praise of the outposts of Empire and his catching calls to a British Imperial mission, appeared in a very different light. In a parody of Kipling's 'Recessional' (dedicated to 'Mr Mudyard Pipling'), F. W. Reitz, President of the Orange Free State from 1889 to 1895 and Secretary of State of the South African Republic from 1898 until its annexation by the British in 1902, described Kipling and his friends, men like Cecil John Rhodes and Leander Starr Jameson who, in the opinion of many Afrikaners, were intent on swallowing them up in the interests of foreign gold, diamond and railway magnates, as

> Gods of the Jingo – Brass and Gold,
>   Lords of the world by 'Right Divine',
> Under whose baneful sway they hold
>   Dominion over 'Mine and Thine',
> Such Lords as these have made them rotten,
>   They have forgotten – they have forgotten.
>
> Drunk with lust of Power and Pelf,
>   They hold not man nor God in awe,
> But care for naught but only Self,
>   And cent. per cent.'s their only Law.
> These are their Lords for they are rotten,
>   They have forgotten – they have forgotten.

To Kipling, the aggression was all on the Boer side. He was no stranger to South Africa, having first visited it in 1891; and, in addressing a dinner of the Anglo-African Writers' Club in London on 20 May 1898, he gave his considered opinion on the Dutch in South Africa. He complained of the conditions under which the 'Uitlanders' (foreigners, mainly English-speaking) were forced to live in the Afrikaner republics. The Boers, whether in the British-ruled Cape Colony or in the Dutch republics, were a backward-looking, obscurantist people, opposed to the coming of civilization. Kipling claimed that the Dutch whom he had observed at the Cape often objected to 'the elementary rudiments of civilization': railways; ' "roads" of all kinds'; 'little things like compulsory education and compulsory inoculation'. The mere observation of the conditions under which they lived had made him 'violently unwell for a week'. The Boers were responsible for discriminating against 'his own countrymen' who had to live 'with the great guns of forts looking into their back gardens'. Nevertheless, he advocated patience with the Afrikaners; and gave to the British in South Africa the typical Kipling advice, 'Be quiet; stop prating about that loaded rifle, and work.'

And yet, as he sat down to the cheers of the guests at this dinner, Kipling could not be sure that his advice would be taken. He concluded by saying that he hoped 'he had not done any mischief by what he had said that night'. But his remarks had been trenchant; and they fitted into and, perhaps, in a small way helped to form a mounting mood of British anger at the Afrikaners. This is suggested by a poem attributed to 'a 'umble waiter' at the dinner who, like Edgar Wallace, could not resist imitating Kipling's style:

> Then I listened to yer speakin' (I was 'id behind the screen),
> An' I said, 'Well, this 'ere Kiplin', 'e's a *man*, an' no mistake';
> An' I said, 'Oh – this waitin', chuck it, let's go out an' fight,
> I should like to punch some fellow's 'ead for good old England's sake!'

War fever intensified in both countries. In May 1899, the British High Commissioner in South Africa, Sir Alfred Milner (into whose social circle Kipling had been drawn when he dined with him, Rhodes and the editor of *The Times* after his election to the select Athenaeum Club in London), sent the Colonial Secretary, Joseph Chamberlain, a telegram for publication in which he declared that Britain had an overwhelming case for intervention in South Africa because 'thousands of British subjects were kept permanently in the position of helots' by the Boers. In September, Britain decided to reinforce its limited army of 12,000 men in South Africa with 10,000 soldiers. On 9 October 1899, Paul Kruger, President of the South African Republic, issued an ultimatum to the British ordering them to withdraw from their colonies in South Africa any troops who had arrived since 1 June and to halt any reinforcements which might be at sea. The ultimatum expired at 5 pm on 11 October. Britain was at war with the Boers; and an Army Corps of 47,000 men was despatched to the Cape.

During this year of drift to war, Kipling himself suffered a series of misfortunes. Instead of wintering in the warm south, as was his custom, in 1899 the Kiplings went to the cold, northern United States for family and business reasons. Kipling's wife was taken ill in February; he nearly died himself in March from inflammation of the lungs; his daughter, Josephine, died on 6 March; his quarrel with his American brother-in-law continued; and Kipling plunged into a lawsuit with an American publishing house for pirating his works. A summer in England did not improve the family's health, and he was ill again at the end of the year. To add to these problems, Kipling, who had long been aware of British unpreparedness in South Africa, experienced the gloom of the 'Black Week' in December 1899, when, in three battles against the Boers, there were 3,000 British casualties.

Indeed, as Great Britain was entering into a turning-point in its history with the Boer War ('our first national and our first Empire War', as it was called by Kipling's friend, L. S. Amery, *The Times*' chief war correspondent), Kipling was going through a critical period in his own life. Because of his well-known reticence it is difficult to know how far his personal crisis coloured his attitude to the national crisis, and vice versa. It is not unreasonable, however, to suppose that there was some mutual influence. In his complex poem on the Boer ultimatum, 'The Old Issue' which was published in *The Times* on the eve of the War, it is possible that such a process was at work. What is clear about this poem, however, is its patriotic stance against the Calvinistic Kruger:

> We shall drink dishonour, we shall eat abuse
> For the Land we look to – for the Tongue we use.

Such unadulterated patriotism was to inspire Kipling's actions in the early weeks of the Boer War. He formed a volunteer company in his village of Rottingdean, Sussex: the beginning of a preoccupation with rifle clubs and 'home guard'-style activities which was to last until the First World War, if not later. And he began to work feverishly for the Soldiers' Families' Fund and other war charities.

The first manifestation of this was his rollicking but socially-conscious poem, 'The Absent-Minded Beggar', with its criticism of those armchair warriors 'killing Kruger' with their mouths, and its spirited call to do something to save the soldiers' families from that ultimate terror of Victorian and Edwardian society: the workhouse. First published in the *Daily Mail* for 31 October 1899, the poem subsequently appeared in a variety of versions: on tobacco jars, ash trays, packages of cigarettes, pillowcases, plates, and many other forms. One of these was a triptych, with the famous Woodville illustration of a British 'Tommy', which was distributed as a souvenir by Lily Langtry in London at the hundredth performance of a play with the title of 'Degenerates'. Lady Tree recited it daily at the Palace Theatre for fourteen weeks and raised £70,000. Set to music by Sir Arthur Sullivan, it went the rounds of barrel-organs, music halls, smoking-concerts, drawing-room recitals, raising at least a quarter of a million pounds. Mark Twain declared that 'the clarion-peal' of its 'great lines . . . thrilled the world'. It led to the offer of a knighthood for Kipling – which he refused. If it is difficult to agree with Mr Peter Porter's claim[1] that 'The Absent-Minded Beggar' 'did actually contribute substantially to the final British victory' in the Boer War, there is no doubt that, both as fund-raiser and morale-raiser, it was no mean contribution to the war effort. It is also no mean poem, in its way; and it is difficult to see why Kipling left it out of the selection of his Boer War verse which he published in *The Five Nations* in 1903.

It has been said of this verse that its 'political flavour' increased 'measurably but steadily during the war years'. This is undoubtedly true, particularly of the famous long poem, 'The Islanders', which Kipling sent to *The Times* before he left to spend the winter in South Africa in 1902. Its attacks on all elements of British society, upper, middle and lower, with their preoccupation with sport, hunting, strikes and similar unpatriotic occupations that diverted their attention from vital issues of national defence, brought him considerable unpopularity. But it led to the verses and other writings that he produced towards the end of and after the Boer War ('The Lesson',

[1] See 'Rudyard Kipling: A Reassessment' in *The Listener*, 8 April 1965.

54 *Opposite* The Boer War: 'The Editors at Work'. Kipling on the right, his friend H. A. Gwynne, later editor of the *Morning Post*, on the left

South Africa

5 *Opposite* Cecil Rhodes, accompanied by
Dr Jameson, on his arrival in South Africa in February
1902, shortly before his death

6 *Below* The Boer War: war correspondents

"TOMMY,"
"The Absent-minded Beggar."

"JACK,"
The "Cook's Son."

RUDYARD KIPLING'S NEW POEM.

The Absent-minded Beggar.

PRINCE CHRISTIAN
OF SCHLESWIG,

"Son of a
Hundred Kings."

LORD
EDWARD CECIL,

"Son of a
Belted Earl."

LORD CHARLES CAVENDISH-BENTINCK,
A "Duke's Son."

MR. RUDYARD KIPLING.

57 *Opposite* 'The Absent-Minded Beggar' was set to
music by Sullivan: the royalties, which were donated to
a fund for buying 'small comforts for the troops at the
Front', came to some £250,000

58 *Below* Pillars of the Empire. Kipling and
Kitchener; drawing by F. Carruthers Gould from
The Struwwelpeter Alphabet (1908)

59 *Overleaf* 'Prediction from Truth', December
1900, of what things will be like in Paardeberg in 1907.
An on-the-spot sketch of Kipling as a Boer War
correspondent

MEN of different trades and sizes
Here you see before your eyeses;
Lanky sword and stumpy pen,
Doing useful things for men;
When the Empire wants a stitch in her
Send for Kipling and for Kitchener.

A Sketch by Our Special Artist on the spot.

LONDON
CAPE TOWN
PRETORIA

CAMPBELL BANN

SPENCER

THE KIPLING

THE
PRESENT
MINDED
BURGHER

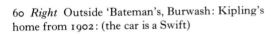

60 *Right* Outside 'Bateman's, Burwash: Kipling's home from 1902: (the car is a Swift)

61 *Below* The mill at 'Bateman's'. 'She has ground her corn and paid her tax ever since Domesday Book . . .'

62 *Opposite* Kipling and his son John on board the yacht *Bantam*, c. 1909

World War One

63 *Right* Kipling appeals for recruits, 1915 (the Mayor of Southport, in volunteer uniform, on his right)

64 *Below* Addressing a meeting at the Mansion House during the First World War

RED CROSS OR IRON CROSS?

WOUNDED AND A PRISONER
OUR SOLDIER CRIES FOR WATER.

THE GERMAN "SISTER"
POURS IT ON THE GROUND BEFORE HIS EYES.

THERE IS NO WOMAN IN BRITAIN
WHO WOULD DO IT.

THERE IS NO WOMAN IN BRITAIN
WHO WILL FORGET IT.

THE SANGERFIELD PRINTING CO. LTD. LONDON.

65 *Top* Wolf Cubs demonstrating the Grand Howl

66 *Left* Anti-German propaganda during the First World War. 'There is no woman in Britain who would do it' – but see 'Mary Postgate'

67 *Above* On the Italian Front, 1917

'Rimmon', 'The Song of the Old Guard', 'The Army of a Dream' amongst others)
which cried out to the British to do something about national defence. Lord Roberts,
the commander of the British forces in South Africa, had seen the trend of Kipling's
thinking when, after the publication of 'The Islanders' he sent him a letter about a
campaign for compulsory military training. We cannot afford to wait, was Kipling's
theme, 'till Armageddon break our sleep'. The state of British military preparedness
at the beginning of the First World War suggests that few heard Kipling's call. But it
was a call which had come to him with renewed and anxious realization during the
Boer War; and this may well have been its most important consequence for him and
those he influenced.

Yet all Kipling's verse during the War was not overtly political in scope. His poems
on the common British soldier in South Africa may not have achieved the popularity
or the range of his verses on the Indian troops in *Barrack Room Ballads*, but some of
them reached heights which even the Indian verses did not attain: the outrageous but
moving onomatopoeia of 'Boots' which no infantryman can fail to appreciate; the
lyrical tribute to the Australian forces in 'Lichtenberg'; the ballad measures of 'Bridge-
Guard in the Karroo'; the poems of reconciliation such as 'General Joubert', 'Piet'
and 'The Settler'. Perhaps the greatest tribute that can be paid to Kipling's South
African verses at this time is that by Dr A. L. Rowse, when he declares that 'it is rare
to be able to express the contemporary as already history, as Kipling did, for instance,
in his Boer War poems, Shakespeare the Elizabethan campaigns in Normandy'.[1]

It is unlikely that a similar tribute could be paid to Kipling's prose of the Boer War:
his two propaganda pamphlets for the Imperial South African association; his short-
lived but spirited journalism for *The Friend*, the troops' newspaper, on whose staff he
served in Bloemfontein from 21 March to 1 April 1900; his handful of short stories;
and his occasional pieces. While not everyone can agree with Mr Edmund Wilson's
assertion that 'the Kipling of the South African stories is venomous, morbid, distorted' a *prima facie* case can be made out for this claim. It is more likely, however,
that there is to be observed in the Boer War tales the transition to the complex symbolism of the Kipling of the later short stories. And, in some of his Boer War tales, an
awakening note of social analysis is to be found: for example, the complicated divisions amongst the whites shown in 'A Burgher of the Free State'; and the commentary
on the white man's war put into the mouth of an Indian soldier-servant in 'A Sahib's
War'.

Yet, neither in his Boer War poetry nor in his prose, did Kipling produce the South
African book which many of his admirers expected of him at the time when Edgar
Wallace was writing his poem in Cape Town, and during and in the immediate aftermath of the Boer War. There is no easy answer to this. South African issues, especially
the Boer War, stirred Kipling profoundly. He often looked upon himself as the
mouthpiece of Cecil Rhodes from his first acquaintance with him in 1897 until his
death in 1902. His winters in Cape Town from 1900 to 1907, in the house that Rhodes

The Kipling Journal, March 1960.

68 *Opposite* British war graves at Abbeville, 1918

built for him on his estate, increased Kipling's affection for South Africa, its country-side and peoples, which had been growing since he first visited it in 1891.

This was intensified by Kipling's South African experiences in 1900. His reputation, which was never higher, preceded him to South Africa; and it was increased amongst soldiers and civilians by his charitable acts, his patriotic journalism, his castigation of the pro-Boer 'Fifth Column' in British territory, and his visits to the front. When he went up early in 1900 to Norval's Point bridge on the Orange River (the setting for his story, 'Folly Bridge'), the excitement 'was surprising'. Almost the whole camp rushed down to see 'the man who put Mr Thomas Atkins on the map'. When Kipling travelled to Bloemfontein for his brief but lively period on *The Friend* newspaper, an editorial claimed that his visit would 'have in it something of the triumph of a conqueror'; and, when he left, the editor wrote on behalf of his staff, 'Great as our readers know him in literature, we know him to be even greater as a man.' Although some critics claimed that the adulation he received in South Africa went to his head, there is no doubt that Kipling had that 'common touch' which he celebrated in his poem, 'If'. No detail of the soldier's life was too small to escape his attention. On his visit to Green Point camp near Cape Town in February 1900, he was described by a soldier as having 'his nose to the ground for subject-matter, and he examined every mortal thing from the Maxims to the officers and privates'. Kipling's attention to the Maxim guns foreshadowed his importation into South Africa of an experimental machine-gun to be tried out in the field.

That Kipling's interest in soldiers' welfare was genuine and not a vehicle for self-publicity was revealed when, after visiting the troops at the Modder River railhead in February 1900, where heavy fighting had occurred, he went back with an ambulance train full of wounded men, and wrote a letter home for one of them who had lost his right arm. Kipling disapproved strongly of the sale of facsimiles of this letter for war charities, and when he tried to get the soldier a job with a town council (the position was given to a former councillor) he excused his intervention on the grounds of the 'well-being of men who have suffered wounds and mutilation for their country'. Injury, disease and death, of which Kipling probably saw more during the British crisis with the Boers than during his days in India, were too serious to be made the subject of stunts – which may be one reason why he left 'The Absent-Minded Beggar' out of *The Five Nations*.

During his short period at Bloemfontein in 1900, Kipling observed soldiers under fire for the first time: in the battle of Kari Siding, at which he was wrongfully accused, by what he called 'the pest-house of propaganda', of helping to shoot down Boer women. In hospitals and at the front, he witnessed outbreaks of typhoid and dysentery, much of which he blamed, with characteristic fervour, on 'our own utter carelessness, officialdom and ignorance'. Kipling never got the images of the dead of the Boer War out of his mind; and when, watching British Army manoeuvres at Aldershot in the late summer of 1913, he had a vision of 'the whole pressure of our dead of the Boer War flickering and re-forming as the horizon flickered in the heat', it was an instance, one amongst several, of the continuity which he saw between the British wars against the Afrikaners and the Germans. His concern for the common soldier was so great and he gave such practical demonstrations of it that, when he claimed during the South African War that his 'position among the rank and file came to be unofficially above that of most generals', he did not exaggerate.

And yet he never produced the great South African book that was expected of him. Was it because, at a time of personal and national distress, his heart and mind, almost in spite of himself, went back to the days of his golden youth in India, and perhaps to the happier times of his childhood? He finished *Kim* in the summer of 1900 after his return from South Africa; and it is clear that it had consumed much of his creative genius in the early and tragic months of the Boer War. He was at work on *Kim*, as one of his comrades on *The Friend* said, 'in the laboratory of his mind – even as he sat with us in Bloemfontein'. Did the creation of *Kim* take too much out of Kipling for a major work on a South African theme to be possible for him?

Certainly, when he returned in the winter of 1901 and 1902 to the house that Rhodes had built him, he stayed close to his family circle – and to Rhodes himself. Kipling fulminated against officialdom, the War Office and the selfishness and short-sightedness of many British civilians. But he never visited the troops at the front nor went up-country again during the War. And, although he was moved by the death of his patron, Cecil Rhodes, and wrote the famous obituary verses about him, Kipling refused an invitation to go north to attend the burial in the Matoppos hills in Rhodesia. During his last winter in South Africa he turned back to the nursery tales which he had told his own children, and finished his *Just So Stories for Little Children* at his house in Cape Town. The Boer War was a long way away from them. A few months later, on 31 May 1902, nearly two years and eight months after it had begun, the War ended with the Peace of Vereeniging, and the Boer Republics ceased to exist as independent states.

To Kipling it was a time of hope. The Boer War had challenged British lassitude and lackadaisicalness. 'We have had,' declared Kipling, 'no end of a lesson: it will do us no end of good . . . It may make us an Empire yet'! He was to write of 'that joyful strong confidence after the war, when it seemed that, at last, South Africa was to be developed'. In less than four years, his hopes were to be destroyed. His friends in power in Britain and South Africa, especially Milner, were forced out of office. Early in 1906, the new Liberal Government in London gave responsible government to the Afrikaners in the Transvaal. It seemed to Kipling that all that the Boer War had been fought for had been destroyed.

A South African historian, Rayne Kruger, has described the Liberal victory of 1906 as the beginning of 'profound change' towards popular democracy in Great Britain, and has attributed many of the reasons for this to the Boer War. 'For one thing,' he writes in *Goodbye Dolly Gray*, 'the war had profoundly shaken people's confidence in the ruling caste, especially as represented by its military officers. Ironically it was Rudyard Kipling [a life-long Conservative] who led the shake-up.' It is unlikely that Kipling would have put it in this way. But in such writings as his poems 'Chant-Pagan' and 'The Return', he saw the social effect of the War on the returned soldiers. 'I started,'

says one of his Boer War veterans, 'as an average kid, I finished as a thinking man.'
And, as another one of them said of himself,

> Me that 'ave seen what I've seen –
> 'Ow can I ever take on
> With that awful old England again . . .
> And the parson an' gentry between,
> An' touchin' my 'at when we meet –
> Me that 'ave been what I've been?

To his pro-Boer contemporaries, who saw in the Afrikaner struggle a battle for
liberty and the rights of small nations, Kipling was often looked upon as 'a sort of
literary bounder who was somehow responsible for the Boer War'; as 'the minnesinger
of the national orgy' of the defeat of the Boers. But was such critics' appreciation of
the Afrikaners more realistic than Kipling's? Their intention, he believed, 'was to
sweep the English into the sea, to lick their own nigger and to govern South Africa
with a gun instead of a ballot box'. 'We put them,' he wrote, 'into a position to uphold
and expand their primitive lust for racial domination.' Kipling was no egalitarian;
but, against the background of events in South Africa since the Boer War, particularly
since 1948, who shall say that his egalitarian critics were right and that he was wrong?

Eric Stokes
KIPLING'S IMPERIALISM

LOOKING back in his seventieth year Kipling could write that every card in his working life had been dealt him in such a manner that he had but to play it as it came. Certainly his imperialism grew upon him effortlessly out of the circumstances of his early life. His birth and infancy in India, his subsequent upbringing by foster-parents in the 'House of Desolation' at Southsea, and then the years at school at Westward Ho! among the sons of impecunious army officers serving overseas, all helped to create a sense of exile from the true centre of his being.

> We have forfeited our birthright
>   We have forsaken all things meet;
> We have forgotten the look of light.
>   We have forgotten the scent of heat.
>
> They that walk with shaded brows,
>   Year by year in a shining land,
> They be men of our Father's House,
>   They shall receive and understand . . .
>
> And Earth accepting shall ask no vows,
>   Nor the Sea our love, nor our lover the Sky.
> When we return to our Father's House
>   Only the English shall wonder why!
>
> (*Song of the Wise Children*, 1902)

His father's summons in 1882 to rejoin the family square in Lahore as assistant editor on the *Civil and Military Gazette* before he was yet seventeen meant a joyous home-coming. But it heightened the contrasts of which his life was composed. In becoming part of the English community in India he paradoxically took upon himself its own sense of exile and its superiority complex over the homestaying Englishman. Because of the need to earn his bread at the earliest moment he had to stifle his inclination to remain in England with his unofficial fiancée, Flo Garrard, or to be entered for Oxford like his wealthy cousin, Stanley Baldwin. From the life of action in the army or the Indian civil administration to which his school friends could look, he was debarred by poor eyesight and scholastic waywardness. His literary aspirations had to be repressed into the career of journalism. It was a long schooling in self-denial, yet in this discipline of imposed limitation he quickly recognized how well the cards had been dealt him.

On the voyage out he passed through the Suez Canal where lay the base camp from which Garnet Wolseley had three weeks earlier struck the single blow that made the British masters of Egypt. This proved to be the first practical essay in the 'new imperialism', touching off the scramble for Africa, and with Gordon's death at Khartoum three years later, fastened the grip of imperialism over the English mind for twenty years. Kipling was in at the start but significantly missed the campaign. He saw just enough to stimulate the imagination, 'the straight line of the Canal, the blazing sands, the procession of shipping, and the white hospitals where the English soldiers lay'. This was but a foretaste of the 'copy' which his seven years in the East were to supply, and for which the English public proved so avid when his name burst like a rocket over London in 1890. But India gave him not only copy; his newspaper training taught him his tight economy of style and turned him to the genre of the short story which became his permanent literary medium. The experience he gained in assessing the weight and colour of words and in using them to convey the physical immediacy of perception – a subtler version of journalistic sensationalism – was never lost. Moreover, the technique of setting a story within two or three widening frames of reference, one of which might be a prefatory motto or verse, enabled him to raise the first *aperçu* in all its freshness and sharpness of detail to progressively higher levels of artistic significance. A tale that could be read at different levels in this way not only assured him of a wide-ranging audience, from railway-travellers to men of letters, but made it possible for him to enlarge his vision within the narrow limitations of his literary form. It might be supposed that his imperialist creed was arrived at in this way, the light inconsequential tales of pathos and satire on Anglo-Indian life with which he began giving way steadily to stories carrying a much heavier frame of symbolism. This is how one of his most perceptive modern admirers, J. M. S. Tompkins, has interpreted him, speaking of 'the coherent and continuous development of his art from the barefaced sallies of immature genius in *Plain Tales from the Hills* to the complex and deeply-considered work of the last two collections'.

Kipling himself says that the larger framework of ideas came only when he had quitted India in 1889 to try his fortune in London. At a stroke he had removed himself from his habitual audience and from his source of copy; inevitably the question of how he should shape his future work pressed upon him. It was as he was riding the first tide of success that there came to him 'the notion of trying to tell to the English something of the world outside England – not directly but by implication. Bit by bit, my original notion grew into a vast, vague conspectus – Army and Navy Stores list if you like – of the whole sweep and meaning of things and efforts and origins throughout the Empire.' The first fruits were 'The English Flag', a set of verses hardly in accord with the oblique conveyance of truth he had resolved upon. Kipling fairly bawled into the public ear, but he struck out a phrase it did not quickly forget and which provided his text for the work ahead:

> Winds of the World give answer! They are whimpering to and fro –
> And what should they know of England who only England know? –

He said the same thing in richer and more splendid verse in 'The Song of the English' two years later in 1893, by which time he had clearly become, in Orwell's words, 'the prophet of British Imperialism in its expansionist phase'.

Even Kipling's most ardent literary admirers have found this overt imperialism an embarrassment and try to shuffle it off. Bonamy Dobrée thought it signified the deformation of Kipling the artist at the hands of Kipling the politician and came to the view that his finest work was completed before the didactic element came to overshadow his writing after 1893. For T. S. Eliot Kipling's imperialism represented an immature phase before the imperial imagination gave place to the historical imagination, and Miss Tompkins looked still later to find the work of Kipling's mature genius in the last twenty years of his life. But there is no agreement on when this rabid imperialist phase began or ended. Edmund Wilson considered that it did not take hold until 1900 and lasted until 1915, but that its effects were fatal. 'How was it,' Wilson asked, 'that the early Kipling, with his sensitive understanding of the mixed population of India, became transformed into the later Kipling, who consolidated and codified his snobberies instead of progressively eliminating them as most good artists do, and who, like Kim, elected as his life work the defence of the British Empire?' Central to his answer was Kipling's over-reaction to the social ostracism he encountered in Vermont after taking his brother-in-law to court for assault in 1896. The death of his daughter on a visit to New York in 1899 sealed the break with America in inconsolable bitterness, and he settled with his family in Sussex as a fierce British race-patriot, for whom almost all other races were 'lesser breeds without the Law'. Wilson's argument for dating the change in Kipling's outlook depends on the thesis that his sensitive understanding of Indian life continued to show itself throughout the 1890s, particularly in the *Jungle Books* (1894 and 1895) and *The Day's Work* (1898), coming to an abrupt end with the completion of *Kim* (1901).

These attempts to explain Kipling's belligerent imperialism by some dateable shift in his fundamental mood are unconvincing, at least so far as his outlook towards tropical peoples is concerned. After leaving India in 1889 his exploitation of Indian material shows a steadily enlarged and not reduced compassion, and the hatred of 'the venomous, morbid, distorted' imperialism of the Boer War period was directed exclusively against white men – Afrikaners, Germans, Americans, and Little Englanders. But the very notion of a radical change of mood and direction in his writing depends on a caricature of the Kipling of the early Indian years. To view him at this period as an exemplar of Keatsian 'negative capability', with that deliberate suspension of judgement that goes with a wide-ranging sensitivity, tolerance and comprehension, is to miss one of the two separate sides of his head by which he explained his own peculiar sensibility, or rather dissociation of sensibility. The note of political prejudice and racial rancour was present from the beginning of his writing and was sounded whenever Kipling felt the security of his Indian world to be under threat, whether from the educated Bengali's ambition for power and place, or from English arm-chair Radicalism typified by Pagett, M.P. And even at the level of artistic awareness there were notes of a still profounder revulsion, when Hinduism became identified in his mind with beastliness and a horror of great darkness that haunted him from his childhood.[1]

So long as India remained an intensely vivid experience and supplied nine-tenths of the material for his stories, he succeeded in keeping the separate elements of his genius in fruitful partnership through the unifying *mise-en-scène*. Whether he put himself into the skin of a British Tommy, an ICS official on leave at Simla, an Afghan

---

[1] Cf. *From Sea to Sea* in Sussex Edition, vol. xxii, pp. 96–7, and my comments in ' "The Voice of the Hooligan": Kipling and the Commonwealth Experience', N. McKendrick (ed.), *Historical Perspectives: Studies in English Thought and Society* (forthcoming).

consumed by a passion for revenge, or an old Hindu Jat recounting the tale of his early illicit love for a Muslim woman, the over-arching Indian sky seems to hold together such wholly discordant moods and attitudes. But his greatest work went beyond the reporter's compartmentalized responses; its achievement was to bring the separate worlds and dimensions into confrontation and to set up a creative tension between them. The contrasted worlds may be those of East and West, or more generally, the world of commonsense rationality as opposed to the underworld of spirituality and magic, or simply the tragi-comic contrast between everyday illusion and pitiless reality. It is the subtle shifts of key between these worlds out of which some of his most impressive stories are constructed, like 'On the City Wall' (*In Black and White*), 'The Man Who Would be King' (*The Phantom Rickshaw*), 'Without Benefit of Clergy' (*Many Inventions*), 'The Bridge Builders' (*The Day's Work*), and 'At the End of the Passage' (*Life's Handicap*).

The change that came over Kipling's writing in the years after the publication of *Many Inventions* in 1893 was partly the result of the growing distance between himself and his Indian experience. Increasingly he was living on memory. As he became a public figure, more politically aware and articulate, it seemed that he became more intent on guarding against intrusion the hoarded treasure-house of his past. The result was to produce idealized images that by their nature tended to exclude genuine tension and conflict. He had always been liable to foreclose his sensibility in this way, producing at times cloying idyllic vignettes like 'Only a Subaltern' (August 1888, *Under the Deodars*), in which his characters observe a perfect cardboard fit. The tendency was now given added impetus by the element of fantasy he introduced in his jungle and animal tales which were written notionally at the level of a child's mentality. But even where he remained in the adult world, and where he continued to wrestle with the two opposed worlds of everyday rationality and the dream kingdom of imagination and unspoiled nature, he excluded the elements of conflict that could not be brought under harmonious control. 'The Miracle of Purun Bhagat' (*The Second Jungle Book*), which foreshadowed *Kim*, was one of the most explicit attempts Kipling made to understand the relationship between the two worlds free of the racial connotation implied in the opposition of East and West. But it achieves its impressive artistic effect by a fairy-tale perfection. To idealize and freeze experience in this way was in the end to kill it, and it is significant that despite the final peroration of *Kim*, with its message of the fertilizing and healing role of Eastern spirituality for modern man, it marks in effect Kipling's farewell to India.

It might be supposed that the counterpart to this idealization of India was a deliberate baring of his teeth in other aspects of his work. That at least would have been nothing new. Even in the wondrously productive year of 1890, after his arrival in London from India, he struck out savagely against what he deemed his political enemies, against the Irish nationalists in 'Cleared', against the Germans in 'An Imperial Rescript' (*Barrack Room Ballads*, 1892), against Gladstonian liberalism and the Indian National Congress in 'The Enlightenments of Pagett M.P.' (*Contemporary Review*, August 1890) and 'One View of the Question' (*Many Inventions*). Yet curiously, even though Dobrée saw him from 1893 as the prey of political didacticism, a study of his actual output scarcely supports the contention. The overtly political verse and stories became less rather than more frequent. The Vermont years (1892–6) were in many ways a retreat from immediacy, punctuated only by the surly snarl against American trade unionism in 'A Walking Delegate' (December 1894, *The Day's Work*). The Jameson Raid in South Africa and the gathering break with his American homestead stirred him in 1896 to sharper consciousness of politics; and with the outbreak of the Boer War in 1899 he determined on giving himself entirely for a few years to the service of the imperial cause. Many of the tales collected in *Traffics and Discoveries* (1904) betrayed the peculiarly vicious streak that his enemies seized upon as proof of the underlying brutality and racialism of his message, but what strikes one on longer consideration is the brevity of this period and the intermittent nature of his political animus. After 1893 Kipling did not seriously falter in his determination to remain a fabulist and to convey the imperial gospel by implication through parable. If there is any deformation of his genius it occurred at a less obvious level, rather in what he failed to accomplish.

But what was the message he sought to convey? In one sense it was no more than the *joie de vivre* that flourished outside the cramped domestic experience of the English middle classes – in the life of the mariner, the settler, the soldier, the colonial official, or even the London cockney. He claimed for art a ground it had forsaken or never occupied, and aimed at recovering the immediacy of elemental experience through the deliberate cultivation of vulgarity – through earthiness, uproarious humour, and a blunt physical assertiveness. One of his main sources of inspiration was the idiom and spirit of the music hall, and it is easy to misunderstand much of his work in the terms of 'Max Beerbohm's caricature of the Bank Holiday cornet virtuoso on the spree'. But there was a more serious purpose. In pointed defiance of the preciosity of the *'l'art pour l'art'* school, he chose to model himself on the ballad-maker who functioned as a mere vehicle of the folk memory and culture, and whose aim was to convey to ordinary men the truths implicit in their own experience. For Kipling was primarily a moralist who reflected contemporary concern at what appeared the debilitating effects of pacific, urban life on human character. Like Machiavelli in the *Discourses*, or Hobbes in the *Leviathan*, he was obsessed with the moral and political disease that seized men once they were secured from the omnipresence of death. That disease was pride and signalled itself in the deluded conceit of the urban intelligentsia who believed themselves to be practising a new, totally altruistic morality while in fact pursuing an egoistic hedonism of the most savage kind. The ordinary people, as distinct from the trade union agitator, were still free of this conceit, possessing as they did the brotherhood and the close knowledge of life and death that came from toil and suffering. In 1890 he sought this lore as the spiritual fount of inspiration, dedicating himself anew in verse with 'The Bell Buoy' (1896) and 'The Wage Slaves' (1902):

> Oh, think o' my song when you're gowin' it strong,
> And your boots are too little to 'old yer,
> And don't try for things that are out of your reach

> And that's what the Girl told the Soldier,
> Soldier! Soldier!

... Some day a man will rise up from Bermondsey, Battersea or Bow, and he will be coarse but clear-sighted, hard but infinitely and tenderly humorous, speaking the People's tongue, steeped in their lives, and telling them in swinging, urging, ringing verse what it is that their inarticulate lips would express. He will make them songs. Such songs! And all the little poets who pretend to sing to the People will scuttle away like Rabbits, for the Girl (who, as you have seen, is, of course, Wisdom) will tell that Soldier (who is Hercules bowed under his labours) all that she knows of Life and Death and Love. And the same they say is Vulgarity![1]

Given this early vision, one needs to ask how successful Kipling was in carrying it into his work. Clearly there was a danger of didacticism, but this was only a superficial indicator of difficulties that lay deeper in his sensibility. His powers as a writer achieve their highest technical skill when he could throw his fertility of imagery and copiousness of verbal resource into a limited frame. But he was constantly threatened by a too ready success that brought in its train the foreclosure of sensibility. Some of his *Barrack Room Ballads*, as T. S. Eliot recognized, are masterpieces of their kind, but all too often they stop short within the limits of artificially contrived vulgarity or pathos. They fall below his ultimate aim of persuading men to see that the ordinary things of life reached upward to a sacramental level. For this he needed to impart a deeper resonance to the delightful verve and spontaneity he could command in such a ballad as 'Loot'. Eliot believed that in 'Danny Deever' Kipling attained the intensity of poetry. But he achieved richer effects for his ultimate purpose in 'The Widow of Windsor', where the earthiness, humour, and tragic pathos of the Tommy is the foundation on which the grandeur of the imperial structure itself is reared:

> Walk wide of the Widow of Windsor,
>   For 'alf of Creation she owns:
> We 'ave bought 'er the same with the sword an' the flame,
>   An' we've salted it down with our bones.
>   (Poor beggars! – it's blue with our bones!)
> Hands off o' the sons of the Widow,
>   Hands off o' the goods in 'er shop
> For the Kings must come down an' the Emperors frown
>   When the Widow at Windsor says, 'Stop!'
>   (Poor beggars! – we're sent to say, 'Stop!')
>   Then 'ere's to the Lodge o' the Widow,
>   From the Pole to the Tropics it runs –
>   To the Lodge that we tile with the rank an' the file
>   An' open in form with the guns.
>   (Poor beggars! – it's always they guns!)

Kipling suffered, however, from a persistent difficulty in finding a suitable literary form to express his imperial imagination. It is not an unfair criticism to suggest that he continued too long with the barrack room ballad, reviving it for his popular Boer

---

[1] 'My Great and Only', *Uncollected Prose I*, Sussex Edition, vol. xxix, pp. 265–6.

War propaganda. His more serious verse, like the Envoi to *Life's Handicap* (1891) 'My new cut ashlar takes the light', the prefatory poem of *Many Inventions* (1893), 'To the True Romance', and 'Recessional' in 1897 suggest he was capable of a more substantial poetic achievement. Similarly, one might fairly argue that he overworked the children's story, going on from the *Jungle Books*, to the *Just So Stories*, *Captains Courageous*, *Puck of Pook's Hill* (1906) and *Rewards and Fairies* (1910). These were media intended to convey truth by implication, but they tended to become arrests in the flow of his sensibility. As a result it has been easy to misunderstand his purpose, and only since Kipling's death have critics begun to recognize the artistic depth of his work.

In recent years Kipling has grown respectable as a student of alienation and of the moral and spiritual predicament of industrial man. We can now see that his imperialism, however questionable superficially in its absolute commitment to dubious persons and causes, at least constituted a serious call to return to the instinctual morality of corporate face-to-face groups in place of the hypocritical moral absolutes of depersonalized society. In essence it was the same as Durkheim's prescription for curing modern *anomie*. And there is a strongly contemporary note in his aim of restoring a balance to over-urbanized, over-intellectualized industrial society by linking it in service with the underdeveloped world and renewing it spiritually by fresh contact there with Nature and 'otherness'; for this is the message of the *Jungle Books* and *Kim*.

Like all the great imperialists Kipling was haunted by a sense of the mortality of empire, so that one is forced to question how essential was empire to his larger philosophy. As early as 1893 he opened 'McAndrew's Hymn' with the line: 'Lord, Thou hast made this world below the shadow of a dream', and he dedicated *Many Inventions* in the same year not to the god of empire but to an unearthly ideal which throughout his life he spoke of as one that could not be consummated except beyond the grave, like the far-off chivalric love of a knight errant for his lady:

> Thy face is far from this our war,
>   Our call and counter-cry,
> I shall not find Thee quick and kind
>   Nor know Thee till I die.
> Enough for me in dreams to see
>   And touch Thy garment's hem:
> Thy feet have trod so near to God
>   I may not follow them . . .
>
> A veil to draw 'twixt God His Law
>   And Man's infirmity,
> A shadow kind to dumb and blind
>   The shambles where we die;
> A rule to trick the arithmetic
>   Too base, of leaguing odds –
> The spur of trust, the curb of lust,
>   Thou handmaid of the Gods!

('To the True Romance', 1893)

Empire then was but the transient shadow of a dream. Like Paul he felt committed to preach the imperial gospel 'that some may be drawn to the Lord – By any means to my Lord!', but he longed to possess his own soul again. The sense of having bound himself voluntarily as a galley slave of empire, of having deliberately sacrificed his talents to 'the day's need' was strong upon him, especially after the Boer War when he murmured for release. In *Puck of Pook's Hill* he identified himself with the colonial-born legionary defending the wall, who after helping to surmount the attack of the northmen declines to serve on under a new emperor. 'In War it is as in Love. Whether she be good or bad, one gives one's best once, to one only. That given, there remains no second worth giving or taking.'

The death of his son at Loos and the shattering of all his horizons by the First World War moved him to a final farewell. At least that is one interpretation which can be put upon the cryptic tale, 'The Madonna of the Trenches' (*Debits and Credits*) first published in 1924. Outwardly this is the story of a sergeant, a model soldier in his fifties, who commits suicide because of a premonition, reinforced by some form of spiritualist manifestation, that the woman he has loved all his life from afar has died and is calling him to be at last united with her. It is this belief in a final union with the ideal in death that has sustained him through the horrors of war; and a quotation from Paul rings in his head: 'If, after the manner of men, I have fought with beasts at Ephesus, what advantageth it me if the dead rise not?' Appended to the story is an act of Kipling's unfinished verse play 'Gow's Watch'. It leaves little doubt about the larger symbolism of the story. The play tells of the corruption of the ancient order of the kingdom, symbolized by the king marrying again. His son, kept too long in palaces instead of being loosed to adventure early, commits incest with the young queen, evidently intended to represent the wantonness of urban democracy. The prince falls to his death from her chamber window; Gow, the faithful servant of the realm, kills the gardener lest he blab. But the king dies broken-hearted, and there follows a struggle for the crown between the young queen and the princess, who appears to signify the uncorrupted stock or moral tradition of Britain and the Dominions. The men of Bargi (the Americans) interpose in the struggle, but the princess emerges victorious. She offers her hand in marriage to Gow, whose fidelity, out of love for the Lady Frances has saved the kingdom. But Gow refuses and, like Godsoe the sergeant, commits suicide on the news that the Lady Frances has died. The princess is left no other choice but union with the traditionless Americans.

Here is a difficult and powerful parable of the decline and fall of the British Empire, but above all, of the otherworldly ideal that sustained it and induced men to lay down their lives for it in war. The princess is told of Gow's love for the ideal, the Lady Frances. Through this love Britain survives the war but neither the ideal nor Gow, its servant, do:

> *Her* wish
> Was the sole Law he knew. *She* did not choose
> Your House should perish. Therefore he bade it stand.
> Enough for him when she had breathed a word:

'Twas his to make it iron, stone, or fire,
Driving our flesh and blood before his ways.
As the wind straws. Her one face unregarded
Waiting you with your mantle or your glove –
That is the God whom he has gone to worship.

The passionate devotion of men to the British Empire as the visible shadow of an invisible ideal was dead. Politics had to take a new shape, the 'craft of kingship' must begin again. Britain had no choice but partnership with the United States, a power which as yet had learned no Law but its own immediate will and to whom world leadership now must pass. But the princess is not to be consoled: 'God and my Misery! I have seen Love at last. What shall content me after?' In the post-patriotic world we are still endeavouring to answer that question.

Robert Conquest
A NOTE ON KIPLING'S VERSE

WITH Kipling we are dealing with what T. S. Eliot describes as 'a type of verse for the appreciation of which we are not provided with the proper critical tools'. The nature of poetic creation, and of the effects on the human mind of the object created, are of an extreme complexity which has not yet yielded its secrets. Attempts to set up 'criticism' as a sort of science in imitation of the success of the physical sciences are premature and pointless – resembling phrenology rather than a genuine study; and, as a result confining the attention to the easily definable, and thus diverting it from the deeper effects. Yet if one holds that at present there can be no such things as either rigour or finality in criticism and that professions to the contrary are merely confusing, one may feel that Kipling, more than most poets, may be illuminated by comments which are admittedly modest and peripheral. All the more so because, in spite of the fruitful essays of Eliot, of C. S. Lewis, of Bonamy Dobrée and (to some extent) of Orwell, large misconceptions persist about not merely the quality, but even the nature of Kipling's verse.

Eliot, in a long eulogy, speaks of Kipling's 'consummate gift of word, phrase, and rhythm', and of his mere skill as a verse writer there can surely be little dispute. But, more generally, Eliot describes him as a 'great writer of verse' rather than of 'poetry' (though conceding that the 'verse' sometimes becomes 'poetry', as in 'Danny Deever'). Rather similarly George Orwell, while holding that 'unless one is a snob and a liar it is impossible to say that no one who cares for poetry could get any pleasure' from 'The Road to Mandalay', adds that all the same it is 'not poetry in the same sense as "Felix Randal" or "When icicles hang by the wall" are poetry'. Eliot's point here (and in effect Orwell's too) is that Kipling is essentially a balladeer – and a writer of hymns, of epigrams, of *vers de société* and occasional poems. If this view is taken there are, as Auden points out, more ballad writers and fewer 'poets' than Eliot implies: he instances Ben Jonson, Dunbar, *Hudibras*, most of Burns, Byron's *Don Juan*[1].

But one may go further: it is not only the balladeer who fails to reach the particular heights implied. And against the Eliot-Orwell view, we may put Lionel Trilling's broader comment: 'Nowadays . . . we are not enough aware of the pleasures of poetry of low intensity, by which, in our modern way, we are likely to mean poetry in which the processes of thought are not, by means of elliptical or tangential metaphor and an indirect syntax, advertised as being under high pressure.' In one sense, at least, this is clearly a parochial defect in contemporary taste. For much English (and foreign) poetry generally recognized to be of the highest type might equally be so criticized – Chaucer and Dryden, La Fontaine and Horace (an affinity with whom is of course to be seen in Kipling's 'translations').

All that Eliot and Orwell are quite truly saying, in fact, is that Kipling's is a poetry of clarification rather than of subtlety and suggestion.

The lapses of clarity are different from the lapses of subtlety, though not necessarily

[1] Auden himself remarks that Kipling's 'poetry is arid; personally, I prefer this to the damp poetry of self-expression, but both are excesses': but this again is to say little more than that Kipling is not except very rarely indeed, a lyricist.

worse. Kipling had, indeed, the vices of his virtues. He was a most prolific writer; and as with almost all English poets who have produced any bulk of work, this means that there are a number of poems on which he could be faulted, just as with Coleridge or Wordsworth or Tennyson.

Much of his verse is of an expository, even didactic nature which it would not be unreasonable to call journalistic. In the role of political rhymester, he sometimes over-simplifies or vulgarizes for the larger audience – the fault (or one of the faults) of modern 'committed' poetry, though often redeemed in Kipling's case by uncommon felicity of phrasing and metre. The reader tends to associate a poet with what is taken, rightly or wrongly, to be the typical tone of his verses, rather than the whole of it, and, in Kipling's case, to generalize excessively from this more journalistic and didactic work. In fact, a selection of a score or a dozen poems could be made which, if read without access to his other verse, would give the impression of Kipling as a poet of sensitivity and sorrow.

All the same, this attention to clarity is at the heart of Kipling's attitude to poetry. In ballad, hymn and epigram the first essential is that they must be readily comprehensible when read aloud. And verse is not readily comprehensible when read aloud unless, generally speaking, the theme is either easy to follow, or non-existent. Again, the aural attention to verbal meaning does not easily stretch back more than a couple of lines, so that a long and complex development involving a different sort of grasp is seldom suitable. This is not to say that this simplicity and apprehensibility is all that matters, nor that profound and subtle effects may not be borne along the lucid stream. Nor, of course, (as Eliot emphasizes), does the audience for the ballad consist only of the simple-minded. But Kipling's usual clarity[1] is not, in any case, any sign of excessive simplicity or crudity of thought. The mind manifest in his fiction is of a brilliant complexity against which the complaint is usually C. S. Lewis's on 'the excess of his art', through being 'too continuously and obtrusively brilliant' – a fault 'only a great artist could commit'. In fact, he has the rather extraordinary characteristic that his prose works are (usually) more subtle than his verse. Much of the verse appears, of course, in the form of epigraphs or codas to the prose, and unlike any other poet's one can think of, his is in a sense inseparable from the prose which produced it, or which it produced. In general, I am here treating the verse in isolation – a procedure justified, I take it, by the republication of the 'story' verses (often in lengthier versions) in the volumes of verse. But as I have said above, it is worth noting that the poems often form a kind of summary, or generalized clarification, of the stories to which they are attached (even if not necessarily at any simple level of direct comment; the relationship of the short version of 'The Prayer of Miriam Cohen' to his 'A Disturber of

[1] The odd obscurities are usually due to a failure to explain in later editions the 'occasion' of occasional verse. For example, 'The Ballad of the Clamperdown' (1892) was intended as a satire on old-fashioned writers on naval tactics. But (in spite of the absurd name of the ship) it is very often taken as quite serious. This is Kipling's own fault. He has become so interested in the problem of what he intended as a *reductio ad absurdum* – the grappling and boarding of an enemy cruiser in modern times – and so taken with the dramatics of a sea battle, that he has gone well beyond his aim. All the same, a footnote might have helped.

Traffic' is notably oblique). And this effect of summarizing often involves a loss of the detail, a certain abdication of the complexity and diversity of the prose; which is only to indicate once more the type of concentration, the type of verse, Kipling was aiming at.

Our 'critical tools' may find this hard to handle (Philip Larkin makes a similar point about John Betjeman). It is also true that the established *Kulturtraeger* of the past couple of generations have trouble with Kipling's content. He never lacked admirers among poets of all types, and has now of course gained considerable rehabilitation even among critics. But the rehabilitation, like the denigration, puts to the fore a rather special aspect of his poetry. Current favourites are, very often, 'The Way through the Woods' and 'A St Helena Lullaby'. These are both reasonably representative of his evocative and constructive skill. But they scarcely seem adequately representative of the more clear-cut, less subtle moods traditionally associated with him (or of the moods of darkness and suffering, of purging and healing, which are also important in his verse). Moreover, leaving aside the *odium politicum* for the moment, the bulk of his work appears to many intellectuals as Philistine. He maintains the prescribed levels of dignity or snobbery or self-importance as little in his themes as in his metres. In him, the childhood component of the adult, so necessary and so fruitful, has not been extinguished by an oh-so-significant adolescence.

Lytton Strachey, Bloomsbury incarnate, could say of Macaulay, 'To write so is to write magnificently, and if one has to be a Philistine to bring off those particular effects one can only say, so much the better for the Philistine.' Kipling, indeed, is incomparably less Philistine than Macaulay, in Strachey's sense. All the same, he lacks many of the characteristics associated with the intelligentsia and thus, however illogically and untruly, with feeling and intellect.

He himself contributed to the mutual ill-feeling, with his talk of 'brittle intellectuals, Who crack beneath a strain'. He sneered at those whose personalities are mere agglomerations of what they have read: 'And this I ha' got from a Belgian book on the word of a dead French lord.' But he has also stated the substance of the clash more plainly and fully:

> Oh glorious are the guarded heights
>   Where guardian souls abide –
> Self-exiled from our gross delights –
>   Above, beyond, outside:
> An ampler arc their spirit swings –
>   Commands a juster view –
> We have their word for all these things,
>   No doubt their words are true.
>
> Yet we, the bondslaves of our day,
>   Whom dirt and danger press –
> Co-heirs of insolence, delay,
>   And leagued unfaithfulness –

> Such is our need must seek indeed
> And, having found, engage
> The men who merely do the work
> For which they draw the wage.

And here we reach the real issue, or much of the real issue. These lines illustrate C. S. Lewis's point that Kipling is 'first and foremost the poet of work'. But even that is not quite accurate. He is, rather, the poet of skilled responsibility, the celebrator of man the artifex.

As Lewis says, this vast area of human experience has been very seldom treated. (Henry James complained of Kipling, how much he left out. True, but then how much he put in which James left out.) And it would be hard to argue – perhaps particularly hard for Kipling's ideological critics – that the theme of working skill is illegitimate in poetry. On the other hand, it is clearly not to be dealt with by the usual resources of poetry.

Among his professionals, the soldier, of course, looms large. But, as Chesterton has said, to see in Kipling a poet of military discipline in particular is a false emphasis: he is a poet rather of all the disciplines and skills, of 'railwaymen or bridgebuilders or even journalists', and, Chesterton might have added, of nurses or jugglers or gardeners. Neither the individuals nor their rather exclusive groupings are likely to be sympathetic. They are hard-bitten, efficient men, touched indeed in their own sphere with following the Gleam, but a little contemptuous of, even offensive to, those who do not accept the harsh discipline of their skills.

Most attacks on Kipling combine sneers at his vulgarity with denunciation of his ethics. His defence, if that is the proper word, is in effect that only deathly refined critics, owing the conditions of their deathly refinement to the hard ethos of the Children of Martha who make their own life possible, are in a position to make such attacks, and in the nature of things are not entitled to do so – are vapid, inane, unreal. And this temperamental antipathy, as Orwell suggests, is consubstantial with the *political* hostility between Kipling and the liberal intelligentsia.

His worst and most fundamental offence is perhaps that while he supports the Sages of Ionia against the obscurantist 'priests and wizards', while he believes in progress, in the potential for change of the machine age, in the advance and spread of civilization, he denies Utopia. He does not foresee a total change in human nature. The Gods of the Copybook Headings who tell us, 'Stick to the Devil you know', and 'If you don't work you die' can be 'transcended' only at the price of eventual disaster. Above all, the Utopia-professing dictatorship is a fraud:

> Holy State or Holy King –
> Or Holy People's Will –
> Have no truck with the senseless thing.
> Order the guns and kill!

Perhaps such general differences of attitude would not more than mildly repel the 'liberal' reader. But there are more specific areas of conflict. At the most superficial level, what could be more offensive to the International Brigade mentality than his

> So, barrin' all that foreign lot
> Which only joined for spite,
> Myself, I'd just as soon not
> Respect the man I fight.

(There were about 2,500 foreigners with the Boers, Germans, French and Irish-Americans being the main offenders.) and similar annoyances are to be seen in what he says on Ulster, or Cecil Rhodes, or half a dozen themes of immediate partisanship. But the vulnerable, or at any rate provocative, targets offered by particular political verses should not be (as they have been) inflated to represent the entirety or the essential core of Kipling – nor even his whole attitude to Empire and patriotism.

Earlier critics of Kipling, Eliot among them, looked forward to the time when political partisanship would not prevent appreciation of his poems. And of course it is as absurd to be bound by these political parochialisms as by the aesthetic ones mentioned earlier: (what a brilliant collection *The Oxford Book of Untrendy Verse* could be). There are probably not many people nowadays who feel a partisan abhorrence of 'The Battle of Naseby' or 'Bonny Dundee'. We are perhaps beginning to reach that stage with Kipling. It is true that there is still much talk of anti-imperialism, but even abroad a good deal of it is of a ritualist nature; and the virtues as well as the vices of the British administration of one-fifth of the world are now recalled. Moreover, the fact that the British Empire was not a precise reflection of Kipling's ideal is rather beside the point, if only because the same applies to the equally idealized institutions of internationalism from the Comintern to the United Nations.

Kipling does *not* see Imperial rule as any sort of perfect system. He is clear, and bitter, about the intrigues among its bureaucracy for power and sex – his Uriah is Jack Barrett. He is clear, too, about administrative and military incompetence. And even his efficient, responsible agents of Empire are not all represented as particularly *likeable* characters. For him the Empire is the embodiment, even if in weak or sinful flesh, of the principle of civilization, of the Law; it is the greatest, or at any rate the largest, of the artefacts of man. As Eliot says, 'he was certainly not aiming at flattery of national, racial or imperial vanity, or attempting to propagate a political programme . . . it was an awareness of grandeur, certainly, but it was more an awareness of responsibility'. In fact, he treats of Empire as the exercise of the skills of rule, of the techniques of extending and defending civilization.

There are a number of overblown poems (particularly in the journalistic period when he wrote for W. E. Henley), which assert Empire at a fairly crude level – though far fewer than is sometimes implied, and even then with little in the way of mere trumpetings of the glory of power. Nor would anyone ordinarily make the error of supposing that what a poet says on a given subject in a given poem is all that he has to say about it: (on which view, one could prove that Catullus merely despised and hated Lesbia). For while it is, of course, reasonable to disagree with Kipling's view of

Empire, it is not reasonable to misrepresent it. And on any fair view, however hostile, there is nothing ignoble in his attitudes.

Auden takes the view that Kipling (and he is writing specifically of his verse) has as his main theme the defence of civilization seen as a continuous emergency, a permanent battle against the forces of darkness and barbarism. His attitude, to a large degree, is that of Yeats, in the first verse of 'Long-Legged Fly'. The motives of the little imperialist wars are crudely known even to the private soldier:

> We broke a King and we built a road –
> A Court-house stands where the reg'ment goed.

The 'White Man's burden' is a phrase of horror these days. But even the phrase is one of responsibilities. And Kipling's interpretation, though still offensive to progressives, can hardly even be called repressive:

> Take up the White Man's burden –
> The savage wars of peace –
> Fill full the mouth of Famine
> And bid the sickness cease; ...

And – a neglected point – he sees the colonial power training the population for eventual freedom, eventual independent participation in civilization, however reluctant they may now be and however ungrateful they may be in future. In the Sudan (a Bengali Muslim tells the locals, while discussing a college built by Kitchener at Khartoum) the purpose of the English is to 'prop' them,

> Till these make laws of their own choice and Judges of their
>   own blood;
> And all the mad English obey the Judges and say that that
>   Law is good.

For 'The Proconsuls' work for 'Power that must their power displace'. One thinks of the abstract idea of an 'imperialist' poet, and then of Kipling greeting the second Jubilee with 'Recessional', a call not to celebrate the imperial power but to remember the fate of Nineveh and Tyre, to ask mercy for 'frantic boast and foolish word'. And with all his belief in the imperial defence of civilization, Kipling, writing for the first Jubilee, sees surviving all the rulers, the ploughman:

> And the Ploughman settled the share
> More deep in the sun-dried clod: –
> 'Mogul, Mahratta, and *Mlech* from the North,
> 'And White Queen over the Seas –
> 'God raiseth them up and driveth them forth
> 'As the dust of the ploughshare flies in the breeze;
> 'But the wheat and the cattle are all my care,
> 'And the rest is the will of God.'

In fact, Kipling calls the English both to pride and to modesty. Excess in Empire would be inappropriate: for the Englishman is above all the technician of power, the artificer of rule. It is he that has developed, over a thousand years, the culture of liberty under law; he is the bearer, over half the world, of political civilization.

This is an important role, but it is not one which implies any inherent superiority over other races except in that particular field. Kipling is no xenophobe. Apart from his cult of the equality of strong or good men, whatever their race, from Kamal and the Colonel's son to St Paul and the Roman Prefect, and the literal inter-racial free-masonry of 'The Mother-Lodge' ('My Brethren black an' brown', all named, with their jobs), he respects other races for their own specific talents.

It is true that he sees bad as well as good in other cultures. Understandably, the Germans come out rather badly. So do others. His 1894 summary, 'An American', is an example of typical admiration for a national temperament different from his own. But he does have occasional bouts of anti-Americanism. This seems at least in part due to his troubles with his in-laws in Vermont. It expressed itself in verse partly in reproaches to America for not coming in to the First World War early enough, balanced to some extent by welcome when they did; and similarly by a sneer at the revolutionaries of 1776 in 'The American Rebellion', again balanced to some extent by a tribute to the dead on both sides.

On the other hand, he is able to put himself into the foreigner's mind, to expose what appear under other standards to be our faults: he shows, for example, in 'Hadra-mauti' the dignified Arab's bleak detestation of what he sees as the vulgarity of the Englishman. More generally, Kipling laughs at callow insularity:

> All good people agree,
>   And all good people say,
> All nice people, like Us, are We
>   And every one else is They:
> But if you cross over the sea,
>   Instead of over the way,
> You may end by (think of it!) looking on We
>   As only a sort of They!

Or, a little more seriously:

> 'Blessed be the English and all that they profess.
> Cursed be the Savages that prance in nakedness!'
> 'Amen,' quo' Jobson, 'but where I used to lie
> Was neither shirt nor pantaloons to catch my brethren by:
>
> 'But a well-wheel slowly creaking, going round, going round,
> By a water-channel leaking over drowned, warm ground –
> Parrots very busy in the trellised pepper-vine – . . .'

He even feels how pleasant it is for men of two races coolly to admit to each other the weaknesses of their own 'codes and customs'. But his final conclusion is that of the mildly pessimistic internationalist, rather than that of the supranationalist to whom the term is nowadays usually applied. Though 'each finds the other excellent', it remains the case that

> The Stranger within my gate,
>   He may be true or kind,
> But he does not talk my talk –
>   I cannot feel his mind.

His patriotism does not imply any particular sympathy for the British social system. His volunteer cannot bear to live in 'awful old England again', feeling

> That the sunshine of England is pale,
> And the breezes of England are stale,
> An' there's somethin' gone small with the lot.

after his experiences in the Boer War.

Many poems express, of course, rage at endemic injustice to the ex-regular. Many more flay the unworthiness of the privileged classes. There is much about English failures and the self-satisfied incompetence responsible. Sometimes he blames the particular clique concerned, as in his 'Song of the Old Guard (Army Reform – After Boer War)'. Sometimes he castigates people and ruler alike, opposing the 'pride' and 'indolence' of the one to the 'insolence' and 'sloth' of the other.

And so Kipling's patriotism, like his imperialism, is not a shallow gang loyalty but a profound sense of a great civilization and its responsibilities:

> Dear-bought and clear, a thousand year,
>   Our fathers' title runs.
> Make we likewise their sacrifice,
>   Defrauding not our sons.

The heritage being, above all, the Law:

> And still when Mob or Monarch lays
> Too rude a hand on English ways,
> The whisper wakes, the shudder plays,
>   Across the reeds at Runnymede.

Though, all the same, that other civilizations have fallen, and so may this, is a constant theme.

He traces the English political heritage (typically enough in a poem which is an allegory of the Boer War) to Saxon times:

> Rudely but greatly begat they the framing of State and Shire.
> Rudely but deeply they laboured and their labour stands till now,
> If we trace on our ancient headlands the twist of their eight-ox plough . . .

For Kipling has an atavistic (i.e. rich and genuine) feeling for the mere land and landscape of England (though even here he admits the right of the man from warmer lands to complain: 'Sirs, it is bitter beneath the Bear'). But the land is not merely the garden, 'the blunt, bow-headed, whalebacked Downs' and so on. The past is stamped into the very countryside:

> See you the dimpled track that runs
> All hollow through the wheat?
> O that was where they hauled the guns
> That smote King Philip's fleet.

Poem after poem, in fact, shows a sense of history, a rootedness, to some degree resembling that of David Jones's *In Parenthesis*. His Britain is that of the Centurion who has 'served in Britain forty years, from Vectis to the Wall'; of Mithras and Sub-Prefects of the Weald; of Eddi, Wilfrid's priest; of the Danes 'waking the white-ash breeze'; of Sir Richard and the jester Rahere; of fifteenth-century shipwrights; of seventeenth-century squires 'In boots as big as milking pails/With holsters on the pommel' and their contemporary 'tinker out of Bedford'; of Oak, and Ash, and Thorn.

It is often a foreigner who is the hero – as with 'Diego Valdez, High Admiral of Spain'. And it is on Rome, more than Britain, that Kipling often projects his views of an impartial and civilizing imperial rule, from Gallio to the 'bored centurions' at Aesica and Hunnum. (With the result, in fact, that our Saxon ancestor takes the barbarian role: 'There was no Count of the Saxon Shore/To meet her hand to hand.')

It is true that Kipling has a few rather dull set-pieces celebrating a sort of generalized British patriotism. What are entirely missing are any patriotic heroics of the type

> Fifteen sail were the Dutchmen bold
> Duncan he had but two ...

Or, let us say, of 'The Ballad of the Revenge', or 'The Charge of the Light Brigade'. On the rare occasions when that tone is touched on in Kipling, it is almost always in a non-British context: 'Thrice thirty thousand men were we to force the Jumna fords' – Marathas, not Englishmen. When a British unit is showing a certain amount of panache it is not in the field but route marching, as in the poem of that name. Not many armchair patriots writing of English history would actually choose the most ignominious scene of all – 'The Dutch in the Medway'. Nor is it easy to imagine a French or other foreign 'patriotic' poet writing (not untypically for Kipling):

> We took our chanst among the Kyber 'ills,
> The Boers knocked us silly at a mile,
> The Burman give us Irriwaddy chills,
> An' a Zulu *impi* dished us up in style:

I would not want to imply that there is no place for a cruder, drum-and-trumpet patriotic verse or battle verse. But, as has often been pointed out, Kipling's war poems, or at any rate those directly dealing with the wars of his time, are scarcely touched with any glorification or even romanticism. Orwell cites the passage beginning 'An' now the hugly bullets come peckin' through the dust.' He also quotes the disgraceful rout

69 *Opposite* 'Mr. Rudyard Kipling takes a bloomin' day aht on the blasted 'eath, along with Britannia, 'is girl'. Max Beerbohm, 1904

of 'That Day', with a British soldier 'squealin' out for quarter as 'e ran'. And there are other similar scenes. 'The Young British Soldier', full of excellent advice to the infantryman, can hardly be said to glorify his prospects, ending as it does with the bleak reference to his best line of conduct when about to fall into the hands of the female anti-imperialists of the time:

> When you're wounded and left on Afghanistan's plains,
> And the women come out to cut up what remains,
> Jest roll to your rifle and blow out your brains . . .

As for incompetence in high places, that too abounds, as in the contemptuous jingle of 'Stellenbosch'.

But, more profoundly, Kipling's envoi to the Boer War is the pathos of the 'Half-Ballade of Waterval' where a British NCO, himself formerly a prisoner of the Boers, is embarking Boer prisoners:

> I'd give the gold o' twenty Rands
>   (If it was mine) to set them free
> For I 'ave learned at Waterval
>   The meanin' of captivity!

It is rare, it must be admitted, not merely for a patriotic balladeer, but for any other partisan of one side in war to express much sympathy for the sufferings of the other. Kipling might have claimed it as a specifically English virtue, however seldom manifested – adducing, perhaps, the wreath that is or was laid by the Navy League under Nelson's Column on Trafalgar Day in memory of the gallant French and Spanish sailors who died in that battle.

When it comes to the First World War, in which his son was killed, Kipling stints no more of horror than did Wilfred Owen:

> That flesh we had nursed from the first in all cleanness
>   was given
> To corruption unveiled and assailed by the malice of
>   Heaven –
> By the heart-shaking jests of Decay where it lolled on
>   the wires –
> To be blanched or gay-painted by fumes – to be cindered
>   by fires –

Or, again, in the strange vision of soldiers gassed, 'Gethsemane'.

He rages like Siegfried Sassoon against the complacent and incompetent leaders:

> But the men who left them thriftily to die in their own dung,
>   Shall they come with years and honour to the grave? . . .

He gives as well, in most unPattonish terms, the fate of the 'shell-shocked':

> For, just because he had not died,
>   Nor been discharged nor sick,

72 *Opposite* A portrait of Kipling in oils by Philip Burne Jones (1899)

> They dragged it out with My Mother's Son
> Longer than he could stick ...

And we get also the hard pathos of 'En-Dor', on wives and mothers trying to contact their dead through mediums.

He wrote, in other tones, on the light-hearted courage appropriate to the English persona, on hatred of the Germans, and similar conventionally patriotic themes; but he also wrote as I have quoted.

For just as he urges empire, with all its blemishes; just as he is a complete patriot, in spite of England's faults; so he is fully alive to the horrors of the War, yet believes it a necessary defence against 'a crazed and driven foe'. For him the truth of

> Who stands if freedom fall?
> Who dies if England live?

is not belied by the equal truth of

> If any question why we died,
> Tell them, because our fathers lied.

This is a position, neither militarist nor defeatist, which it is hard for many liberal intellectuals to understand. And it has been wildly and inexcusably misunderstood.

It is sad to have to concentrate so on Kipling's 'imperialism', 'chauvinism' and 'militarism', just in order to clear up the main misunderstanding of his work – particularly as he is himself in part responsible for that misunderstanding in his cruder verses. Yet the crudities prove not that he had a crude mind, but that he had a subtle mind capable of crudity, a sensitive mind capable of insensitivity. On the other hand, the well-known 'vulgarity' of Kipling seems partly due to his being more or less consciously, and quite paradoxically, a spokesman for the inarticulate to whom inarticulateness is actually a virtue. Only Kipling would have written a poem praising English modesty, as has rightly been pointed out of 'The English Way'. (The annoying part about this is that, until the five final verses in which he rubs in the moral, it is a most effective ballad.) And, at equal length, he applauds their reticence: 'The English – ah, the English! – don't say anything at all.' (More broadly this seems to be a part – an odd pert – of his celebration of the idiosyncracies, the distinctivenesses, however minor, of a given culture or 'race'. He gives equal prominence, for example, to the on the face of it ethically and aesthetically neutral English custom of being specially polite just before losing their tempers.)

To explain Kipling's lapses, and to insist that they are usually peripheral or venal, is not to justify all of them, not to say that the crudities are simply to be dismissed. Both Edmund Wilson and T. S. Eliot defend Kipling on the charge of moral obtuseness (to say the least) in such poems as 'Loot' – and, one might add, even if not so strikingly, in poems like 'Screw-Guns'. Their argument, in effect, is that Kipling is not speaking *in propria persona*, but for the soldiery. There is, of course, something to this defence: nor can anyone be expected always to be working at the same level. All the same, 'Loot', at least, does seem hard to justify, even thus. But many of Kipling's critics are in any case estopped from complaining of such things, since they often admire Ezra Pound, incomparably more shallow and vulgar, with his vicious, scatological anti-Semitism.

Merely to think of such comparisons is at once to differentiate Kipling from the 'literary' poets of recent generations. This was true of his whole output. For example, the contrast between the poets in vogue in the 1890s with their generalities about love, religion and sin, and Kipling's insistence on factual detail is remarkable. This applies, indeed, even as to sex. Where Dowson tells us vaguely that 'The kisses of her bought red mouth were sweet', Kipling has his Scottish engineer saying:

> Judge not, O Lord, my steps aside at Gay Street in Hong Kong!
> Blot out the wastrel hours of mine in sin when I abode –
> Jane Harrigan's an' Number Nine, The Reddick an' Grant Road!

Indeed, Kipling's matter-of-fact attitude to sexual relations is one of the very many pieces of evidence available, though not often admitted, that Victorian puritanism did not go very deep. 'The Ladies' takes it for granted that the 'I' of the poem, not represented as being in any way out of the ordinary either in his moral tone or in the extent of his experience, has lived in turn with a half-caste widow, a young Burmese girl and the wife of a native head groom, though decent enough not to seduce a sixteen-year-old convent girl on the ship:

> Love at first sight was 'er trouble,
>   *She* didn't know what it were;
> An' I wouldn't do such, 'cause I liked 'er too much,
>   But – I learned about women from 'er!

For the artifex, however worldly his morals, has his code. More usually Kipling deals with this artifex at his major concerns, reserving romantic love to his own personal poems. And on the work-life of his characters he is again always fascinated by detail – ('Life, like autumn silence,/Is always deep in detail', Pasternak was to write). 'McAndrew' addresses his Lord:

> The crank-throws give the double-bass, the feed-pump sobs
>   an' heaves,
> An' now the main eccentrics start their quarrel on the
>   sheaves:
> Her time, her own appointed time, the rocking link-head
>   bides,
> Till – hear that note? – the rod's return whings glimmerin'
>   throught he guides . . .
>
> Uplift am I? When first in store the new-made beasties
>   stood,
> Were Ye cast down that breathed the Word declarin' all
>   things good?
> Not so! O' that warld-liftin' joy no after-fall could vex,
> Ye've left a glimmer still to cheer the Man – the Arrtifex!

In sorting out Kipling's attitudes on more or less public themes, I have given inadequate attention to this type of thing, and even more inadequate attention to, for example, his skill as a poet of the sea: the sea, that is, both in visual description, as imagery, and as a venue of battle, exploration and other romance: (even a torpedoing:

> Till, streaked with ash and sleeked with oil,
> The lukewarm whirlpools close!)

Nor, except barely, have we touched on his concern with suffering and healing, as in 'Helen All Alone'; nor on the light *vers de société* of *Departmental Ditties*; nor on the richer poems of old Indian history; nor on such intensities as those of 'Azrael's Count'; nor the mere descriptive felicities:

> Whether the broken, honey-hued, honey-combed limestone
> Cream under white-hot sun; the rosemary bee – bloom
> Sleepily noisy at noon and, somewhere to Southward,
> Sleepily noisy, the Sea.

nor the bare Hugonian sentiment:

> Here where men say my name was made, here where my work
>   was done,
> Here where my dearest dead are laid – my wife – my wife and
>   son.

We have not developed, at least in quotation, the full scope and variety of technique and mood, nor yet the full range of intelligence, in his verse.

I must, however, not end without stressing the strong power in all his work of the feeling of romance. Just as he sees the political world as (at any but a superficial level) concerned with the defence of civilization and its values against the various bestialities within and outside, so in the sphere of feeling and ideas he is concerned to defend against cold-blooded corruptions the romantic motivations. His world, where stoicism is on duty without any noticeable metaphysical support against the inhuman, is also a world relieved by humour and romance. The monochrome of Zeno here has its saving admixture of variety and delight.

As Lewis points out, to say that Kipling does not cover certain areas of experience, carry out certain styles of writing, and so forth, is true, but without significance. There is no rule to stop one reading the other types of poetry before or afterwards. And such criticism would apply, *mutatis mutandis*, to almost all poetry. But in the areas in which Kipling prefers to work he is, as Eliot puts it, so far from being 'shallow' that at times he 'is not merely possessed of penetration, but almost "possessed" of a kind of second sight'.

Gillian Avery
THE CHILDREN'S WRITER

ALTHOUGH Kipling's stock has risen enormously over the past generation, his popularity with children appears to have declined. Rosemary Sutcliff, second to none in her admiration, her own writing profoundly influenced by him, sadly admitted this in her monograph on Kipling as a children's writer (1960); my own contact with children had suggested it, and questioning of librarians bore it out. Only the *Just So Stories* survive as a universal favourite. The first *Jungle Book* is borrowed by Wolf Cubs, or by those who have seen the Disney film, but is usually returned without enthusiasm, while I have not found anyone now at school who has ever read the Puck stories. Kipling's reputation as a children's writer is 'artificially kept alive' – the phrase is not mine, but a librarian's – by the fact that he is on the reading-list of teachers' training colleges and the Wolf Cub and Brownie movements.

Perhaps he has never really been popular with the common run of children, perhaps we delude ourselves in assuming that he was from the qualities that we recognize in the stories as adults; from the enthusiasm of a few specially perceptive readers, and from the tributes by writers who remember the intensity with which they read him in childhood. J. M. S. Tompkins, in *The Art of Rudyard Kipling*, prefaces her chapter on the children's tales with a recollection of what they meant to her fifty years before. Rosemary Sutcliff was brought up on them too, and the spell has never left her. 'Good hunting!' her Roman legionaries call to each other, and salute another affectionately as 'cubling', echoing the greetings of the *Jungle Books*. Her novels of Roman Britain take up the story at the point where Kipling laid it down: the disintegration of the Empire, the withdrawal of the legions from Britain. Her account of the last galley leaving Rutupiae Harbour and the extinction of Rutupiae Light must have sprung from the sadness of 'On the Great Wall', the second of the Roman stories in *Puck of Pook's Hill*, when the young centurion, proud of the greatness of Rome, sees the humiliating word 'finish' on the bricked-up arch over the Great North Road. And admirers of E. Nesbit's Bastable family will remember how they acted the *Jungle Book* with such vigour – borrowing the odd tiger-skin rug – that a timid visitor turned a dreadful green colour and fainted.

But the ordinary child – what is it that defeats him? The trouble may partly lie in the way that Kipling tells his historical tales. Children love reading about going back in time, of present-day children being magicked into the past. But Kipling brings his historical characters forward, and somehow the magic vanishes. There they sit in Edwardian Sussex – Sir Richard Dalyngridge the Norman knight, with a horse real enough to break away clods from the bank where it crosses the stream, Parnesius the centurian fingering Dan's catapult – and tell the children their adventures. Where these are difficult Puck, who is the convenor of the proceedings, supplies a gloss, and Dan and Una ask questions. They are not ghosts, there is no nimbus of mystery about them, and they seemed to me as a child like dressed-up figures from a pageant. I felt too that the history was all too grown-up, and that it lacked the delicious magic of E. Nesbit. Like many other children, I was also prejudiced against stories told in the first person. I still feel that too many people get in the way of the narrative, and that the interruptions do it no good.

This was *Puck of Pook's Hill*. It is rare to hear of anybody who made much of its sequel, *Rewards and Fairies*, as a child. Technically the stories are superb, but Kipling's virtuosity is almost oppressive here. With immense élan he identifies himself with the various narrators, at one moment a seventeenth-century astrologer talking like a character out of *The Alchemist*, neolithic man at the next. He whirls his readers round the centuries. The effort of adjustment is considerable, and many of the stories are too compressed, too subtle for a young reader. In 'The Knife and the Naked Chalk' he considers how a stone-age man from the chalk downs might dread the unknown, fever-infested forest lands below, and their inhabitants:

I was afraid of the terrible talking Trees. I was afraid of the ghosts in the branches; of the soft ground underfoot; of the red and black waters. I was afraid, above all, of the Change. It came! . . . A fire without a flame burned in my head; an evil taste grew in my mouth; my eyelids shut hot over my eyes; my breath was hot between my teeth, and my hands were like the hands of a stranger. I was made to sing songs and to mock the Trees, though I was afraid of them. At the same time I saw myself laughing, and I was very sad for this fine young man, who was myself. Ah! The Children of the Night know magic.

The finest is the last story, 'The Tree of Justice', incomprehensible to children, yet neglected by the adult enthusiast because it falls in what is assumed to be a children's book. It is, in fact, a development of 'The Man Who Was'. Into a deer hunt staged for Henry I strays a demented old man, the protégé of Rahere the King's Jester (whom Kipling imagines with 'a sad priest's face' – own brother, as it were to the Fool in *Lear*). At the banquet that follows Rahere identifies him to Henry and his court as Harold the Saxon king, whom he has found wandering mad by the wayside. A flicker of light penetrates the poor confused mind; Harold remembers his royal past:

[Henry] turned to the tables, and held him out his own cup of wine. The old man drank, and beckoned behind him, and, before all the Normans, my Hugh bore away the empty cup, Saxon-fashion, upon the knee.
'It is Harold!' said De Aquila. 'His own stiff-necked blood kneels to serve him.'

It is more difficult to understand why the *Jungle Books* are not more widely enjoyed. Perhaps the official hand of the Scout movement has helped to deaden them. All the ritual of the Wolf Cubs is derived from the first *Jungle Book*, and a drab re-telling of 'Mowgli's Brothers' appears in the Wolf Cub Handbook. Cubs weekly stalk and kill Shere Khan the Tiger and Tabaqui the Jackal, so that for many the jungle is overlaid by the thought of a dusty church hall and little boys in green caps chanting 'Akela, we'll do our best'.

Still, Kipling should certainly never be thought of as the type of the official writer to Baden Powell. Even his *Land and Sea Tales for Scouts and Guides*, where he is described on the title page as 'Commissioner, Boy Scouts', contains much that is hardly in the spirit of the Scout and Guide laws. There is, for instance, a light-hearted further adventure of Stalky, who gets himself out of a tight corner by locking up a farmer and his men and lobbing stones at the cattle in the farmyard until they are frantic with fear and pain. Most of the stories, except for the fact that they are adventurous, are completely irrelevant to Baden Powell's movement, and 'His Gift', which alone does treat of Scouts, shows that the Commissioner has not really grasped all the technicalities of the organization. It also turns on one of his favourite themes, hatred. Here 'raging hate against a too-badged, too virtuous senior' at last stirs the buffoon of the troop out of his torpor.

The Mowgli stories make up only a proportion of the two *Jungle Books*; there are three of them in the first, and five in the second. The remainder are all stories about animals, but they have not that savage enchantment which held the imagination of people who remember loving Mowgli as children. The Bastable family indeed despised their timid visitor long before she fainted, because she skipped the Mowgli stories and read 'Rikki-Tikki-Tavi' and 'The White Sea' instead, the very ones that children of today are said to prefer.

Considered as an animal story, 'Rikki-Tikki-Tavi' is a better one than any about the jungle. It really does convey the character of the mongoose and the cobras without a touch of the anthropomorphism that lies so heavily over the other. So does the macabre 'Undertakers', a conversation between a crocodile, a jackal, and an adjutant bird concerning various sorts of carrion flesh, with the crocodile wistfully recalling his satiation in the Mutiny days. But the Mowgli stories possess what the others do not, a fantasy and a wonder and a sadness. 'The grip of the stories was extraordinary,' recalls Miss Tompkins, 'and a sense of something wild and deep and old infected me as I listened.' As a child I myself could never understand Mowgli's tactics when he trapped Shere Khan, I was bored by his visits to the Human Pack, and missed most of the point of the superb 'King's Ankus'. But my imagination was seized by the description of the monkey-folk carrying Mowgli between them in their headlong flight through the tree-tops: 'the terrible check and jerk at the end of the swing over nothing but empty air brought his heart between his teeth' (a marvellously convincing detail that). And I went back time and again to the description of Cold Lairs, the lost city in the jungle where the monkeys hold court and where they fight and lose the battle with Kaa the python.

But Baden Powell did not just choose the *Jungle Books* because the fantasy appealed to small boys. They do have something of the primness of the conventional Victorian children's book mingled with the wild strangeness of the jungle. Kipling's wolves are not cowardly and treacherous like other story-book wolves. Their great virtue is their solidarity and loyalty to the Pack, and the family that adopts the infant Mowgli maintains to the end, when he is a grown man, a touching domestic unity, as safe and certain as in one of Charlotte Yonge's families. Kipling also imposes a curious gentlemanly code upon the jungle. He provides Mowgli with two mentors, Baloo the Bear and Bagheera the Panther, disconcertingly like public-school masters, who teach him the Law of the Jungle. There are hints at Kaa's superior moral status to other snakes because as a python he uses his strength to kill and despises poison-snakes as cowards. The inferiority of the Bandar-log is emphasized, the monkey-folk who have no law. They are outcasts. They have no speech of their own, but use the stolen words which they overhear when they listen, and peep and wait up above in the branches. Their way is not our way. They are without leaders. They have no remembrances. They boast and chatter and pretend they are a great people about to do great affairs in the jungle, but the falling of a nut turns their minds to laughter and all is forgotten.

The people of the jungle are bound by law, and one of those laws is that they may not eat man – it is *unsportsmanlike*.

Baden Powell made much of the moral patches, and slid over the episodes that were alien to his purpose. Kipling, even when he was writing for children, was still attracted to hatred, here seen at its most ferocious in 'Letting in the Jungle'. Mowgli, offended by the behaviour of the village towards the woman who has sheltered him, lusts for revenge. It is a community that lives 'year in and year out as near to starvation as the Jungle was near to them', but he incites Hathi the elephant to destroy it, knowing that if the crops perish it will be death for the people. Even Hathi demurs: 'We have no quarrel with them, and it needs the red rage of great pain ere we bear down the places where men sleep.' But Mowgli is inexorable:

I do not wish even their bones to lie on the clean earth. Let them go and find a fresh lair. They cannot stay here. I have seen and smelled the blood of the woman that gave me food – the woman whom they would have killed but for me. Only the smell of the new grass on their door-steps can take away that smell. It burns in my mouth. Let in the Jungle, Hathi!

It is often asserted that the best children's books come from authors who are not writing deliberately with children in mind, but for themselves. It is also said that the best children's authors are those who have their own childhood in mind, or who still retain in some respects a child-like outlook. But when the point is made it is usually assumed that the childhood was a happy one. Kipling's was not. In 'Baa Baa, Black Sheep' the tormented and lonely Punch, alias ten-year-old Rudyard, 'brooded in the shadow that fell about him and cut him off from the world, inventing horrible punishments for "dear Harry", or plotting another line of the tangled web of deception that he wrapped round Aunty Rosa'. The story concludes: 'When young lips have drunk deep of the bitter waters of Hate, Suspicion, and Despair, all the Love in the world will not wholly take away that knowledge; though it may turn darkened eyes for a while to the light, and teach faith where no Faith was.'

This experience left its mark on *Stalky*, and on the *Jungle Books*. The Puck stories escaped, but these were written with his own children in mind. So were the *Just So Stories*, and it is undoubtedly these which nowadays have the greatest success with children. He had always loved the company of small children, and telling them stories. The *Just So Stories* began some time during the 1890s when the Kiplings were at their Vermont home. Their first daughter Josephine had been born in 1892, and to her and her little cousin Kipling used to tell tales about camels and whales and the cat that walked in the wet, wild woods up the road. By 1898 Kipling was telling them to two small daughters, and Angela Mackail, another cousin, remembered the joy of hearing them in the study at Rottingdean:

The *Just So Stories* are a poor thing in print compared with the fun of hearing them told in Cousin Ruddy's deep unhesitating voice. There was a ritual about them, each phrase having its special intonation which had to be exactly the same each time and without which the stories are dried husks. There was an inimitable cadence, an emphasis of certain words, an exaggeration of certain phrases, a kind of intoning here and there which made his telling unforgettable.

They were not written down, it seems, until a late stage, and were not published until 1902. They are, thus, like *Alice*, one of the very few children's books which actually have been told to children first. It is probably because of the questions of Josephine, Elsie and their small cousins that we get explanations such as, what the Rhinoceros's skin was like when he took it off ('it buttoned underneath with three buttons and looked like a waterproof'), and their delighted horror at other people's naughtiness that was responsible for the Elephant's Child going home and spanking all his relations. And it is certain that the eldest Kipling child would have heard the sonorous chant 'Change here for Winchester, Ashuelot, Nashua, Keene, and stations on the *Fitch*burg Road', for these are all stations near Brattleboro, the old Vermont home.

The *Just So Stories* are far more than a family joke, though; they have the universal touch which his other children's books lack in some measure, however good by adult literary standards. You do not have to be specially perceptive to love them, you do not have to skip bits. They are wonderful to read aloud, of course. But if you read them to yourself you have the pictures. Kipling drew them himself, two to a story, the best illustrations any of his books had, and embellished them with illustrations that answer every question any one could want to ask. 'This is the Parsee Pestonjee Bomonjee sitting in his palm tree . . . he has a knife in his hand to cut his name on palm trees. The black things on the islands out at sea are bits of ships that got wrecked going down the Red Sea but all the passengers were saved and went home.'

There is humour and a smacking good moral to each story (it is always pleasant to feel smug when the naughtiness is not your own), there is cumulative repetition and a wild logic, and long words that sound good and are only put there for their sound. But it is their humour that is so endearing. Small children's humour is crude; a joke that pleases them usually makes adults wince. It is Kipling's triumph that in *Just So Stories* he found a vein of humour that captivates both the old and the young.

Roger Lancelyn Green
THE COUNTRYMAN

ONE outstanding quality of Kipling's work, which has often been pointed out, was his ability to 'get beneath the skin' of so many of his characters, making them talk and act as though he had direct personal experience of their very varied professions and backgrounds, when he had in fact usually gained this expertise simply from observation and enquiry, by pumping his informants dry and storing up their words, accents, and turns of phrase in his amazingly retentive memory. Yet relatively little attention seems to have been paid to his comparable understanding of English country life, in particular that which came under his personal observation in Sussex – at Rottingdean from 1897 to 1902, but more especially after he had bought Bateman's, Burwash, with thirty-three acres of land about it, and moved there in September 1902, after which it became his home until his death thirty-four years later.

Kipling came to this new life of a country gentleman as a complete outsider. He was the son of an artist and a Methodist minister's daughter. He had no family link whatsoever, so far as is known, with the landed aristocracy – even, for several generations, with the yeoman or peasant classes. His childhood was divided between a bungalow in Bombay and a semi-detached lower-middle-class lodging-house in Southsea, followed by the rigours of Westward Ho!; from the age of seventeen to twenty-three he was slaving as a journalist in India; from the autumn of 1889 to the spring of 1892 he lived in lodgings in London, when not seeking health in southern Europe or voyaging via South Africa and Australasia on the way to his last brief visit to India.

As his reputation soared during the two years when his home was in London, Kipling was doubtless invited to several 'stately homes' – where, as often as not, he may have found his reception both constrained and uncomfortable (like that accorded to the minor poet so brilliantly described in F. Anstey's *Lyre and Lancet* serialized in *Punch* in 1894). The recollection of this first contact with an alien and rather self-contained way of life may have recurred to him when writing the story of the American who couldn't fit in, 'An Error in the Fourth Dimension' in 1894.

Only after an increasingly uncomfortable four years as a landed proprietor in Vermont (perhaps 'stranded' would be a better adjective as it became more and more apparent that he too had made an error in the Fourth Dimension, American version), did he begin to experience English country life as one of the wealthy few in the village of Rottingdean. This was, however, already becoming a suburb of Brighton, and he seems to have come in close contact only with the inhabitants of the other two 'big houses' across the green, the Burne-Joneses and the Ridsdales.

It was only after he bought Bateman's in September 1902 that he found himself settled in a big country house, owning land (he increased his estate to three hundred acres in 1903 by the purchase of Park Mill Farm and Rye Green), employing agricultural labour, and called upon by his new position to fulfil many of the duties incumbent upon a 'landed proprietor'.

'We began with tenants – two or three small farmers on our very few acres – from whom we learned that farming was a mixture of farce, fraud, and philanthropy that stole the heart out of the land,' he wrote in *Something of Myself* (p. 192) in 1935. 'After many, and some comic experiences, we fell back on our own county's cattle – the big, red Sussex breed who make beef and not milk. One got something at least for one's money from the mere sight of them, and they did not tell lies. Rider Haggard would visit us from time to time and give of his ample land-wisdom.' (Haggard besides his romances was also, it should be remembered, the author of *A Farmer's Year* and *Rural England*.)

Here was every ingredient calculated to produce the situation of an outsider looked down upon and pitied or ridiculed, according to the background of his neighbours, by the real or would-be real country gentry of the rather exclusive county of Sussex. Was there ever any danger of him being classed at once and forever with 'bounders' like 'Sangres – he's a Brazilian gentleman, very sunburnt like', who turned three good farms into parkland and drove to church every Sunday in a 'silver-plated chariot'?

We do not, I think, know for certain what the local gentry really thought of Kipling – the landowner rather than the author – between 1902 and the end of that particular civilization they typified, which came with the First World War. But we do know that Kipling in two of his best stories captured for ever the whole ethos, outlook and sentiment of the old landed gentry once and for all, absolutely and authentically, with such understanding and conviction that any survivor of that particular 'Inner Ring' knowing nothing of him but these two stories would place him unhesitatingly as the scion of an ancient house with many centuries of ancestral background in the same spot and enough authentic quarterings to satisfy Mr Pine himself.

These two stories are 'An Habitation Enforced', written in March 1905, published in *The Century Magazine* for August of the same year and collected in *Actions and Reactions* (1909), and 'My Son's Wife', written in October 1913 and first published in *A Diversity of Creatures* (1917). To them may be added 'Friendly Brook', written in November 1912, published in *The Windsor Magazine* of December 1914 and also collected in *A Diversity of Creatures*, which captures with as great a feeling of authenticity the mental outlook of those who laboured on the old estates and formed an important part of the same hierarchy.

To most readers the world which Kipling describes in these stories is as distant and as hard to recapture as the Simla of *Plain Tales*; to do so demands as much of a mental metempsychosis as the stories of Romans and Normans in *Puck of Pook's Hill*. But many of us at least remember old people met in our youth who knew Kipling's India as and when he knew it – soldiers, administrators, political residents, civil engineers, with their wives or widows from 'the Colonel's lady to Judy O'Grady' – who bore witness to the fidelity with which he had caught and preserved the background, and often to the minuter details of the stories themselves.

In the same way there is still time – but only just – to test the reliability of his grasp of the people and their outlook and way of life in the rural England – the Sussex in particular – which he got to know so well between 1902 and 1914.

His approach to both India and England was surprisingly similar. He came to each as an outsider, studying a foreign culture – and became a part of it. 'We discovered

England, which we had never done before,' he wrote to his American friend Charles Eliot Norton in November 1902 at the beginning of his adventure, 'and went to live in it. England is a wonderful land. It is the most marvellous of all foreign countries that I have ever been in. It is made up of trees and green fields and mud and the gentry, and at last I'm one of the gentry.'[1]

One is reminded at once of Midmore's first letter from his unexpected country inheritance in 'My Son's Wife', and his rather superior attitude to 'Ther Land, as they call it down here . . . Ther Land is brown and green in alternate slabs like chocolate and pistachio cakes, speckled with occasional peasants who do not utter. In case it should not be wet enough there is a wet brook in the middle of it. Ther House is by the brook.'

In both this story and 'An Habitation Enforced' we are shown how 'Ther Land' and 'Ther House' grow upon their unwilling or unsuspecting captives, Midmore and the Chapins, until they become a part of it – return, in a sense, to the clay from which they were digged. It is in their discovery of the land and its people and their absorption into it that Kipling shows the depth of his own exploration and the completeness of his own discovery of the inner meaning of what at first seems so incomprehensible.

As old Iggulden (the Hobden of *Puck*, Isted in real-life Burwash) tells of the empty house and of 'the lives and deaths and doings' of the family which had held it down the ages, the mystery is made manifest.

The motives that swayed the characters were beyond their comprehension: the fates that shifted them were gods they had never met; the side-lights that Mrs Cloke [the tenant-farmer's wife] threw on act and incident were more amazing than anything in the record . . . 'But why – why – *why* – did So-and-so do so-and-so?' Sophie would demand from her seat by the pothook; and Mrs Cloke would answer, smoothing her knees, 'For the sake of the place.' 'I give it up,' said George one night in their own room. 'People don't seem to matter in this country compared to the places they live in' . . .

But as with the best of Kipling's mature stories the whole closely packed accumulation of detail and insight is needed, and the only valid quotation is the story in its entirety. And that entirety in 'An Habitation Enforced' and 'My Son's Wife' may be accepted as being as accurate in every detail and character – from the squire to the village idiot – as it could possibly be – bearing in mind that Kipling, however great a writer, was a writer first and always; and that he was compressing what he had learnt (as a journalist maybe, but a journalist of genius) into two short stories, each of which might have served a writer of different inspiration for the plot of a whole novel.

We all, according to our own temperaments and backgrounds, have our own favourites among Kipling's stories – not necessarily those we think his greatest, but those which touch us most nearly. Chance has made me able to feel in this way about the two stories in question and given me the touchstone that proves them to be pure gold. Although not fully a member of that lost world, for simple chronological reasons,

[1] Quoted by Carrington, p. 369.

I grew up on a small country estate – of no importance, but with a background of nearly nine centuries. It, like others, tried to continue in 1919 as if the previous five years had not taken place – and of course failed utterly, but only when the approach of 1939 brought on the main phase of 'the greatest change in recorded history'.

Others still living can remember the days before 1914, and can speak with even greater authority: but I am enough of a dinosaur (as C. S. Lewis styled himself in a similar context) to 'know in my bones' the authentic ring of the true metal in this case. It is all true: the loyalty to the estate and the family which puts 'the places they live in' before merely personal or temporal considerations – for we are no more than life-tenants in a place that belongs not to us but to the family; the loyalty which binds the squire, the tenants and the labourers complete with their families into one greater family. Sophie (and Kipling) feel this at one remove: 'It's *not* our land. We've only paid for it. We belong to it, and it belongs to the people – our people they call 'em.'

Midmore's London friends could not understand his relationship with the truculent tenant farmer Sidney – and he realized it only by degrees: but Sidney is as true to life as any character in the stories. I can remember his counterpart – or the composite counterparts that make for the greater basic truth. And such instances could be multiplied endlessly.

It took Kipling longer to get fully into the minds of the more humble countrymen in 'Friendly Brook', but he seems to have achieved it as perfectly; and for the villagers too in such stories as 'The Wish House' (1924) and 'Fairy-Kist' (written 1925, published 1928).

In *Puck of Pook's Hill* (begun September 1904, published 1906) Kipling captured Sussex and the country in a different way. The historical grasp and understanding which he displays in this and the later *Rewards and Fairies* (1906–10) is apt to be overlooked, since the stories, in the first volume particularly, are told to children – even after his direct statement in *Something of Myself*: 'Since the tales had to be read by children, before people realised that they were meant for grown-ups . . . I worked the material in three or four overlaid tints and textures, which might or might not reveal themselves according to the shifting light of sex, youth, and experience.'

But as eminent an historian as G. M. Trevelyan declared in his Clark Lectures to the University of Cambridge in 1953 his belief in the outstanding excellence of these stories:

When he fell under the charm of rural Sussex, its folk like old Hobden and their traditions, he had a sudden vision of the whole length of our island history. *Puck of Pook's Hill* is natural, beautiful, gentle – if you like, childlike. In a setting of fairyland and childhood the very opposite of brutal [Trevelyan was answering Raymond Mortimer's condemnation of Kipling as a 'boy who never grew up' with 'a morbid interest in cruelty'] he tells us tale after tale of the ancient history of England, as he imagines it, with a marvellous historical sense, I think . . . Above all the tales are alive and they are beautiful. The story about Drake called 'Simple Simon' and the story about Harold called 'The Tree of Justice' in *Rewards and Fairies* are very striking. As a piece of historical imagination I know nothing in the world better than the third story in *Puck*, called 'The Joyous Venture', in which the Viking ship coasts Africa to find gold and fight gorillas in the tropical forest. I can see no fault in it, and many a merit.[1]

Kipling's 'marvellous historical sense' is given an even more vivid reality by the Sussex background so subtly woven into the fabric of the Puck stories. Thus, for example, the Roman centurion Parnesius is on his way to Hadrian's Wall but camps for the night in the valley below Pook's Hill. England is conquered by Duke William, but the clash between Norman and Saxon and the beginning of their fusion into 'English' is shown happening on the Manor of Pevensey, while the most moving story of the series 'The Tree of Justice' is set in the very spot near Bateman's where the children are hearing about it – though the actual legend of King Harold's survival after Hastings places his death at Chester. And you may still find 'Panama Corner' in Burwash church, where Una and Dan met St Wilfrid, the patron Saint of Sussex. In the same way Kipling adds an extra touch of reality to one of his best tales with a historical background, 'The Eye of Allah', by the suggestion of Sussex or Hampshire scenery that identifies the medieval abbey in it with Romsey or Beaulieu.

He was not perhaps quite as successful in that painful appendix to the stories of country life, 'Beauty Spots' (written 1928, published 1932), in which he tried to capture that warped and tragic period between the Wars which fell to pieces under the hands of those who could not accept the change and the new 'generation that tolerates but does not pity', neither recognizing fully the extent of the cataclysmic revolution both spiritual and economic which Kipling did not live long enough to capture really convincingly from our side of the Second World War – which he prophesied, but was spared from seeing.

Kipling was not on very sure ground in 'Beauty Spots', and perhaps his earliest stories with a country setting are also presented rather from outside: 'My Sunday at Home' with its somewhat overwritten opening in a Hardyesque Wessex, and 'An Error in the Fourth Dimension' (they both date from 1894). Even 'The Brushwood Boy' of the following year achieves little more than a superficial sketch of country life.

Only after settling at Rottingdean in 1897 did Kipling begin to strike roots into the Susses soil and reach the conclusion that he had come home at last – a feeling which he was able to express once and for all in verse six months before moving into his real kingdom at Bateman's, with the poem 'Sussex' (written in March 1902):

> God gives all men all earth to love,
>   But, since our hearts are small,
> Ordained for each one spot should prove
>   Beloved over all;
> Each to his choice, and I rejoice
>   The lot has fallen to me
> In a fair ground – in a fair ground –
>   Yea, Sussex by the sea!

By 1904 he could already have said, with his Norman Knight in *Puck* 'But now

[1] *A Layman's Love of Letters*, 1953, p. 33.

Alan Sandison
A MATTER OF VISION
Rudyard Kipling and Rider Haggard

On this occasion might have been seen the spectacle – probably unique – of a learned judge seated upon the bosom of a furious person who was swearing loudly and trying to bite him, while a less learned Master of the High Court tackled his arms and legs!

I T reads like a projection of the knockabout fantasies of Study Five into an ambiguously adult world. However, the description is Haggard's not Kipling's and the occasion was real enough.[1]

At the age of twenty-one, totally innocent of any legal training, Haggard had been appointed Master and Registrar of the High Court of the Transvaal, and at this point was on circuit with Judge Kotze and the Court Usher. The latter turned out to be exceptionally bibulous, and having got raging drunk and not a little violent had to be first restrained and then solemnly discharged 'in the midst of the open veldt'.

The incident is worth mentioning because it serves to show that, in the British Empire, Kipling and Haggard found themselves possessed of a dimension to operate in which afforded them a physical and mental freedom almost beyond our conception. Because the term 'imperialism' still survives in common usage we think we know what Empire meant in the last quarter of the nineteenth century: in fact, its real significance for those who actually lived and worked within it can only be reached now by a strenuous effort of the imagination. Perhaps least of all do we realize its astonishing capacity for fulfilling fantasies.

Thus Haggard, who had arrived in South Africa at the age of nineteen, accompanies some of the most impressive colonial administrators of his day – Shepstone and Osborne, for example – on missions of very considerable danger; escaping ambushes, confronting the massed Zulu *Impi*, being accorded the extraordinary royal salute, all much in the manner of *King Solomon's Mines*. Returning from one of these expeditions he is just in time to raise the flag at the Annexation of the Transvaal, his twenty-second birthday still some two months away. Clearly the Earl's Court Tournament isn't an entirely adequate surrogate for such a period or its ethos.

Though Kipling himself did not take part in the actual process of empire-building (and it is a notable difference between the two men), he lived in the most intimate association with it for many years where the field was even more exciting and the possibilities still more dazzling. There he watched the 'food-for-fever', as he called the administrators, committed to the great organization of which they were a humble and insignificant part, sacrificing themselves to a cause which brought them no material benefit in any way commensurable. He saw, too, the men who performed prodigies of valour on the unpacified frontiers – young men, for it was particularly the day of the subaltern when a mere lieutenant could build the Ganges canal and another could be appointed Political Officer to the Maharajah of Jammu. 'How you will laugh,' the latter wrote to a friend on the day of his appointment, 'a Lieutenant of Foot advising the King of the Mountains! Such is India.'

[1] The quotation comes from Lilias Rider Haggard's biography *The Cloak that I Left* (p. 83) to which I am generally indebted in this essay; as I am to Morton Cohen's *Rudyard Kipling to Rider Haggard, The Record of a Friendship*.

Such was Empire for both Kipling and Haggard: a milieu where young men could perform outsize tasks in outsize circumstances, with life constantly in hazard. To function in such an environment was to have one's existence imbued with an epic quality. Courage and loyalty were demanded of these youths in sacrificial measure, and an appropriate *mise en scène* was furnished for their translation. Life in the active service of the imperial idea was rendered more intense, noble and simple: so much so, that it was an encouragement never to grow up and very many of those who participated in it bore to the end of their days the indelible, Empire-made mark of arrested adolescence.

Into this elemental scale Haggard's quasi-mythical heroes – so much in contact with a Homeric and a Norse past – fit easily and naturally. The epic scale of empire readily accommodates – if it does not, indeed, inspire – a moral and spiritual vision of proportional simplicity and grandeur, and human activity is prompt to identify itself with eternal verities. Man is more starkly presentable in permanent confrontation with the Lords of Life and Death, to use Kipling's phrase, and the Great End becomes a question of perpetual moment.

Kipling and Haggard had, then, the Empire in common; but there was little real identity in the deeper *moral* significance it had for the two men. The picture of Haggard and Kipling sitting opposite each other in the quiet of the latter's study companionably occupied with their gloomy speculations on human destiny, or, alternatively, overcoming together some knotty problem of composition, while it says a lot about the closeness of their personal friendship, does not signify a unity of vision.

Haggard's favoured world is one of heroic men and deeds, a world full of 'the din/ Of victories; gods revealed; supernal calls' as Ronald Ross put it. But the world he creates is simultaneously vanishing – and he with it, for he is intimately involved in this 'fictional' universe. In fact, by associating his own life-cycle with the decline of the Zulus, which he does continually, Haggard very successfully blends the individual with the cultural cycle, postulating in the process the notion that if any meaning is to be discovered in existence, it must be sought in time.

This brings us to the heart of Haggard's moral vision and also to the heart of what distinguishes him fundamentally from Kipling. His consuming preoccupation is with time: the words of the burial service 'Man that is born of woman hath but a short time to live, and is full of misery. He cometh up and is cut down like a flower; he fleeth as it were a shadow and never continueth in one stay', are directly quoted at least once in his work, but, paraphrased, they are the verbal stock-in-trade of his characters, in particular of his sententious Zulus.

Implicit in such reflections – and very often explicit too – is a continual questioning of purpose. His characters find it very difficult to square the notion of a beneficent providence with the amount of human suffering they see around them; the only hope lies in the possibility that the pattern may be too big for man's strictly limited perspective. Again it is his Zulus who seem best able to express this with the desired rhetorical sonority which is the only way Haggard knows of achieving emphasis: 'All things are a great pattern, my father, . . . and our lives, and what we do, and what we do not do, are but a little bit of the pattern, which is so big that only the eye of Him who is above, the Unkulunkulu, can see it all.'

Haggard was deeply influenced by the evolutionary argument but it is clearly his own mystical bent that impelled him to find solace in reflections upon the vast process of time.[1] And most of what is characteristically the Haggard 'voice' has its source in this preoccupation: such as his fatalism, or his cultural relativism which saved him from his contemporaries' racial exclusiveness and condescension. As an instance of the latter, one thinks of his regard for 'black' culture in all his African books, or of his contemptuous dismissal of those who see the native African as 'just a native, a person from whom land may be filched upon one pretext or another, or labour or taxes extracted and who if he resists the process and makes himself a nuisance must be suppressed'. But there are plenty of other examples. In the introduction to *Allan Quatermain* we find this:

Civilisation is only savagery silver-gilt. A vain glory is it, and like a northern light, comes but to fade and leave the sky more dark. Out of the soil of barbarism it has grown like a tree, and as I believe, into the soil like a tree it will once more, sooner or later, fall again, as the Egyptian civilisation fell, as the Hellenic civilisation fell, and as the Roman civilisation fell ...

Given this cyclical view of history, Haggard's instincts constantly urged him to pierce the veil that drops between one cycle and another. Ayesha is perhaps the most conspicuous – even blatant – example of this, but nearly all his major characters at one time or another teeter on the brink of their own apotheosis: conversely, goddesses appear and divulge secrets of past and future with a garrulous disregard for the professional inscrutability of the divine.

The ready resort to allegory is further testimony to the strength of his desire to find a greater reality beyond the finite human vision. As Kipling wrote to him after reading *Wisdom's Daughter*: 'You are a whale at parables and allegories and one thing reflecting another'; and for once his schoolboy colloquialism is quite appropriate. One immediately thinks of the 'celestial barmaid' Ayesha, though in *She* Ayesha is not wholly allegorical – that is clear from the discovery of the real thing in the Moneta-like sculpture in the ruined city of Kôr, 'perhaps the grandest allegorical work of Art that the genius of her children has ever given to the world'. The figure is Truth, beseeching mankind to draw the veil from her face but carrying etched on the base a tart rebuke from an anonymous authority to the effect that by death alone can the veil be drawn. There is, of course, a teasing similarity between Ayesha and Truth, but she has to be individualized, temperamental Ayesha as well, since Haggard was thoroughly convinced that sanctified or not – and Ayesha is often a thorough-going no-nonsense sceptic – human nature is eternal: '... it is the one fixed unchangeable thing, fixed as the stars, more enduring than the mountains'. 'Time hath no power against Identity' says Ayesha grandly, expressing Haggard's own view that individual personality was immeasurably ancient, capable of being born again and again.

No other aspect of Haggard's vision so completely differentiates him from Kipling,

---

[1] An extended critique of Haggard's writing, including an appraisal of the effect on it of Darwinian theory, can be found in my book *The Wheel of Empire* (Macmillan, 1967).

one of the two men with whom he found himself to be 'in supreme sympathy'. Such an extraordinary stability of identity was not only what Kipling lacked even in ordinary measure; its absence and his consciousness of it is precisely what distinguishes his own creative vision.

The individual self for Kipling was a precariously sustained artefact, and its integrity was necessarily the end of all one's calculations. Of self and society, for example, he has this to say in *A Book of Words*: 'For the eternal question still is whether the profit of any concession that a man makes to his Tribe, against the light that is in him, outweighs or justifies his disregard for that light.' Practising such a careful economy of self he offers the sharpest contrast with Haggard: in fact, someone who sought to find his answer in the fluidity of time could never be at one with Kipling *au fond*.

It is no mere playing with words to suggest that where Haggard is preoccupied with time, Kipling is preoccupied with space. All his efforts are bent towards building and defending structures in order to appropriate something of their substance and pattern, and so define his own being. Anything lacking a name or a form inspires contempt or fear: the déclassé drunk in 'Her Little Responsibility' is simply 'the Thing', having spurned the social conventions which gave it its shape. 'The Thing,' he says in a Conradian moment 'had long been divided from all social and moral restraint' and being so had foregone its identity and could only be repudiated by those who would remain whole. It is not that Kipling believed in society for its intrinsic value: there is no Burkean view of society as the temple of the living God. In the same story where he disparages the Thing for its betrayal of its caste he refers with studied casualness to 'that carefully trained menagerie of wild beasts, Decent Society . . .' Nevertheless, whatever one thinks of society at heart, its structure is a necessity and its rules must be duly observed if men are not to disintegrate.

The underrated story 'Beyond the Pale', with its extremely well-sustained and quite complex irony, tells the same tale: strange and morally destructive experiences await anyone who goes beyond his given limits. Or, as he puts it elsewhere:

> A stone's throw out on either hand
> From that well-ordered road we tread
> And all the world is wild and strange.

The title of the story and the Hindu proverb used as epigraph – 'Love heeds not caste nor sleep a broken bed. I went in search of love and lost myself' – point the moral.

There is more than a clue in this as to why so many of Kipling's favourite characters are the administrators and men of the Public Works Department, who submit uncomplainingly to the harsh discipline of their arduous routine, menaced by 'great, grey *formless*' India and what that hostile force can do to break them. Where Haggard's heroes are continually raising their eyes to the hills and well beyond, Kipling's keep theirs firmly on the ground. This allows them to absorb themselves in the task nearest to hand and do something useful to assist suffering humanity – but, of course, it also holds them together morally. They are cogs in a great machine and so long as it goes on they have a function and an appointed place. As cogs they will wear out, but they can be replaced, and in the meantime they will have sustained their integrity – albeit at enormous cost – and helped to create the necessary conditions for others to survive in the continuous warfare between self and chaos.

Where Haggard at most rises to a gloomy pathos Kipling comes near achieving a truly tragic vision. Moreover, at some point the former's heroes are always to be found on tip-toe aching with aspiration, whereas Kipling's never are: they *know* they are doomed. For them the struggle is to secure a space, an identity, for the brief moment of their problematic existence. These men are persecuted by the gods almost in the classical manner, unlike Haggard's characters who tend to make chums of their divinities. In the following extract the paraded lightness of tone – a device of some subtlety in Kipling's writing – should not be allowed to mislead us: 'The Gods had no mercy but the Government and the men it employed had no fear. This annoyed the Gods who are immortal, for they perceived that the men whose portion was death were greater than they. The Gods are always troubled even in their paradises by this sense of inferiority.' However, in this story, 'The Last Relief', the gods get their man, though, as we might guess, their victory is not complete.

Thus while space for Haggard rolls outwards and upwards towards the infinite, for Kipling, in his scheme of things, it must necessarily remain altogether finite. This is what makes his literary use of the imperial idea so much more subtle and interesting than Haggard's, furnishing as it does such an apt metaphor for the tensions of his own moral universe. There the confrontation is stark ('One of the many curses of our life in India is the want of atmosphere in the painter's sense. There are no half-tints worth noticing'); space *must* be pegged out and the wild and strange domesticated ('. . . in India where everyone knows everyone else . . .'). Despite the structural network of categories and compartments, however, there will never be complete security; and one is made continually aware of the menace in the darkness – or the blinding sun – beyond the established order of the cantonment.

Interestingly, Kipling defines the role of the artist in very similar terms, making art nothing if not committed. In two allegories, 'The Children of the Zodiac' and 'Teem', he requires the artist to serve humanity by helping man to realize his fate and to come to terms with it. 'Outside his Art,' we are told in 'Teem' 'an Artist must not dream', and if Teem is occasionally tempted to 'return to my lost world' such nostalgia, it is made clear, is no good to him nor anyone else, and Teem and the sheepdog with his quite different art devote themselves to the needs of their human dependents – the meeting-point of all the arts. In the allegory there is also the clear option on a very wide meaning for Art: certainly wide enough to include all daily crafts.

Outside his art an artist must not dream, but that Kipling could conceive the dream gives a depth to his vision and a tension to his art which very nearly lifts it out of the minor rank. His imaginative preoccupation with the problems of integrity is a mature and creative one, immediately calling to mind the finer yield of a very similar concern in the work of Joseph Conrad.

Unfortunately in the last instance Kipling is too afraid of the dream, too fearful for the precarious self to give the devil of potential destruction his artistic due: keeping

73 *Opposite* 'The first Court of the Season: Mr and Mrs Rudyard Kipling', 1925,

The Later Years

74 Honorary degrees at the Sorbonne, 1921. From left
to right, Sir James Frazer, Kipling, the Rector of the
Sorbonne

5 Kipling's installation as Rector of St Andrew's,
1923. Stanley Baldwin ('Cousin Stan') second from
left, Lord Haig second right

Friends and Contemporaries

76 *Right* Proconsuls: Lord Curzon and Lord Milner, 1918

78 *Opposite* Henry Rider Haggard (1856–1925)

77 Lord Roberts visiting Vernet-les-Bains, 1911, Kipling in attendance

79 *Opposite* Field-Marshal Lord Roberts of Kandahar ('There's a little red-faced man/Which is Bobs . . .')

80 *Left* W. E. Henley. 'I had the fortune to know him only as kind, generous, and a jewel of an editor . . .' (*Something of Myself*)

81 Henry James (1843–1916), was close to Kipling and the Balestiers during the 'nineties

82 Sir John Bland Sutton, Kipling's doctor and close friend in later years

83 HMS *Kipling* (launched by Kipling's daughter, Mrs Bambridge, two years earlier) at Alexandria in 1941, after picking up survivors from Crete

the square intact comes to be an obsession with him, leaving an insufficient gap, in Eliot's famous phrase, between the man who suffers and the mind which creates.

Truth for Kipling was not a veiled and alluring enigma to whose seduction he was only too willing to submit: he knew too much for that: '. . . Truth is a naked lady, and if by accident she is drawn up from the bottom of the sea, it behoves a gentleman either to give her a print petticoat or to turn his face to the wall and vow that he did not see.' Unlike Haggard, who was for ever nipping behind the Veil to catch the Animating Spirit at a disadvantage, Kipling prayed for

> A veil 'twixt us and thee, dread Lord
> A veil 'twixt us and thee
> Lest we should hear too clear, too clear,
> And unto madness see.

And when others seemed to threaten the defences he had erected between himself and 'the edge of nothing', he savaged them without mercy. 'Lesser breeds without the Law' were not so much to be pitied as feared, for they kept alive the principle of law-lessness and so menaced those who depended morally on a rigorous observation of the rules.

'Even your imagination is out of the fifth form,' Andrew Lang once wrote to Haggard with unusual bluntness. Kipling's is certainly not, though for purposes of camouflage he often made it sound as though it were. It is a tactic he uses even in his letters to Haggard, which are full of slang and schoolboy persiflage reflecting his essential closeness and reserve and inability to give freely of himself.

Haggard, on the other hand, despite his recurrent pessimism, could be described as spiritually expansive. It is significant that it was not the man for whom service and discipline were concepts *necessary as concepts* to his imaginative and moral life who involved himself in actual service to his country. It was Haggard, the writer with the strong inclination to mysticism, who, in addition to writing over fifty novels, a massive and highly-regarded study of the state of English agriculture, and a number of other substantial works, served on several important commissions, touring the Dominions at least twice in a semi-official capacity and eventually getting his knighthood for public services – something which pleased him greatly.

There can, of course, be no doubt about Haggard's inferiority to Kipling as a writer: despite his ability to work on us through a vividly deployed image of arche-typal force, he continually fails to provide a full literary communication with the primitive and elemental. Yet he, too, had vision of a sort – a sympathy, a largeness of soul which raised him above the materialism, the complacency and the shallow-minded paternalism of many of his contemporaries. And it was this quality of soul which – in contrast to Kipling – he sought to communicate, ultimately allowing the end to take precedence over the means. With a revealing, if typical, choice of vocabu-lary he frankly states his position: 'In an adventure story . . . the substance is, as it were, the soul of the matter; the style is its outward and visible body. I prefer a creation with a great soul even if its form is somewhat marred, to one with a beautifully finished form and very little soul.' He himself was aware of the difficulty. Some five years before he died he wrote: 'In these latter days – thank Heaven I do seem to be grasping the skirts of vision – though they slip from the hand like water. But to describe – to set down! – There's the rub! – '

Both Kipling and Haggard cared intensely about what can only be called the human condition, and for both it was acutely focused in the death of a beloved son from which neither ever fully recovered. 'A long talk with Kipling is now one of the greatest pleasures I have left in life,' Haggard wrote in 1918, and the two imperialists remained the staunchest of friends until Haggard's death in 1925, linked by the largeness of their view and their consequent pessimism and suffering.

Bernard Bergonzi
KIPLING AND THE
FIRST WORLD WAR

R UDYARD KIPLING began as the chronicler of a peace-time army. The early stories which made him famous described life in the British Army in India during the 1880s, with occasional references to wars off-stage, on the North-West Frontier or in Burma. It was not until the Boer War that Kipling saw anything of war at first hand. And for Kipling, as for many of his fellow-countrymen, the Boer War – and specifically the early defeats of the British – came as a profound shock. The British Army, for all its proud traditions, was badly organized and ill supported by the nation at home. In 'The Islanders', with its famous attack on 'The flannelled fools at the wicket or the muddied oafs at the goals,' he berated the English for their indifference to the soldierly virtues, and like other writers of the early 1900s – such as Erskine Childers in *The Riddle of the Sands* – he had a keen sense of the possibility of invasion:

> But ye say, 'It will mar our comfort.' Ye say, 'It will minish our trade.'
> Do ye wait for the spattered shrapnel ere ye learn how a gun is laid?
> For the low, red glare to southward when the raided coast-towns burn?
> (Light ye shall have on that lesson, but little time to learn.)

In one of his stories about the Boer War, 'The Captive' (*Traffics and Discoveries*), a general remarks, 'It's a first-class dress-parade for Armageddon', and during the next few years the possibility of Armageddon was often in Kipling's mind. Its likelihood was emphasized in his story, 'The Edge of the Evening' (*A Diversity of Creatures*), written in 1913, an improbable account of the capture and death of two foreign spies who have been surveying British military installations from a silent aeroplane.

For Kipling, the outbreak of war in August 1914 was something long expected, which he greeted with a sense of grim fulfilment, as in 'For All We Have and Are':

> For all we have and are,
> For all our children's fate,
> Stand up and take the war,
> The Hun is at the gate!

Despite Edmund Wilson's account of the importance of Kipling's childhood in his imaginative development, he remains one of the most impersonal of authors, offering few clues about the relation of the life to the work. Kipling responds to the First World War in several poems and stories, in a lively set of impressions of life with the Navy called *Sea Warfare*, and in the two-volume *The Irish Guards in the Great War*, published in 1923. Only the last of these directly relates to the major personal event of the war for Kipling: the death in action of his son. John Kipling was not quite seventeen at the outbreak of war, the only son of a man famous for his love of children and his skill as a writer of children's books: John and his sister Elsie had appeared as 'Dan' and 'Una' in *Puck of Pook's Hill* and *Rewards and Fairies*. Now, in August 1914, John hastened to answer Lord Kitchener's call for volunteers. He at first proposed to enlist as a private soldier, but helped by Kipling's influence with Lord Roberts, an old family friend, he was given a commission in the Irish Guards. In March 1915 Rider

Haggard wrote in his diary, after a visit to the Kiplings: 'Their boy John, who is not yet 18, is an officer in the Irish Guards and one can see that they are terrified lest he should be sent to the front and killed, as has happened to nearly all the young men they know.' It was not a fate that could be averted nor, in that time of absolute, unfaltering patriotic commitment, in any sense wished away. In September 1915 John Kipling, serving in the Second Battalion of the Irish Guards, took part in the Battle of Loos. Casualties were heavy, and on 2 October a War Office telegram announced that John Kipling was wounded and missing. Hope lingered painfully for a few weeks, but by 12 November Kipling had given up believing that his son might be a prisoner. He wrote to Brigadier Dunsterville: 'He was reported as one of the best of the subalterns and was gym instructor and signaller. It was a short life. I'm sorry that all the years' work ended in that one afternoon but – lots of people are in our position – and it's something to have bred a man.' It was to be another two years before Kipling received an eye-witness account of John's death. His principal monument to his son was the large regimental history on which he worked for several years, where Lieutenant John Kipling appears merely as a name on a casualty list, illustrating, to the end, his father's stoical reticence.

Their son's death caused the parents to withdraw into the privacy of grief. As Charles Carrington writes, 'Neither Rudyard nor Carrie ever talked much about their son, but their life without him was never the same; it had lost a motive force.' Kipling's bitterness about the war became more pronounced, and was expressed in a series of angry propagandist poems, directed at such targets as 'The Pope, the swithering Neutrals, 'The Kaiser and his Gott'. Pope Benedict XV, who had made proposals for ending the war, was savagely condemned in 'A Song at Cock-crow'; Kipling believed that the Pope was pro-German and trying to ensure Roman Catholic dominance over Europe. The publication of Kipling's wartime poems was curiously punctuated by the appearance in *The Times* in May 1918 of a poem ascribed to Kipling called 'The Old Volunteer', which turned out to be a forgery by an unknown hoaxer. Of all Kipling's war poetry, it is the 'Epitaphs' that now seem most moving and authentic. He called them 'naked cribs of the Greek Anthology', and it is evident that Kipling used the terse, controlled form of the classical epigram to touch on feelings he was unable or unwilling to express more fully and directly. Thus 'The Beginner' shows the lover of children reflecting on the deaths of young men who, like John Kipling, were scarcely more than children themselves:

> On the first hour of my first day
> In the front trench I fell.
> (Children in boxes at a play
> Stand up to watch it well.)

There is a comparable theme, treated very differently, in Kipling's short story, 'Mary Postgate' (*A Diversity of Creatures*), probably his best-known piece of fiction about the war, and certainly the most controversial. It brings together public events, like the development of the Royal Flying Corps and the first German air-raids during 1914–15, and some of Kipling's deepest preoccupations: a concern with the more extreme manifestations of feminine psychology ('The female of the species is more deadly than the male'), with the suffering and death of the young, and the ethics of revenge. Mary Postgate is a middle-aged spinster, who acts as lady's companion to the ageing, crippled Miss Fowler. She is devoted to Miss Fowler's orphaned nephew, Wynn, who is being brought up by his aunt. He is a cheerful, shallow youth who is fond of Mary, though he subjects her to a great deal of crude teasing. At the outbreak of war Wynn joins the Flying Corps, and after a few months is killed on a training flight:

'I never expected anything else,' said Miss Fowler; 'but I'm sorry it happened before he had done anything.'

The room was whirling round Mary Postgate, but she found herself quite steady in the midst of it.

'Yes,' she said. 'It's a great pity he didn't die in action after he had killed somebody.'

The faded but determined maiden lady – 'quite steady in the midst of it' – takes up the task of accomplishing the death that Wynn died too soon for. After the funeral Mary Postgate prepares to burn all the boy's treasured possessions; she makes a funeral pyre of them – in describing it, Kipling takes a page to give a lovingly exact inventory of toys and books and sporting equipment – and then walks into the village to buy paraffin. She thinks she hears the sound of an aeroplane overhead, recalling the flights that Wynn used to make over the village while he was in training. Then there is an explosion. A bomb has fallen, bloodily killing one of the village children: 'It was little Edna Gerritt, aged nine, whom Mary had known since her perambulator days.'

Returning home Mary sets fire to Wynn's funeral pyre. As she does so she hears a groan and discovers a badly injured German airman lying nearby. Her response is neither fear nor pity, but simply anger; she goes into the house to fetch a revolver, and threatens the man with it. She ignores his cries for a doctor, and gets on with burning Wynn's things, deliberately letting the man die. *This* is to be the death that Wynn had failed to accomplish, and it is specifically an act of revenge for the death of Edna. Kipling, in fact, relates the man and the child in a bizarre but striking image: 'When she came through the rain, the eyes in the head were alive with expectation. The mouth even tried to smile. But at sight of the revolver its corners went down just like Edna Gerritt's. A tear trickled from one eye, and the head rolled from shoulder to shoulder as though trying to point out something.' When he calls for help, Mary musters her small German to tell him, *'Ich haben der todt Kinder gesehn.'* As the pyre burns through, Mary waits for the German's final death agony; she hears it, at last, with orgasmic satisfaction, and returns to the house glowing with unfamiliar fulfilment: ' *"That's* all right," said she contentedly, and went up to the house, where she scandalized the whole routine by taking a luxurious hot bath before tea, and came down looking, as Miss Fowler said when she saw her lying all relaxed on the other sofa, "quite handsome!" '

The presentation of the heroine's state of mind is masterly, and 'Mary Postgate' is one of Kipling's most brilliant stories. Nevertheless, some readers have understandably found it too horrible to take seriously, while others have tried to defuse its morally problematic quality by arguing that Kipling by no means endorses Mary's behaviour. It has also been suggested that the bitterness of the story is a result of the death of John Kipling, which is verifiably untrue, since Kipling wrote the story six months before John's death, though it is possible that the anxiety he felt about his son's future was a contributory element. I do not, in fact, think one can make very much of the story without some sympathetic understanding of Kipling's attitudes. It is well known that he was deeply interested in revenge; it forms the basis for many of his stories, such as the crude and boisterous 'Village that Voted the Earth was Flat' and the late and complex 'Dayspring Mishandled'. Kipling seems to have had not merely a detached interest but a real commitment to the ethics of revenge, considered both as a tragic destiny and a necessary ritual; his own values may have been closer to those of the Sikh soldiers so sympathetically portrayed in 'In the Presence' (*A Diversity of Creatures*), than to those of the post-Christian liberal. Furthermore, 'Mary Postgate' was written when hatred of the Germans, because of reported atrocities in Belgium, and the first civilian deaths in air-raids, was raging uncontrollably. A *Punch* cartoon by Bernard Partridge of that time shows the Kaiser rebuking a German aviator for not having killed any children: 'Well, then, no babes, no iron crosses.' The key sentence in 'Mary Postgate' is, I believe, '*Ich haben der todt Kinder gesehn.*' It points, too, to the theme of another and slighter story, also written early in 1915, 'Swept and Garnished'. This is about a prosperous, self-satisfied middle-aged lady in Berlin, who takes to her bed with influenza and is haunted by the ghosts of young children killed in the German advance into Belgium. At the end of the story the woman is out of bed and on her hands and knees, trying to wipe spots of blood from the floor. In these stories, Kipling is not merely expressing anti-Hun hysteria, though that is present, but is touching on something more profound and more obscure. The sociologist Peter Berger, discussing 'signals of transcendence' in his book *A Rumour of Angels*, has referred to 'the argument from damnation', which he says 'refers to experiences in which our sense of what is humanly permissible is so fundamentally outraged that the only adequate response to the offence as well as to the offender seems to be a curse of supernatural dimensions'. And, says Berger, the massacre of the innocents is an archetypal instance of such an offence. There were good reasons why such a subject was particularly sensitive for Kipling: '*Ich haben der todt Kinder gesehn*' is also the theme, though expressed with serenity and not disturbance, of one of his finest stories of the previous decade, the deeply poignant 'They' (*Traffics and Discoveries*), in which a traveller finds a beautiful country house that is haunted by the happy ghosts of dead children, including, as he discovers by a fleeting touch of the hand at the end of the story, his own dead child. And 'They' is certainly a transmutation into art of Kipling's own sense of loss for his beloved eldest child, Josephine, who died at the age of seven in 1899.

Revenge was a perennial theme in Kipling's fiction, though it may well have been sharpened by the war. It is dominant in another story written early in 1915, 'Sea Constables' (*Debits and Credits*), which is full of Kipling's hatred for the 'swithering neutrals'; four naval reserve captains reminiscing after a long spell of duty are told how one of them pursued a neutral vessel that was trading with the enemy and yet relying on the protection of the Royal Navy, and in the end left its owner to die of bronchial pneumonia. 'Sea Constables', though sharing in the same extremity of feeling as 'Mary Postgate', is far less effective. Yet the revenge theme, basic though it was in Kipling's imaginative world, was balanced by an opposed theme of reconciliation and healing. And this pervades several stories written during or after the war. One such is 'On the Gate', a curious but tender fantasy about the problems posed in heaven by the arrival of so many dead during the war. In May 1918 Rider Haggard recorded having this story read to him by Kipling: 'he read me a quaint story about Death and St Peter, written in modern language, almost in slang, which his wife would not let him publish. It would have been caviare to the General if he had, because the keynote of it is infinite mercy extending even to the case of Judas.' Kipling did not, in fact, publish 'On the Gate' until 1926, when it appeared in *Debits and Credits*. In the same volume there are several stories set in a masonic lodge in South London, where injured and shell-shocked men gather to relive their experiences and give each other help and support. The masonic element shows Kipling's conviction that ritual is a necessary element in preserving order in human affairs, especially at times of stress, and it reminds us of his love of in-groups of men united by a common purpose and with shared values and language, something that had fascinated him ever since as a youth he had been a privileged visitor to British Army messes in India. These stories – which in my view are often marred by an arch falsity of tone – include 'A Madonna of the Trenches', which occultly reveals the transcendent power of human love, and 'The Janeites', where a group of soldiers – not all educated men – find in the novels of Jane Austen both a satisfying source of arcane knowledge and reference, and a scheme of values that can help them withstand the horror of front-line existence. In some of these stories the theme of healing merges with another that preoccupied Kipling: the sense of man being taxed beyond endurance, which underlies several late stories in *Limits and Renewals*.

As a member of the War Graves Commission Kipling was very familiar with the great military cemeteries in France and Flanders, and it was after visiting one at Rouen in March 1925 that he wrote 'The Gardener' (*Debits and Credits*). Like 'Mary Postgate' this fine story is deeply concerned with the psychology of a middle-aged woman; in all other respects it is opposed but complementary to the extreme negative emotions of the earlier story. 'The Gardener' opens with the words, 'Everyone in the village knew that Helen Turrell did her duty by all her world, and by none more honourably than by her only brother's unfortunate child.' The unmarried Helen brings up the boy, Michael, after the death of his parents. But in fact he is her illegitimate son; she preserves the fiction that he is her nephew, though many people suspect the truth. He joins the army on the outbreak of war, and is killed after the Battle of Loos. Most of the story describes Helen's first visit to his grave in a huge military cemetery; she is somewhat repelled by her fellow mourners, and is deeply disturbed by a hysterical woman who wants to talk about her dead lover. At the end of the story Helen is looking for Michael's grave, and a casual encounter dispels the pretence which she has sustained for so many years:

A man knelt behind a line of headstones – evidently a gardener, for he was firming a young plant in the soft earth. She went towards him, her paper in her hand. He rose at her approach and without prelude or salutation asked: 'Who are you looking for?'

'Lieutenant Michael Turrell – my nephew,' said Helen slowly and word for word, as she had many thousands of times in her life.

The man lifted his eyes and looked at her with infinite compassion before he turned from the fresh-sown grass toward the naked black crosses.

'Come with me,' he said, 'and I will show you where your son lies.'

When Helen left the Cemetery she turned for a last look. In the distance she saw the man bending over his young plants; and she went away, supposing him to be the gardener.

The last words echo St John's gospel, where Mary Magdalene supposes that the risen Christ 'must be the gardener'. (Mary Magdalene was forgiven much because she had loved much, and seems to have had a particular appeal for Kipling: in 'On the Gate' St Peter is accustomed to invoking what he calls 'a most useful ruling' under the initials QMA, which stand for '*Quia multum amavit*'.) Together 'Mary Postgate' and 'The Gardener' show the range of Kipling's imaginative response to the war: hatred is countered with a hint of 'infinite compassion', and both are involved with the memory of a dead child. Kipling's writings about the war remind us of the strange complexity of his art, and show how completely it resists any neat and limiting formula.

John Raymond
THE LAST PHASE

WHEN the First World War ended, Kipling, a world-famous literary figure and a Nobel prize-winner, was still only fifty-two. He had always, at least from the age of twenty onwards, seemed incredibly old for his age, a best-selling omniscient prodigy when Shaw, nine years his senior, was only just making his name. Though his sales and popularity were still enormous, his reputation, like the faith and gospel that he preached, had been dwindling since long before the War. In May of that year, the young 'T.S.E.', reviewing *The Years Between* in the *Athenaeum*, could write that 'Mr Kipling is a laureate without laurels. He is a neglected celebrity. The arrival of a new book of his verse is not likely to stir the slightest ripple on the surface of our conversational intelligentsia.'

Charles Carrington – to whose biography everyone concerned with the life of Kipling owes such a debt – gives us a sombre, muted picture of the writer corralled down at Bateman's, jealously guarded, watched over and protected from prying eyes by Carrie Kipling:

Not only did she guard his health; she opened his letters, dictated replies to the secretary, corresponded with the literary agent, managed the household and eventually farmed the land, watching all expenditure with a prudent eye; and it was commonly said in the neighbourhood that she would have got more out of the estate if she had put more into it ... His autograph was now so strictly guarded that no unauthorized scrap of his handwriting was allowed to leave the house; even his personal letters were checked in and out by the secretary ...

The secretary herself noted that Kipling had lost his buoyant step and that his physical condition was worsening. The gastric attacks, which were increasing, were ascribed to 'suppressed anxiety'. (As his daughter [Mrs Bambridge] has testified, it was not until 1933 that a Parisian doctor discovered that for fifteen years Kipling had been suffering from duodenal ulcers: so much for that exuberant and companionable tycoon of surgery, Sir John Bland-Sutton.) Only four years had passed since the War Office telegram had announced Lieutenant J. Kipling to be wounded and missing – one of the 20,000 who fell in the battle of Loos. A few months previously Rider Haggard, his father's great friend, had noted:

Poor old boy, John's death has hit him very hard. He said to-day that I was lucky to have lost my son early, when I still had youth to help me to bear up against the shock ... I pointed out that this love of ours for our lost sons was a case of what is called 'inordinate affection' in the Prayer Book which somehow is always bereaved. 'Perhaps,' he answered, 'but I don't care for "ordinate" affection and nor do you.'

Haggard was ten years older than Kipling ('then you have less time left in which to suffer', his friend told him). Judging by his journals and Kipling's letters, he was right to declare that 'I believe honestly that outside of his own family there is no one living to whom Rudyard opens his heart except myself'. The record of their friendship – it began in the early nineties and lasted until Haggard's death in 1925 – makes lively and, for the last years, moving reading. It also throws much light on Kipling's delvings into the numinous and the unseen during this period, his questioning of the problems of pain and disease, of love, suffering, separation and survival after death –

all themes that play such a powerful and disturbing part in the last two volumes of his short stories. Such speculations awoke a warm and uninhibited response in Haggard. Whenever they met, at Bateman's, Ditchingham or in the Athenaeum, the two men habitually 'talked till we were tired about everything in heaven above and earth beneath' – about ancient Egypt, the Ice Age, Lord Curzon and the newly-ennobled 'Squiff' ('dead in the dug-out that he spent his mischievous leisure in deriding'), Kipling's cousin Baldwin ('Stanley is a Socialist at heart'), smallholdings, emigration, the Americans' attitude to war debts and the pro-German policy of the Vatican. They had most of their public obsessions in common, including the common enemy, and it was in 1920 that, in company with Lord Sydenham and backed by *The Times*, they sponsored The Liberty League, a campaign against Bolshevism; this hopeful but short-lived organization collapsed in the following year through financial mismanagement. Meanwhile, Haggard raged at the trade unions and his friend at supposed Jewish international politicking. Kipling also foretold a second Mutiny. On learning that Haggard's niece Phyllis had accepted a Sapper and was marrying into the Indian Army, he declared that if she were his daughter he would not allow her to go ('as though', Rider commented, 'he could prevent it if she was another man's wife'). Together they condemned the optimistic claptrap of Lloyd George ('him with his sunsets and his mountains and his banners of dawn'), Northcliffe's 'stunts' and the internationalism of Woodrow Wilson. Grimly and proudly they agreed that 'we were both of us out of touch with the times'.

Meanwhile, there was the copybook round of duties to be observed: visits to and from the Baldwin cousinhood and the other relatives, Sussex neighbours to be entertained, the farm's herd and yield to be logged, deaths of friends and acquaintances lamented, New Year Honours perused and their recipients congratulated, Royal Commands to be attended, doctorates and a Rectorship (Edinburgh, Paris, St Andrew's) to be accepted and acknowledged. Twice the Order of Merit was declined (1921, 1924), Lord Stamfordham being asked, 'while presenting my humble and loyal duty . . . to pray that His Majesty may hold me excused'. (The King understood: 'he could do better service without a title or award than with one'. Gradually, over the years, Kipling had become a friend of George V's, one of that inner circle of old men who, in Betjeman's phrase, 'never cheated, never doubted'.) And, above all and always, there was that part-pilgrim, part-guardian duty of keeping troth, Kipling's work as a War Graves Commissioner, 'to visit and report upon the cemeteries where the million dead of the British Armies were re-buried'. As Carrington tells us, 'he made careful inspections of more than thirty cemeteries in northern France, and, on his first tour, turned aside to see the battlefield of Loos and to identify the shattered stumps and brambly undergrowth of Chalk-pit Wood'.

His two-volume history (one for each battalion) of *The Irish Guards in the Great War* was published in 1923. He had been gathering material for this since 1917, endlessly and meticulously questioning and comparing notes with John Kipling's brothers-in-arms for every bloody or humdrum detail of those four years. At last he had discharged his debt of piety. It is a curious *memento mori*, the collection, assembly and re-presentation of men's scattered memories, 'edited and compiled from their diaries and papers'. Supremely factual, massive in its detail, it seems, at a first glance, to be a miracle of understatement, telling everything and nothing about the fragment of Hell it describes. The narrative is mostly written in a heightened mixture of company- or platoon-commander's report-style and *Gazette* citation English, flavoured with unnatural Irish OR reminiscence (scant breath of the authentic Mulvaney in these 650 pages!) The tone, when not subaltern-facetious ('As one youngster wrote home triumphantly, "I was never *actually* sick" '), is clipped and even, with every piece of trivia recorded, e.g. 'at Béthune they enjoyed a nine days' rest ... and a Divisional football competition for a cup presented by the Bishop of Khartum'. This, after all, as Kipling rightly pointed out in his introduction, is the stuff of a wartime regimental narrative, not written for the outside and uncommitted reader. Perhaps the strangest features of the book were the attractive maps of Armageddon – the woods and villages beautifully inked-in like a geography of folk-myth, the borders elegantly embellished with skulls and hour-glasses, and only the thin neat trails of red-inked dots and arrows to mark the carnage of 'actions and billets', the miniature reproductions of salients and 'Pushes'.

As a remembrance monument, a masque of death decently camouflaged to assume the form of a sculptured battle-frieze, this reticent, ordered narrative serves its purpose perfectly. Yet its pages contain all the ingredients and raw material of those astonishing short stories based upon the war that Kipling was later to include in *Debits and Credits* and *Limits and Renewals*. The horror and camaraderie of trench-life, the hellish glow of the braziers in the dug-outs, the shell-shock and trepanning, the smell of poison-gas, the stench of long-dead bodies creaking beneath duck-boards or stashed like sandbags around the walls of re-occupied positions – it is all here in embryo, indicated but unexorcized, not yet purged by the writer's power of catharsis. Only in the meagrest glimpses – in this eerie shot of No Man's Land, for instance – do we see what Miss Tompkins, in her fine study of Kipling, calls 'his spontaneous imaginative stroke', vaguely groping:

... The trenches were full of such mysteries. Strange trades, too, were driven there. A man, now gone to Valhalla, for he was utterly brave, did not approve of letting dead Germans lie unvisited before the lines. He would mark the body down in the course of his day's work, thrust a stick in the parados to give him his direction, and at night, or preferably when the morning fog lay heavy on the landscape, would slip across to his quarry and return with his pockets filled with loot. Many officers had seen C—'s stick at the back of the trench. Some living may like to know now why it was there.

Two contemporary reactions to *The Irish Guards* are interesting, though predictable. In his *War Books* (1930), that invaluable survey of 1914–18 literature, Captain Cyril Falls, later the Military Correspondent of *The Times*, awarded Kipling's narrative two stars – a score equal to Ian Hay's *The First Hundred Thousand* and one pip up on *Goodbye to All That* ('his attitude ... leaves a disagreeable impression') and Colonel Repington's War Diaries. Though professionally discriminating ('regarding certain matters of detail he is inaccurate'), the captain was respectfully enthusiastic ('a noble tribute to the great regiment in the ranks of which he lost his son'). But the view of another who had survived the trenches (and received three pips from Falls for *Undertones of War)* was very different. Writing when the book appeared, Edmund Blunden (Kipling's successor on the War Graves Commission) declared roundly:

The fact is that Mr Kipling appears not perfectly to understand the pandemonium and nerve-strain of war; it seldom surges up in his pages of that appalling misery which brought seasoned men down in the shell holes beyond Thiepval, as they went up to relieve the Schwaben Redoubt, crying and 'whacked to the wide'. He makes constant stern attempts at actuality; he constantly falls short, in expressions merely strained, in sheer want of comprehension. To those who were in the line, his technical phraseology will seem incongruous now and then; but the deeper defects may be exemplified by such expressions as – touching pill-box warfare – 'the annoying fights and checks round the concreted machine gun posts' . . .

Land and Sea Tales for Scouts and Guides by 'Rudyard Kipling, Commissioner, Boy Scouts', also appeared in 1923. A year later, at the Imperial Jamboree at Wembley, 6,000 Wolf Cubs were at last given the chance to show their literary inspirer 'how Baden Powell had made the characters of his *Jungle Books* come alive'. Two breaches, one within the family, the other of friendship, occurred about this time. Charles Carrington writes that Oliver Baldwin 'had meant much to the Kiplings when they lost their own son . . . That he should change sides in politics was his own affair, but conduct which they thought unfilial they could not forgive.' The other break was with Stanley Baldwin's opponent, Lord Beaverbrook. Later (in 1931) Kipling was to supply his cousin with the words that lashed the conspiring press lords – and helped to get Duff-Cooper in at the St George's, Westminster by-election: 'What the proprietorship of these papers is aiming at is power, and power without responsibility – the privilege of the harlot throughout the ages' – a condemnation that still echoes across the years.

In March 1925 Kipling was away touring in France – and telling Rider Haggard, in one of the last of those long, richly descriptive travel letters, that

. . . motoring *ain't* wearisome. It's all the fun of the road compressed into a few hours; with leisure at one end at least . . . and consider now a day that gives you a couple of hours in the morning among the caves of the Dordogne – incised and painted Cromagnon piccys of bison, horse, wolf and Rhino traced on the irregularly dimpled roofings and sides of those limestone grottoes, as smooth as candle-drippings . . . the rest is all warm stone walled stillness and these inexplicable figures . . . Your Egypt is merely a parvenu beside them.

Then, a couple of hours later, you are at Lourdes. Same sort of smooth bluish-white rock grotto in a hill side but instead of incised totems, a lavender and white presentment of Our Lady just on the spot where Bernadette, the peasant girl, aged fourteen, had the visions of her in '58. And all the smooth nodular scarped rock below smeared and covered and runnelled with the gutterings of countless candles . . . lighting up and going out like the children of men.

And at the evening's end, soft, quiet, relaxing, *most* English Pau, full of elderly birds with doubtful lungs in plus fours! That's a fairly large octave to stretch . . .

A few weeks later Haggard was dead – the day after Lord Milner, a friend of both men and one of Kipling's greatest admirations, had also died. (He was later to praise what he regarded as Milner's 'selfless statesmanship' in his poem, 'The Pro-Consuls'.) Two more stewards who had laid down their burdens. Meanwhile, as events in India, Ireland, Egypt and elsewhere seemed to indicate, the heritage that men like Milner had striven to preserve was undergoing erosion. Kipling's public heart hardened and he moved further to the right – and to the policies of his friend, H. A. Gwynne, editor of the *Morning Post* and its proprietor, Lady Bathurst, with both of whom he was friendly about this time. When the Liberal and internationalist Philip Kerr (later Lord Lothian) was appointed a Rhodes Trustee, he himself resigned from the Trust in public protest. One could say of Kipling in these years what the DNB was to say later of his friend George Lloyd, Allenby's successor as High Commissioner in Egypt (1925–9), the resolute and rearguard proconsul broken by Arthur Henderson during the second Labour Government – that 'his vision of his country's imperial destiny was not compatible with prevailing sentiment'. Kipling's own public sentiments remained what they had always been – for patriotic service in the many forms it still took for a man with his convictions: Scouting for the young, the Navy League, the Territorials, the Royal Society of St George, the British Legion for the adult and middle-aged, the ideals of Freemasonry and comradeship for all, but especially for the old, the lonely, the shell-shocked and disabled.

Kipling had been a Mason ever since he was admitted (under age) to the Lodge of 'Hope and Persuasion' at Lahore. In *Debits and Credits* (1926), his formidable imaginary Lodge ('Faith and Works, 5837 E.C.') came into being, both as the subject of a tale itself ('In the Interests of the Brethren' is heavy with the Craft) and as the setting of 'A Madonna of the Trenches' and 'A Friend of the Family' (as also of 'Fairy-Kist' in *Limits and Rewards*). How much these stories and others in the last collection owed to the material gathered for *The Irish Guards* can only be measured by those who have read both the fact and the fiction – plus the Kipling-Haggard record. There are strange equations, relationships and correspondences between all three. For example, remembering (in 'A Friend of the Family') Bevin's nervous gesture, a scar from Gallipoli (' "Oh, there was fun in Hell, wasn't there, Australia?", and again his hands went down to tighten the belt that was missing') we recall Haggard's noting, after a long and deeply personal talk at Bateman's, that '. . . In one way R. is a very curious man – when he talks he always likes to be doing something with his hands. "I must occupy my hands," he said, and went to fetch a holly-wood stick he had been drying and peeled and sandpapered it . . . Last time we talked in this fashion he employed himself with a fishing rod and line.'

As far back as May 1918, Kipling had read Haggard a story[1] which embodies 'a conception of transcending mercy', as Miss Tompkins puts it, the after-life as conceived by Wesley rather than Calvin, an echo of the Psalmist's 'If I go down to Hell thou art there also'. Besides the stories already mentioned and two Stalky episodes, this volume contains five unforgettables – 'The Wish House', 'The Janeites', 'The

[1] 'On the Gate: A Tale of '16' (see p. 140 above).

Bull that Thought', 'The Eye of Allah' and 'The Gardener'. Of all of these one can safely say that only Kipling could have written them (incidentally, much that is most original and strange in the art of Muriel Spark is prefigured mysteriously in 'The Wish House').

Captain Falls, that faithful literary barometer, was delighted. Three-starring *Debits and Credits*, he voiced the previous misgivings of all Kipling's literate admirers when he wrote that the book 'is notable because it represents what the sporting reporters call a "come-back". Certain of the master's works had shown a falling off distressing to the faithful and a cause of scoffing to the lesser breeds, so that it was a triumph for the former and discomfiture for the latter when he returned to his best vein . . .'

Though the stories included in *Limits and Renewals* were not collected until 1932, they were mostly written in 1927 and 1928. The book contains yet another dog story, 'The Woman in His Life' (*Thy Servant a Dog*, 1930, had sold one hundred thousand copies in the first six months of publication), and two more tales of disease and medical life ('Unprofessional' and 'The Tender Achilles'). It also included 'The Church that was at Antioch' and 'The Manner of Men', two remarkable stories in *Rewards and Fairies* vein centering round St Paul, the latter specifically based on the episode of the shipwreck at Malta in Acts 27, the former also concerned with Valens, the young police lieutenant and worshipper of Mithras who pleads for his assassins, 'don't be hard on them . . . they get worked up . . . they don't know what they're doing'. St Paul, busy as ever, suggests that Valens should be baptized but St Peter, looming 'vast and commanding' beside him, countermands this suggestion and, in doing so, unconsciously voices his primacy: 'Think you that one who has spoken Those Words needs such as we are to certify him to any God?'

Of the other stories in this collection, 'A Naval Mutiny' and 'Beauty Spots' are high-spirited comedies, the one with a typological, the other with an obliquely but genuinely sentimental difference. And if we regret the inclusion of 'The Tie' – 'an ill-natured anecdote', as Professor Carrington rightly describes it – the superb 'Dayspring Mishandled' more than atones. Carrington describes this tale as 'a profound, obscure, and singularly unpleasant story about a vindictive feud between two expert bibliophiles, or rather the vindictive persecution of a sham expert by a genuine expert', and this has, indeed, long been the general view. But it is surely more than that. For here, as nowhere else in his work, Kipling has, so to speak, revenged himself upon all his own hates and revenges. 'There are no flourishes in it; every sentence tells and matters,' writes Miss Tompkins, whose seven-page analysis of this strangest of all Kipling's stories is one of the high points of her own study. 'The upas crumbles, and Manallace is left "emptied out" by hate, as he had been by his sacrificial love. It is a Limit but there is no sign of another Renewal.'

In 1927, after an illness, Bland-Sutton recommended a long sea voyage and Kipling sailed to Brazil. He recorded his impressions for the *Morning Post* in a remarkable series of *Brazilian Sketches* (reprinted in Vol. 35 of the Sussex Edition, 1938), in which he paid tribute to the Portuguese empire-builders, men with just 'as little fear, reason or what is called common-sense' as their Tudor contemporaries. He visited

Bahia and felt, without telling, that it was 'the Mother City – the hearth of all that flaming energy when Brazil was being born'; he found Rio ('enormous, opulent, spotless') preparing for Carnival and stalked the Victoria Regia Lily in its Botanical Gardens (she 'lived in a pond and was all the books had said. Five to six feet across were the pads and turned up at the edge in three-inch rims ... the Gardens cried aloud – just like politicians – that they could produce everything man requires between certain degrees of latitude'). A snake farm, a power factory at São Paulo ('The Father of Lightnings') and a coffee estate all drew his reporter's eye. On Pernambuco quayside he caught a last glimpse, prosaic and unadventurous, yet in its own way touching, of what had once been a semblance of the White Man's burden:

And as one stared, there unrolled itself a length of well-known film – a shoreboat with a man in white kit that had been often washed. He came aboard and introduced himself to a very young man in quite new London 'whites', with the creases still down the front of the trousers, who turned to his companions and bade them farewell. It was just a Pernambuco Bank taking over a new clerk. When the pair were gone – the young figure looking all ways at once – and I had finished estimating the number of shore-boats of different makes, in different ports, at that hour, with allowance for change of time, conveying just the same suit of whites – I asked a man, 'What do you think he'll make of it?' 'He'll like it no end, and he'll talk about his first commission at Pernambuco as long as he lives. They all do. I know *I* did. It's a dear little place.' Which may be good news to some mother, the far side of the sea.

In this same year (1927) the Kipling Society, envisaged by J. H. C. Brooking as long ago as 1919, was formally constituted, with Major-General L. C. Dunsterville ('Stalky') as president and George Beresford ('M'Turk') on the committee. Needless to say, 'the object of attention' regarded it 'with gloomy distaste'. Since then, the society has steadily increased its membership (something under a thousand at the present time) and, as readers of its quarterly journal have reason to know, has made many original contributions to Kipling studies, in the last few years especially.

In January 1928, Hardy died and Kipling, along with Shaw, Galsworthy, Housman, Gosse and Barrie, was among the pall-bearers. The year 1930 was disastrous for Carrie Kipling. 'Her eyesight failing, racked with rheumatism and diagnosed as a diabetic,' she collapsed with appendicitis while on a cruise to Bermuda, and the Kiplings returned home by way of Canada. This was their last sight of that New World in which they had enjoyed such exhilarating experiences and suffered such ghastly public moments. It is good to know, from Professor Carrington's book, that Beatty Balestier, Kipling's errant brother-in-law and the source of all his troubles in Vermont, 'when he came to die in 1936, expressed regret for the harm he had done them, and a wish that they could have met again in friendship'.

'Proofs of Holy Writ', a conversational tour-de-force in which Shakespeare and Ben Jonson assist in the perfecting of the Authorized Version, was published in 1932. The idea appears to have been suggested by John Buchan, a companion of Kipling's at 'the Club'. (Buchan's *The Long Traverse* (1941), on its author's admission, is a Canadian *Puck of Pook's Hill*, intended to supplement the 'perfectly deadly' textbooks of

Canadian history.) It was also in 1932 – the year before Hitler came to power – that Kipling published his prophetic poem, 'The Storm-Cone'. In Year One of the Third Reich his Horatian tribute to Pepys appeared – with a hint, in the fourth verse, that the readiness is all.

Ever since the spring of 1878 when, as a schoolboy, he had accompanied his father to the Paris Exhibition, his feeling for France and the French people had deepened and increased. Her common-sense and professionalism, her imperial mission (in the manner of Lyautey's achievement in North Africa), the comradeship and 'shop' of conscription, the nation's very 'sou-mindedness' appealed vastly to Kipling – 'it makes for simplicity; the acceptance of hard living which fortifies the moral interior as small pebbles assist the digestion of fowls'. 'What of civilization was to continue,' he felt, 'lay in our united hands.' In 1933, as if to hearten himself about the beloved ally, he published his *Souvenirs of France* – as brief and moving a tribute to the French genius as Winston Churchill's essay on Clemenceau, written at about the same time (*Great Contemporaries*, 1937). Both men had been friends and admirers of the Tiger, embodiment of the embattled Republic.

Kipling celebrated his seventieth birthday at the end of December 1935, and he and his wife planned to go to Cannes early the following month. On the 12th, he had a severe haemorrhage in the night and was rushed to the Middlesex Hospital. He died soon after midnight on 18 January, the forty-fourth anniversary of his marriage. His death preceded George V's by a few days, the cocktail critics remarking smartly that the King had taken his Trumpeter with him. But already, unrecognized as yet, the ebb tide that had carried his work so far from fashionable literary consciousness was on the turn. In the shadow of the aftermath at Poets' Corner, a small but lively and determined voice was already remarking in the *New English Weekly* that the imperialism of the eighties and nineties

was sentimental and ignorant and dangerous, but it was not entirely despicable ... It was still possible to be an imperialist and a gentleman, and of Kipling's *personal* decency there can be no doubt. It is worth remembering that he was the most widely popular English writer of our time, and yet that no one, perhaps, so consistently refrained from making a vulgar show of his personality ...

... Now that he is dead, I for one cannot help wishing that I could offer some kind of tribute – a salute of guns, if such a thing were available – to the story-teller who was so important in my youth.

George Orwell's was the first salute of many, heralding the final recognition of Kipling's genius.

J. I. M. Stewart
KIPLING'S REPUTATION

Evenshually we *puckarowed* wan man. 'Trate him tinderly,' sez the Lift'nint. So I tuk him away into the jungle, wid the Burmese Interprut'r an' my clanin'-rod. Sez I to the man: 'My paceful squireen,' sez I, 'you shquot on your hunkers an' dimonstrate to my frind here, where *your* frinds are whan they're at home.' Wid that I introjuced him to the clanin'-rod, an' he comminst to jabber; the Interprut'r inturprutin' in betweens, an' me helpin' the Intelligince Departmint wid my clanin'-rod whan the man misremimbered.

THIS is the first passage of Kipling's prose to be quoted by a reviewer in an English periodical.[1] He is writing in the *Saturday Review* of 9 June 1888 in praise of *Plain Tales from the Hills*, and his conclusion is notable:

One advantage in the extreme shortness of the stories is that, as they are read in a few minutes, their incidents are easily forgotten, and they may be read again with fresh pleasure after a short interval. For this reason, and because it is small, the book is one to buy, and not merely to get from the library.

Truth and error are rather comically mingled here. Kipling's six volumes of garnered anecdotes and yarns in Wheeler's *Indian Railway Library* were indeed small and inexpensive, and few of their constituent units were too long to be read between – we may almost say – shifting from one uneasy posture to another as one chugged across the interminable immensities of the sub-continent: and it may well be that this was a point in their success. But that the 'incidents are easily forgotten' is assertion of a different order. Few readers, glancing however hurriedly at the contents of one of these volumes on a bookstall, are likely to have been in doubt as to whether they had read it before. They might buy it because their first copy had been thumbed to tatters or disappeared on permanent loan to untraceable friends, but assuredly not (as happens with detective stories) because they had forgotten all about it.

Certain it is that these paperbacks enormously took the fancy of the sort of people who had to travel about none too comfortably – even if 'soft' and at the expense of government – on Indian trains: subalterns and field officers, rank-and-file administrators, and such nondescripts as Kipling's father, who was an artist and scholar and therefore by no means exalted in the scheme of things established by the Raj. But the stories were not only attractive and memorable on their home ground. Nearly all of them were to prove to carry well, and some were soon declaring their quality as nurslings of immortality. Devised by an uncomfortable young man yet in his nonage – a young man resentful of having been educated not at Harrow but at a cheap and scruffy school, of not belonging in the least to any sort of 'inner ring', of having endured circumstances which had (in the gloomy phrase of a slightly later reviewer) 'thrown him into journalism' – devised by such a young man, these volumes contained, in other words, writing which was to contribute permanently to the fame of a major English author.

Something of the reputation he had precociously gained in India accompanied

---

[1] I am greatly indebted throughout this essay to *Kipling: the Critical Heritage* (1971) edited by Roger Lancelyn Green.

Kipling to England when he returned there in his twenty-fourth year. But nobody could have foretold the brilliant success story that thereupon immediately followed. It is legendary in the annals of literature – and moreover was, on a long-term view, as daunting a situation as ever faced a young writer. Quite soon, people were to be writing of him – indeed, publicly *to* him – stuff like this:

Now while a nation is grovelling at your feet, will you display an English contempt towards such servile adulation, or the kindly forbearance with a tinge of deeper brotherhood that, we fancy, underlies all your cynicism? For you write of 'niggers' and children with a loving pen – not sentimentally, not patronisingly, but with the manlier tone of kinship with the least of these, that whined as it may be by specious hypocrites, is yet the noblest truth of our common life . . .

Where does a young man go from here? And what, most specifically, had *got* Kipling here? The answer to the second question, crudely expressed, is that cleaning-rod – which had been wielded by a certain Mulvaney, a private soldier who, together with his comrades Learoyd and Ortheris, stalks prominently through these virtually adolescent imaginings of Kipling.

In the main, Kipling suggested himself at the start to the English public as commanding two Anglo-Indian territories. The first was that of Simla, which he presented – precociously, cynically, knowingly – as pervasively given over to philandering and adultery. Kipling's mother (who is said to have done a little society-reporting of a politer sort for a newspaper) disapproved of these sketches, and in England reactions to them varied. When Edmund Gosse surprisingly recorded, *viva voce*, 'the troubling thrill, the voluptuous and agitating sentiment', which Kipling's early writing prompted in him he may or may not have had these improper but scarcely stirring chronicles in mind. Andrew Lang, another pillar of the literary establishment and an early and diffuse celebrant of Kipling's genius, thought that the stories collected in *Under the Deodars*, exhibiting as they did 'the misery, the seamy, sorry side of irregular love affairs', might serve to 'convert a man or woman on the verge of guilt'. But in fact, whether for good or ill, readers do not much frequent fiction for a purpose like this, and on the Simla type of story Kipling might not have got very far. Professional critics, indeed, must have been fascinated by the spectacle of so young a man, and one who might be presumed so imperfectly educated, evincing before this particular spectacle a cool and detached regard more characteristic of Gallic than of Anglo-Saxon attitudes. But a larger public these things would scarcely have gained, and certainly not kept.

It was on his second territory, then, the barrack square, that the young Kipling most securely triumphed. His soldiers went on parade in both prose and verse: first in *Soldiers Three* and secondly in the long series of ballads which appeared for the most part in Henley's *National Observer*. The double impact was tremendous. What one critic has called 'the stab and glitter of the first Kipling furore' must have been largely due to it.

1890, the first full year of his return to England, saw him writing at an astonishing pace. He produced the equivalent of a volume of verse, and in prose 'The Courting of Dinah Shad', 'The Man Who Was', 'Without Benefit of Clergy', and 'On Greenhow Hill'. With this rapidly accumulating evidence before them, people wondered whether Kipling would develop into a novelist or into a fully-fledged poet, or whether he would perhaps continue to double-bank like Meredith (or like Hardy: only nobody yet knew about that). As it turned out, *Barrack Room Ballads* was pretty well to represent the twitch of Kipling's tether so far as metrical composition went. We may reflect that had he advanced as far from that volume in verse as he was to do from *Soldiers Three* in prose, he would rank today among the greatest English poets.

What is chiefly interesting about the three soldiers, together with the whole press of persons and incidents more immediately surrounding them, is the breadth of the appeal they proved to command. The *Spectator*, a periodical at that time going in for a little moral tone, found that Kipling happily did not belong to the school of so-called realists. And so 'The actualities of barrack-room life are not extenuated, but the tone of the whole is sound and manly. The author does not gloss over the animal tendencies of the British private, but he shows how in the grossest natures sparks of nobility may lie hid.'

Lang in the *Saturday Review* took a more robust line. 'Gemini' in *In Black and White* might 'make a Radical Indophile laugh'. And of 'On the City Wall' in the same volume (in which we learn how 'the dog-whip cracked across the writhing backs, and the constables smote afresh with baton and gun-butt') he remarks 'How the British soldiers quell a multitude of yelling fanatics, without drawing a bayonet or firing a shot, is pleasant to read.'

But the three soldiers captivated more fastidious critics than these, notable among them being Henry James. Of Mulvaney, the hero of the cleaning-rod, James in 1891 wrote in almost lyrical terms: 'He is a piece of portraiture of the largest, vividest kind, growing and growing on the painter's hands without ever outgrowing them. I can't help regarding him, in a certain sense, as Mr Kipling's tutelary deity – a landmark in the direction in which it is open to him to look furthest.' And in general – James adds of Kipling's 'Indian impressions' – 'the most brilliant group is devoted wholly to the common soldier, and of this series it appears to me that too much good is hardly to be said'.

James's attitude to Kipling was in fact, and as we shall see, highly ambivalent; he renders fully articulate much that can be sensed as latent in the more sophisticated discussions of Kipling's work throughout the 1890s and beyond. And here it is necessary to note that the problem of Kipling's reputation in this period is bound up with the problem of his relation with literary London as a whole. On the one hand we can discern him as generously received from the start by an impressive array of men of letters distinguished in their time: Lang, Henley, Whibley, Barrie, Gosse, Saintsbury, Besant, Dowden, and many others. With the exception of the equivocal James, indeed, the great are absent; but it is still a formidable reception committee or jury. Kipling was properly grateful – yet it is clear that he was ill at ease, alienated, even antagonized before and by the society in which he was enjoying so brilliant a success.

> But I consort with long-haired things
>   In velvet collar-rolls,
> Who talk about the Aims of Art,
>   And 'theories' and 'goals',
> And moo and coo with womenfolk
>   About their blessed souls.

These lines are from a snort of mysteriously angry and resentful contempt which, very soon after his arrival in England, he sent back to India to be printed in his first stand-by, the *Civil and Military Gazette*. What had gone wrong may well have been, fundamentally, something amiss in his private life. But there must also have been something he didn't like in the very basis of the reputation growing around him.

Why those scornful capital letters and inverted commas? Why the succeeding childish gibe that what the long-haired things call 'psychology' is simply 'lack of liver-pill'? Roughly put, the answer seems to me to be that Kipling resented the assumption that he was merely the next thing to come along in the aesthetic movement of the time.

There is much to suggest that I cannot possibly be right in this. Time and again one finds him hailed in those early years as a crude and vulgar writer with a strong dash of genius. Lang himself runs some such line on his protégé. Of the early stories, he says, the 'defects are a certain knowingness and familiarity, as of one telling a story in a smoking-room rather late in the evening'. According to Humphry Ward, Kipling 'though an admirably direct writer, is comparatively wanting in style', and it is to be hoped he will improve in this department of literary art. W. E. Henley (a very genuine admirer) finds Kipling's English, other than his dialect English, liable to be inadequate, pert, and common; his style has 'a savour of newspaperese and is . . . unworthy of the matter it conveys'. Charles Whibley is solemn on 'the line which divides art from reporting'. Stevenson sees Kipling as a portent of 'trouble coming' for those who would uphold the sanctities of 'style'. There is a lot about 'style' in this whole critical debate. Its obverse is 'slang'. Kipling's lack of the first and abundance of the second tend to be equally deprecated. 'Mr Kipling,' a severe person pronounces in 1898, 'has still to vindicate his title to be considered as a model of English style.' And Professor Sir Arthur Quiller-Couch sternly pronounces the words 'facile vulgarity'.

All this might persuade us that Kipling was exclusively received as an inspired monster or portent from a barbaric beyond. ('Infant monster', indeed, is almost Henry James's first word on him.) He may well have seen himself as that – or as a fresh, clean wind, a violent cross-wind blowing the long-haired things, as in Milton's poem, into Limbo. But it was not, at least, as simple as that.

Dixon Scott, an able critic who died young and whose posthumously published *Men of Letters* (1916) deserves to be better known than it is, was, I believe, the first to discern another and significant relation in which Kipling stood to the period:

A new star had arisen, a rival to Loti, and the elect were at once in full song. Perhaps the hour was specially apt for such an overture. It was the hour of the eighties, the ineffable, amateur eighties, when a recondite vulgarity was the vogue; and aesthetic London was not at all unanxious to display its capacity for enjoying raw sensation. Hedonism had deserted the Oxford of Pater for 'The Oxford' of Marie Lloyd and Walter Sickert. If you were a poet you were ashamed not to be seen in cabmen's shelters; and a little hashish was considered quite the thing. A superior hour! And so, when the rag-time chords of the *Departmental Ditties* flicked and snapped an introduction to the laconic patter of the *Tales*, and when the *Tales* themselves, with their parakeets and ivory, their barbaric chic and rubricated slang, proved a mixture of Persian print and music-hall, then the 'ten superior persons scattered through the universe' were persuaded that their hour had found its very voice, that they were listening to the last delicious insolence of aesthetics . . . The youngster was bracketed with Beardsley, was bracketed with 'Max' . . . The little sun-baked books from Allahabad seemed if anything more golden than *The Yellow Book*. The proof of the literary epicure was his palate for the Kipling liqueur.

'And then,' Dixon Scott goes on, 'the exasperating fellow became popular.'

That Kipling was thus ineptly co-opted by the aesthetes explains the unanimity of his first acclaim; explains too, it may be, one occasion of his uneasiness, since he was not a man to relish a false position; and may be viewed, finally, as a factor in that decline of his reputation which marked the later 1890s. He had turned out to be *not* an aesthete, but a writer widely hailed by a vast public not much given to hailing writers at all. And the critics – Dixon Scott concludes – found it 'impossible to watch their liqueur being drained like Bass without having doubts about its quality'.

But there must have been more than this to Kipling's eventual decline into the position of 'a neglected celebrity', which was T. S. Eliot's description of him in 1919. It was not merely aesthetes who lost interest in him. Henry James was not in the least an aesthete – or not if we cling to any meaningful use of that term. But from the first we can see James paving the way for a withdrawal of all interest or approval from Kipling. This – curiously enough in so apolitical a creature as James – has a little to do with politics: he goes on record as unable to take Kipling's 'patriotic' verse. But it is much more a revolt of the sensibility and the intelligence; when it comes to a show-down he simply cannot bring himself to admit Kipling to the club. (Nor, really and truly, can Eliot, who in 1919 called Kipling 'very nearly a great writer' and at the same time placed him among those 'who are not or hardly artists'.) James tries hard; tries to be honest before the fascination Kipling had initially exercised over him. The 'infant monster' has 'genius'. He has a 'prodigious special faculty'; 'his bloom lasts from month to month'; he owns an 'active, disinterested sense of the real'; we ought to be 'thankful for any boldness and any sharp curiosity' – and so on. But it all won't quite do. The genius is something 'distinct from fine intelligence'. The prodigious special faculty is 'without a dream of nuance or a hint of "distinction" '. The active, disinterested sense of the real is turned upon 'the coarse, receding edges of the social perspective'. (This last reminds one of James's verdict on *Sons and Lovers*: 'a nearer view of commoner things'.) There is a reductive use of diminutives: 'an embodied little talent, so economically constructed for all use and no waste'; 'a singularly robust little literary character'. (This too carries its reminiscence: James contrived to speak of 'the good little Thomas Hardy'.) Finally there is a letter to Grace Norton, written in 1897, in which James says of Kipling:

In his earliest time I thought he perhaps contained the seeds of an English Balzac; but I have given that up in proportion as he has come down steadily from the simple in subject to the more simple – from the Anglo-Indians to the natives, from the natives to the Tommies, from the Tommies to the quadrupeds, from the quadrupeds to the fish, and from the fish to the engines and screws.

After this sally (which so decidedly dismisses Mulvaney) James appears to have lost interest in Kipling altogether. And so, in fact, did what may be called the literary intelligence at large. Both in England and America, he was left with very much the sort of public he had first gained in India. His sales were not affected, although the faithful may not always have got to the end of his later stories, some of which are a tax upon as much literary intelligence as any man is likely to possess. But in a sense he had – as Edmund Wilson was to put it in a celebrated essay – 'been dropped out of modern literature'.

The cause of his long eclipse must, as has been hinted, be complex. Partly, at least, it came from within the writer and the man. There are a good many signs that, after his first phenomenal success (and phenomenal outpouring of imaginative energy), Kipling suffered some disabling loss of confidence. From the first a novel was expected of him. 'One would gladly see him at work on a larger canvas,' a very early review concludes; and on this theme, only a few months later, Lang struck a slightly foreboding note: 'People will probably expect Mr Kipling, with all these graces of his, to try his hand at a long novel. We are a nation that likes quantity. But it may very probably turn out that Mr Kipling is best at short stories and sketches.'

It did so turn out. That *The Light that Failed* was a failure even before it was published is apparent from the fumbling after an ending which its textual history declares; and neither the collaborated *The Naulahka* nor *Captains Courageous* nor the incomparable *Kim* is significantly a novel in the more substantial sense. For some years, indeed, Kipling bore the appearance of having turned himself into a writer for children.

The obverse of this uncertainty of stance, and doubtless connected with it, was an increasing positiveness, a dogmatism of political opinion, apparent in his prose and verse alike. Wilson speaks of 'the deliberate cultivation of the excommunicatory imperialist hatreds' as having made an adverse impression even on the general public, and it certainly alienated an articulate liberal class. This seems to have been particularly true in America. Thus Professor Lionel Trilling, in *The Liberal Imagination* (1943), while able to tell us that Kipling 'is not properly to be called a Fascist', detects in his Toryism 'a lower-middle-class snarl of defeated gentility'. I do not myself believe that Kipling's snarls are quite like this. Still, they are undeniably *there*; and I think it true that something which must have been unsympathetic in the man percolates indefinably into much of his art. There is a marked lack of amenity, for one thing: something that Lionel Johnson early distinguished in him as an inability to 'feel the common sentiments of natural good breeding', so that it is more often 'bad manners' than 'brutality' that mars his work. All this we can feel. However cunningly Kipling can conjure up the atmosphere of yarning into the small hours in a smoking-room, we yet suspect that his was a voice which would break up any party.

But there remains an element of the unaccountable about Kipling's long eclipse. A very little chronological study will invalidate the notion that there was, throughout his later career, any very substantial period of time in which he failed to vindicate his ability to produce a masterpiece. It may be true, as Professor W. W. Robson suggests, that 'what insights Kipling had, he seems to have had from the beginning', and that we do not get from his later work 'the sense of a profound and radical change of out-look, the discovery of a new spiritual dimension'. But why ever should we? The cardinal fact is that the writer who produced 'The Man who would be King' when he was twenty-two produced 'The Wish House' some thirty-six years later. Almost to the end of his days, we may say, Kipling was never far out of reach of the top of his form. But he was – and this is surely the point – for many years substantially out of touch with his time, and with the spirit of that time as the art of his contemporaries and juniors was interpreting it. This total isolation from what was happening creatively was surely symbolized at his funeral in Westminster Abbey. No member of the pro-fession of letters was among those who bore his ashes to Poets' Corner.

Kipling as Eliot's 'neglected celebrity' or Wilson's writer 'that nobody read' now belongs to past history. Even Eliot's 'very nearly a great writer' sounds quite wrong. We have come to see that Kipling's verse and his politics alike clouded the issue, and that when we focus upon his real achievement any question of placing him in a second rank becomes absurd. He is, quite simply, the first short story writer we have had. This was too patent a fact to lie obscured for long: indeed, do we not have a sense of having known it all the time? What has been more elusive is the gravity, as distinct from the brilliance, of his art.

A clearer view of Kipling here constitutes our principal debt to more recent criti-cism. In 1941 Edmund Wilson had seen only the brilliance. ('As his responses to human beings became duller, his sensitivity to his medium increased.') But in the following year George Orwell paid tribute to what he called Kipling's 'sense of re-sponsibility'; and already Professor Bonamy Dobrée had published the first of several considerations of Kipling's underlying thought which have culminated in *Rudyard Kipling: Realist and Fabulist* (1967). This book, with Dr J. M. S. Tompkins's *The Art of Rudyard Kipling* (1959), Professor C. A. Bodelsen's *Aspects of Kipling's Art* (1964) and numerous able essays by younger academic writers all attest the rehabilitation of Kipling in the regard of professional critics. The common reader, one suspects, has never very drastically written him down.

Philip French
KIPLING AND THE MOVIES

KIPLING was an established author well before the rise of the commercial cinema and was never placed in the position, as so many writers have since been, of having to turn to the film industry to supplement his income. His direct involvement in the movies was slight: his own adaptation of 'Without Benefit of Clergy' was announced for production in 1921 but never filmed; shortly before his death he worked on treatments of *Soldiers Three* and *Thy Servant a Dog* which also failed to reach the screen.[1] Although he never evinced an interest in the cinema comparable with that of his contemporaries Bernard Shaw and H. G. Wells, both of whom wrote seminal essays on the potential of the new medium and later became personally involved in film-making, Kipling did show an imaginative grasp of the power of motion pictures in his story 'Mrs Bathurst' as in other stories he revealed his fascination with flying and radio.

Written in 1904 and published in *Traffics and Discoveries*, 'Mrs Bathurst' is a strangely compelling tale, unfolded almost entirely in dialogue, concerning the mysterious desertion in South Africa of a British sailor, 'Click' Vickery, eighteen months before his retirement from the navy. What triggers off his flight is the sight of an old flame, the New Zealand landlady of the title, whom he accidentally sees for a brief forty-five seconds on the platform of Paddington station in a newsreel called 'Home and Friends' shown as part of a travelling circus in Cape Town. The story is told to a party of drinkers on Simonstown waterfront by the shipmate whom Vickery had dragged along night after night to catch an elusive glimpse of the lady from Auckland, and Kipling captures superbly the experience of early movie audiences and the hypnotic effect of the flickering images on the screen. No explanation is given of Mrs Bathurst's presence in London or of why Vickery should have been so disturbed by seeing her in the newsreel, but what is strikingly conveyed is the quality of his desperate obsession and anguish which eventually leads to his hideous, lonely death in Rhodesia.

'Mrs Bathurst' is notable in several ways – for the pared-down, elliptical modernity of its style, the now fashionable device of an eponymous figure who remains off-stage, and of course the early reference to the cinema. The tale also anticipates the contemporary cinema's concern with the hallucinatory impact of its own image, the recurrent present-day use of films-within-films. Indeed the picture that 'Mrs Bathurst' most brings to mind is Alain Resnais' *Muriel, ou le temps d'un retour* (1963), another

---

[1] Another unfilmed Kipling script is perhaps more significant. In August 1926 S. G. (later Sir Stephen) Tallents, Secretary to the Empire Marketing Board, met Kipling at Burwash to discuss publicizing the Board's activities. Kipling pressed on him the desirability of producing a propaganda film and recommended as its maker Major Walter Creighton who had worked with Sir Herbert Tree and C. B. Cochran. Creighton developed a scenario with Kipling which came to nothing – and anyway Kipling did not want to be publicly associated with the Board. Subsequently Creighton studied film-making and three years later, in 1929, brought in John Grierson to direct *Drifters*, the first major British documentary picture. The Empire Marketing Board Film Unit became in the mid-thirties the General Post Office Film Unit, and later the Crown Film Unit which survived until it was killed as a penny-pinching economy measure by the Tory government in 1952. It could be said therefore that Kipling played a crucial role in founding the British documentary film movement, the brightest, most controversial, star in the crown of British cinema.

complex, highly elliptical work dealing with memory and the impossibility of fully understanding human actions, and which also has an eponymous heroine who doesn't appear and a character obsessed by a silent movie that he keeps watching over and over again.

It is perhaps a little curious that an internationally popular writer of Kipling's stature should have attracted the film companies so relatively little – until, that is, the very last year of his life, when, according to Charles Carrington's biography, he was busily negotiating film rights with Hollywood agents. Nevertheless he has a significant place in the history of the movies. Hardly surprisingly, however, the movie Kipling is not the Kipling of 'Mrs Bathurst', not Edmund Wilson's 'Kipling that Nobody Read', but rather the Kipling that everyone knows: the man who wrote about children, animals, patriotism, the Empire, the mystic East and the White Man's Burden. In terms of box-office returns, the producers of films derived from his works cannot but bless his name. From the torrid triumph of *A Fool There Was* in the second decade of the century (for which Kipling presumably received nothing as he hadn't copyrighted the work on which it was based) to Walt Disney's *Jungle Book* in 1967, Kipling pictures have been big business. Yet strangely enough, *A Fool There Was* seems to have been the only Kipling movie of the silent period, apart from an unsuccessful remake of the same picture and a long-forgotten 1923 version (made by the same man, George Melford, who had directed Valentino in *The Sheik*) of *The Light that Failed*, while *The Jungle Book* has been the only substantial Kipling production of the past twenty years. In artistic terms, neither picture can be taken seriously.

The Jungle Book had been filmed before in Hollywood – by Zoltan Korda in 1942, with the Indian actor Sabu as Mowgli. Sabu had been discovered working in the stables of the Maharajah of Mysore by Robert Flaherty in 1935 and cast in the title role of *Elephant Boy*, a film based somewhat remotely on Kipling's 'Toomai of the Elephants'. This generally disastrous attempt by the American documentary-movie genius Flaherty to crash the world of big-budget feature films was not without its sequences of visual power and grandeur. And whereas the Eskimoes, South Sea islanders and Irish peasants, whose struggles against nature Flaherty had celebrated in his earlier films, returned to their traditional pursuits after the cinematic caravan had passed, Sabu came to Britain where *Elephant Boy* was re-written and re-made at Denham studios. The producer Alexander Korda had made his brother Zoltan co-director of *Elephant Boy*, and subsequently Sabu became Zoltan's protégé for the early stages of his movie career, appearing in *The Drum* (1938) and *The Thief of Baghdad* (1940), a picture started in Britain and, due to the exigency of war, completed in Hollywood. Korda's *Jungle Book* was shot on a ten-acre jungle-set in southern California with a menagerie of trained animals, and though a picture of little distinction, it at least had some feeling for Kipling and the Indian subcontinent. The same cannot be said for the Disney re-make. This seventy-eight-minute animated cartoon was the last picture to be personally supervised by Walt Disney before his death, and in the words of his unofficial biographer Richard Schickel, 'it is not, of course, for purists.' Less pretentious, less sentimental than many recent Disney products, *The*

Jungle Book is a likeable if unstimulating children's entertainment with the usual Disney line in cute anthropomorphism, half-a-dozen facile pop songs, and everything cosily Americanized. This unabashedly vulgar film couldn't even be said to be a contemporary middle-American law'n'order version of Kipling's Law of the Jungle, and were it not for the movie's phenomenal success, one might agree with Disney's reported remarks after viewing some of the rushes: 'I don't know, fellows. I guess I'm getting too old for animation.'

At the other end of the spectrum, *A Fool There Was* is just as ludicrous. The genesis of this silent melodrama was Kipling's poem 'The Vampire' which appeared in the catalogue of an 1897 exhibition at the New Gallery, London, to accompany a painting of the same name by the author's cousin Philip Burne-Jones, depicting a pale, predatory woman with her male victim. The poem, which related in six stanzas the grisly tale of a man brought low by a callous woman, was adapted for the stage (and as a novel) by Porter Emerson Browne under the title *A Fool There Was* from the poem's first lines:

> A fool there was and he made his prayer
>   (Even as you and I!)
> To a rag and a bone and a hank of hair
>   (We called her the woman who did not care)
> But the fool he called her his lady fair –
>   (Even as you and I!)

The combination of prurient melodramatic scenes and stern morality no doubt accounted for its Broadway success in 1909. The screen rights were acquired by the movie pioneer William Fox under whose auspices it became an enormously successful six-reeler (roughly an hour and rather a long film for its day) in 1915 as 'adapted and picturized by Frank Powell'. This risible picture launched the brief, meteoric career of Powell's Cincinnati-born discovery Theodosia Goodman under the screen-name Theda Bara. In consequence she became the cinema's first and archetypal 'vamp' and introduced that word, as noun and verb, into the language.

Kipling's principal association with the screen spans the years 1935 to 1940. In 1937 there were film versions of *Captains Courageous* (in which Spencer Tracy won an Academy Award for his moving portrayal of Manuel, the Portuguese fisherman), *Wee Willie Winkie*, and Flaherty's *Elephant Boy*; in 1939 adaptations of 'Gunga Din' and *The Light that Failed* (starring Ronald Colman). But more importantly these pictures formed part of a cycle of Kiplingesque movies that sought to celebrate the British Empire and its achievements, and English heroism, with films drawn from A. E. W. Mason, Francis Yeats-Brown, P. C. Wren and Alfred Lord Tennyson, not to mention the febrile imaginations of numerous anglophile (or cynical) Hollywood screenwriters.

There had been a steady trickle of pro-British imperial and First World War movies, including two silent Hollywood versions of *The Four Feathers* and such pictures as *The Black Watch*, John Ford's first full-length talkie, before the great wave of them broke in the thirties. Then in 1935, for example, there was *Clive of India* and

Stage and Screen

84 *Opposite* 'From my desk I could look out of my window through the fan-light of Gatti's Music-Hall entrance, almost on to its stage' (*Something of Myself*)

85 The Chairman at Gatti's, 1890

86 *Opposite* Leo Dryden, 'the Kipling of the Halls'

THE LIGHT THAT FAILED.

Torpenhow Mr. AUBREY SMITH.   Dick Heldar Mr. FORBES ROBERTSON.
"Don't let 'em think you're afraid."

88 *Above The Light That Failed* as a play,
with Mr Forbes Robertson and Mr C.
Aubrey Smith (as he then was)

87 *Right The Light That Failed* as a film,
Ronald Colman and Ida Lupino (1939)

90 *Overleaf left* Gatti's *Hungerford Palace of Varieties* painted by Walter Sickert

89 *Wee Willie Winkie* (1937) with Shirley Temple and Sir C. Aubrey Smith

91 *Overleaf right* 'Mandalay Waltz', published by Charles Sheard in 1893

MANDALAY WALTZ.

By the old Moulmein Pagoda, lookin' eastward to the sea,
There's a Burma girl a-settin', & I know she thinks o' me;
For the wind is in the palm-trees, & the temple-bells they say:
'Come you back, you British soldier; come you back to Mandalay!'
Rudyard Kipling

BY
BEWICKE BEVERLEY
LONDON

CHARLES SHEARD & Co. MUSIC PUBLISHERS, 196, SHAFTESBURY AVENUE, W.C.
(Bloomsbury End)
COPYRIGHT, 1893, BY CHAS SHEARD & Co

SOLO	4/-
DUET	4/-
OCTUOR	1/-
FULL ORCHESTRA	2/-
MILITARY BAND	2/6

92 A rag and bone and a hank of hair. Theda Bara in
A Fool There Was (1915)

93 *Opposite top Gunga Din*: Cary Grant, Victor
McLaglen, Douglas Fairbanks Jr.

94 *Opposite left* Errol Flynn and Dean Stockwell in
Kim (1949)

95 *Opposite bottom right Captains Courageous*: Spencer
Tracy and Freddie Bartholomew

96 *Opposite* and 97 *Above* Sabu in *The Jungle Book*
(1942)

98 Mowgli in Disneyland: *The Jungle Book* (1967)

99 Sabu in Robert Flaherty's *Elephant Boy* (1937)

Lives of a Bengal Lancer, in 1936 *The Charge of the Light Brigade* (most of which is set on the North-West Frontier, a massacre there providing Errol Flynn with the revenge motive to order the attack at Balaclava) and in 1938 *Suez* (where Disraeli provided Tyrone Power as de Lesseps with money to build the canal). Even Laurel and Hardy found themselves accidentally defending the British Raj against frontier tribesmen in *Bonnie Scotland*, and dressed in kilts too! In Britain the Hungarian romantic Zoltan Korda played his part with *Sanders of the River* (1935), *The Drum* (1938), and *The Four Feathers* (1939), though in the post-war years he was to take a rather less exotic view of Africa with the Hemingway-derived *The Macomber Affair* (1947), and a sober version of Alan Paton's novel *Cry the Beloved Country* (1951).

A number of different, often contradictory, factors, influenced the development of this cycle, and fortuitously they worked together. And of course once a Hollywood cycle is under way it has a built-in, bandwagon momentum of its own. Obviously the East offered colourful subjects not entirely removed from the Western genre and capable of being shot on similar local terrain. Then in the thirties, one might suppose, there was a desire to escape from the horrifying uncertainties of the American present to a world of fixed values remote from the Depression era. The apparently unchanged Victorian or Edwardian atmosphere of imperial India was tinged with a paternalistic, nostalgic view of life that suited the movie moguls who in the face of the New Deal and the threat of socialism were shifting rapidly to the political right, especially after the 1934 campaign they waged against the left-wing writer Upton Sinclair when he ran (unsuccessfully) for the governorship of California. At the same time the studios had under contract numerous British actors who formed a little colony in Hollywood: C. Aubrey Smith, Ronald Colman, Cary Grant, Victor McLaglen, Errol Flynn, Basil Rathbone, Charles Laughton, David Niven, Herbert Marshall, to name but a few. Not many of these performers could be plausibly cast in Westerns; on the other hand American actors could quite easily be placed on the North-West Frontier with the right explanation. In *Lives of a Bengal Lancer*, for example, Richard Cromwell was introduced as the American-reared son of the regiment's commanding officer (Sir Guy Standing) and Gary Cooper established as a Scots-Canadian. In these roles, the American actor would invariably be presented as an insubordinate rebel who eventually came to appreciate, in the final reel, the unwritten code of the regiment and the demands of the Empire.

It was not just a case of adult performers either. Child actors were all the rage at the time; from 1935 to 1941 Shirley Temple or Mickey Rooney topped the annual 'Money Making Stars Poll'. *Wee Willie Winkie* was re-shaped as a vehicle for Miss Temple at Twentieth-Century-Fox and *Captains Courageous* was acquired by M-G-M to star Freddie Bartholomew. As the 'unaffected' innocent arriving at the Khyber Pass, Miss Temple showed how easy it would be for a child to solve apparently irreconcilable political differences with a little love and common-sense; conversely, Master Bartholomew, as the spoilt rich boy accidentally fallen among Grand Banks fishermen, demonstrated the way in which a touch of discipline and physical labour could straighten out the rebellious, discontented young.

Fundamentally then, these pictures can be viewed as conservative, reactionary and escapist in cast. But early on another element was to enter into the picture which in a way might be thought to run counter to the original intention of the cycle. If the initial thrust was towards a nostalgic celebration of the British Empire on the part of the studio owners, it was turned by some of their underlings into a political weapon against Hitler's Germany and the rising tide of European fascism. By the end of the decade their predominantly Jewish employers were to support this aim, although they were naturally disinclined to make pictures that were overtly anti-fascist in a frankly controversial, combative fashion, or which fell outside the bounds of conventional entertainment.

The most determined exponent or exploiter of this aspect of the Kipling cycle was Douglas Fairbanks Jr, a committed anglophile and outspoken advocate of American support for Britain and of US intervention in the Second World War. His biographer Brian Connell traces the clear course by which Fairbanks deliberately set out to put pro-British propaganda into entertainment pictures, such as a 1938 re-make of *The Dawn Patrol* (with Errol Flynn, Basil Rathbone and David Niven) and *The Sun Never Sets* 'a didactic piece about the colonial service in West Africa in which Fairbanks was won over to the idea of Empire, as personified by C. Aubrey Smith). His greatest triumph in this vein was *Gunga Din* (1939), a vigorous knockabout adventure yarn that comes across today with undiminished force. Directed by George Stevens, who was much later to become a major Hollywood figure through such films as *A Place in the Sun*, *Shane* and *Giant*, the picture was the highwater-mark of the cycle: 'Kiplingesque' perhaps rather than Kipling, in a way that an equally crude, though pessimistic and pretentious, type of entertainment is 'Kafkaesque' rather than Kafka. Fairbanks himself developed the story along with the top screenwriting team of Charles MacArthur and Ben Hecht, and the former Oxford Rhodes Scholar Joel Sayre of *The New Yorker* wrote the final screenplay. Hecht was at the time a passionate anti-fascist, devoted to bringing America into the war against Nazi Germany; ironically, in view of his pro-British activities during the Second World War, he was later to be black-listed in Britain as a result of his intemperate remarks about the post-war Palestine situation.

Basically *Gunga Din* combined the characters of *Soldiers Three* – with Fairbanks, Cary Grant and Victor McLaglen playing Sergeants MacChesney, Cutter and Ballentine (clearly derived from Kipling's Mulvaney, Otheris and Learoyd) – and the poem 'Gunga Din', with the fine actor Sam Jaffe as the trio's long-suffering 'regimental *bhisti*'. The film has battles galore, a sinister anti-imperial conspiracy (led by the invaluable shaven-headed Italian character actor Eduardo Cianelli, who may at the time have invoked Mussolini), a pit of hissing cobras, and a climax in which Gunga Din lays down his life by sounding the alarm that saves the regiment from an ambush. In a concluding sequence, we are presented with a glimpse of a journalist bearing a strong resemblance to Rudyard Kipling drafting a poem (though in fact Kipling never heard a shot fired in anger in India) followed by the posthumous award of the Victoria Cross to Gunga Din and the recital of the poem, during which Sam Jaffe as Din is superimposed on the screen saluting the flag. This echoes the scene at the end of *Lives of a Bengal Lancer* where a posthumous VC is pinned on Gary Cooper's horse.[1]

An incidental irony of Hollywood's Kipling cycle is worth noting, for it concerns the film *Wee Willie Winkie* and a British admirer of Kipling's, Graham Greene. Twentieth-Century-Fox changed the sex of Kipling's eponymous hero in order to make Shirley Temple the grand-daughter of the unbending North-West Frontier commandant C. Aubrey Smith, and the plot was altered to present her achievement as greater in scale – reconciling a warrior chieftain (Cesar Romero) and the British Raj, instead of merely saving a reckless woman from a ruffian band. But it would not be unfair to say that the excruciating sentimentality and sheer incredibility of the original were faithfully rendered by the director, John Ford. Mr Greene, in his capacity of film critic for the magazine *Night and Day*, reacted so strongly to Miss Temple and her producers that a libel action was brought against the journal. The action brought about the demise of the short-lived *Night and Day*, and Greene temporarily left the country to undertake a travel book about Mexico, *The Lawless Roads*: this led on in turn to what Greene himself and many of his critics regard as his most satisfactory novel, *The Power and the Glory*.

Pearl Harbor, the reality of war and America's involvement with itself brought an end to the Kipling cycle. Suddenly the achievements of the British Raj, the struggles of *Mrs Miniver* and the problems of *A Yank in the RAF* gave way to challenges on the domestic front, to the defence of *Wake Island* and *Bataan*, to entries in a *Guadacanal Diary*. The Bureau of Motion Pictures, a branch of the Office of War Information, was established to counsel Hollywood on the political aspects of its patriotic efforts; it was especially concerned about the feelings of America's fighting allies, and one of the steps it took, as Richard R. Lingeman tells us in his social history of the American home front, *Don't You Know There's a War On?*, was to veto a proposed version of *Kim*: '*Kim*, with its pro-Empire, white-man's-burden philosophy, was thought to give aid and comfort to those who were criticizing the British for fighting the war solely to keep their colonies (a favourite theme of German propaganda, as well as of editorials in the Chicago *Tribune* and *Life* magazine).'

The rights in *Kim* had been acquired by M-G-M and announced as a 1938 vehicle for Freddie Bartholomew and Robert Taylor for production in India. In 1942 the property was on the stocks once more, to feature Mickey Rooney, Conrad Veidt and Basil Rathbone. This was the version the Bureau of Motion Pictures aborted. M-G-M eventually got around to filming the novel in 1950 with the British director Victor Saville at the helm, Errol Flynn as the red-bearded Mahbub Khan and Dean Stockwell, last of the M-G-M contract child stars, as Kim. The notion of Russian agents intriguing on the North-West Frontier must have seemed a timely ingredient, but the picture was in most respects a disaster, not only because a feeble script dodged the

---

[1] There is an interesting essay by Bertolt Brecht in which he admits to having been stirred by *Gunga Din* when he saw it, like the rest of the audience, and consequently finds the way in which 'it perverts our picture of the world' all the more dangerous. See *Brecht on Theatre*, translated by John Willett (London, 1964), p. 151.

original's complexities, but also because the company attempted a cut-price epic by unduly restricting the location shooting in India.

With *Kim* the old Kipling cycle died with a post-war whimper. Whether Robert Flaherty would have made a better job of the film we cannot tell. In 1926 he had proposed a version of *Kim* to be made in colour on Indian locations, but failed to raise the money. It would be unfair to judge this project against the glorious failure of *Elephant Boy* a decade later.

Between Saville's *Kim* and Disney's *Jungle Book* there were to be only a couple of Kipling films. The first was a frightful M-G-M version of *Soldiers Three* (1951), directed by the veteran Tay Garnett, and featuring a largely British cast of Stewart Granger, Robert Newton, David Niven, Cyril Cusack, Robert Coote and Greta Gynt, that could surely only have been made in order to honour (and conclude) a variety of long-standing contracts. The other was a 1961 re-make of *Gunga Din* called *Sergeants Three*, a ramshackle vehicle designed to accommodate the Sinatra Clan having fun at the public's expense.

For no apparent reason there was a string of North-West Frontier movies during the fifties including *King of the Khyber Rifles* (1954), which was a re-make of Ford's *The Black Watch*, *Zarak* (1956), *The Bandit of Zhobe* (1959), and *North-West Frontier* (1959). Their roots were only too obviously in Kipling but they offered sad fruit, soon withered on the branch. Some were actually made in India, but the true cinematic explorers of the Indian subcontinent are now of course Satyajit Ray, the only major director India has yet produced, and his American protégé James Ivory, in whose work the influence of Kipling is clearly discernible and who is perhaps the man to undertake serious adaptations of Kipling in the future.

Kipling has also provided film-makers with a number of evocative titles, the most striking instance, and ultimately the most engaging of Kiplingesque movies being Lindsay Anderson's *If* (1968). The screenplay was written by David Sherwin and John Howlett and based on their own experiences as public schoolboys; originally it was called *Crusaders*, and was apparently an exposé of the public school system. The script passed through several producers' hands and numerous drafts before its propitious arrival in the lap of Anderson. Like Kipling, Anderson was born in India – in 1923, in Bangalore, where his father was an officer with the Royal Engineers. Also like Kipling, he was educated in England and then returned to India, though in his case as a wartime army officer: in 1945 he raised the Red Flag over the officers' mess to celebrate the Labour Party's electoral victory. An unswerving left-wing socialist, Anderson nevertheless retains a certain ambivalence on class issues, and this is apparent in *If*. Fundamentally the film is Kipling's *Stalky & Co.* as filtered through the anarchic surrealism of Jean Vigo and the alienation techniques of Bertolt Brecht. The rebellious activities of the public schoolboys Mick, Johnny and Wallace in *If* inevitably recall *Stalky & Co.*, the division of the film into eight didactic chapters is consciously Brechtian, and the climactic fantasy sequence in which Mick and his friends turn on their school with machine-guns deliberately evokes the liberating end of Vigo's *Zéro de Conduite*.

Few foreign commentators have recognized how essentially British and indeed how Kiplingesque this picture is. For *If* is steered along a parallel course to *Stalky* until just before the moment of Kipling's surprise affirmation, when Anderson steps aside to make a quite different, though for him no less positive, point. He has protested in several interviews that he didn't dislike his own schooldays and isn't attacking the public-school system directly. It is perhaps not too fanciful therefore to see his latter-day Stalky and Co. as training themselves for another kind of warfare. The equation that Kipling makes between schoolboy pranks and serious North-West Frontier tactics, in the two sections of *Stalky* entitled 'Slaves of the Lamp I' and 'Slaves of the Lamp II', has its counterpart in *If*, where public-school antics prepare their partici-pants for contemporary guerilla warfare on lines laid down by Che Guevara, a heroic portrait of whom graces the wall of Mick's study. In effect this reverses the end of *Stalky & Co.*, which many critics over the past seventy years have found unconvinc-ing in its endorsement of the establishment. (Whether they would care for this new, more consistent conclusion is another matter.) Of course, for all Anderson's commit-ment to egalitarianism, the film proposes an essentially élitist vision of the future, the White Man's Burden transformed as it were into the public-school man's responsi-bility to make revolution at home and in the Third World. And it is as mystical and romantic, and ultimately as unattainable, as anything Kipling himself had in mind, as Anderson underlines by using the 'Missa Luba' as the film's theme music.

Questioned about changing the title of the film to *If*, Anderson remarked:[1]

It was related to Rudyard Kipling's poem, *If*, which expresses the good side of the public school ethos. It begins 'If you can keep your head when all about you are losing theirs' and ends with 'What's more you'll be a man my son'. I think these boys, particularly Mick, are traditional heroes. They become men. They stand up for their convictions and for them-selves against odds that may be overwhelming. The hero of *If* is a very responsible man. He finds the right solution. Now, because the film is *not* literal, the end is plainly a metaphor.

Finally, of course, the nature of that metaphor remains elusive both to the audience and the director. But in *If* Anderson perhaps gets closer to the central core of Kipling than anyone has previously done in the cinema.

The Film Director as Superstar by Joseph Gelmis, London, Secker and Warburg, 1971, p. 104.

Index

Edwardes, Major-General Sir Herbert: *A Year on the Punjab Frontier* (1850), 39–40
Egypt, British Imperialism in, 90, 148
Eliot, T. S., 132; on RK, 91–2, 95, 100, 101, 104, 110, 112, 144, 158, 160
Emerson, Ralph Waldo, 72
Empire Marketing Board Film Unit, 162n
England, RK's feelings for, 107–8, 122 *and see* British Empire, Sussex

Fairbanks, Douglas, Jr, 166
Falls, Captain Cyril: *War Books* (1930), 146–7, 149
Fielding, Henry: *Tom Jones*, 10, 28, 29
films of RK's works: *see* Kipling, Rudyard, works
Flaherty, Robert, 163, 164, 168
Flynn, Errol, 165, 166, 167
Ford, John, 164, 167
Four Feathers, The (film, 1939), 164, 165
Fox, William, 164
France, RK visits, as a boy, 151; in 1925, 145, 147
Freemasonry, RK's membership of, 140, 148–9
Friend, The, RK works for (1900), 85, 86, 87

Galsworthy, John, 150
Garnett, Tay, 168
Garrard, Florence ('Maisie'), 3n, 90
Gatti's-under-the-Arches (music hall), 59
George V, friendship with RK, 145; death of, 151
Germans, RK's attacks on, 92, 93, 104, 106, 110, 137, 138–9; in 1st World War, 44, 137, 138–9; in 2nd World War, 167
Goodman, Theodosia, *see* Bara, Theda
Gordon, General Charles George, 90
Gosse, Edmund, on Balestier, 64, 65, 69; at Hardy's funeral, 150; and RK, 155, 156
Gosse, Mrs Edmund, 69
Granger, Stewart, 168
Grant, Cary, 165, 166
Graves, Robert: on RK, 44; *Goodbye to All That*, 146
Green, Roger Lancelyn: *Kipling: the Critical Heritage* (1971), 154n
Greene, Graham, 54, 167
Grierson, John, 162n
Guevara, Che, 169
Gwynne, H. A., 148
Gynt, Greta, 168

Haggard, Phyllis, 145

Haggard, Sir Henry Rider: friendship with RK, 121, 129, 130, 134, 136–7, 144, 147, 148; life in South Africa, 128–9; work of, 129–34; death of (1925), 134, 148; *Allan Quatermain*, 130; *Farmer's Year, A*, 121; *King Solomon's Mines*, 128; *She*, 130; *Rural England*, 121; *Wisdom's Daughter*, 130
Haileybury school, 8, 16
Hakluyt, Richard, 11
Hardy, Thomas, 155, 158; *Jude the Obscure*, 5; RK at funeral of, 150
Harris, Joel Chandler, 72
Harte, Bret, 72, 73
Hay, Ian: *The First Hundred Thousand*, 146
'Hauksbee, Mrs', 12, 54, 55
Hecht, Ben, 166
Heinemann, William, 68
Henderson, Arthur, 148
Henley, W. E., 104, 155, 157
Hill, Mr and Mrs, RK visits in Pennsylvania, 72, 73, 74
Himalayas, the, 31, 32, 33, 52, 53
Hinduism, 30, 32, 33–5, 49, 92
Hitler, Adolf, 151, 166
Hobbes, Thomas: *Leviathan*, 94
'Hobden' (Isted), 122, 125
Hollywood, 163–8
Holt, Maud, *see* Tree, Lady
Horace, 11, 100
'House of Desolation', 2–3, 90 *and see* Southsea
Housman, Alfred Edward, 150
Howells, William Dean, 66, 67
Howlett, John, 168
Hughes, Thomas: *Tom Brown's Schooldays*, 14

If (film, 1968), 168–9
Imperial South Africa Association, 85
imperialism, *see* British Empire
India: John L. Kipling in, 20, 21–5; RK in, 11, 87, 90, 120 *and see* Bombay, Lahore; source for RK, 30–5, 38–44, 47–50, 52–6, 66, 68, 87, 90–3, 121, 131, 132, 154–5, 157–8 *and see* Simla; British in: 28–9, 30, 32, 38–44, 47, 50, 52–6, 121, 148; RK's attitude to, 12, 14, 15, 28, 30, 32, 38, 41, 43–4, 47–50, 55–6, 91–2; subject for films, 164–6
Indian Civil Service, 48–9, 50, 131
Indian National Congress, RK attacks, 93
Irish nationalists, 148; RK attacks, 93, 104
Isle of Wight, 67

INDEX